D0371815

# Exit Interview

# EXIT INTERVIEW

# DAVID WESTIN

SARAH CRICHTON BOOKS | Farrar, Straus and Giroux   New York

Sarah Crichton Books
Farrar, Straus and Giroux
18 West 18th Street, New York 10011

Distributed in Canada by D&M Publishers, Inc.
Printed in the United States of America
First edition, 2012

Library of Congress Cataloging-in-Publication Data
Westin, David, 1952–
    Exit interview / David Westin. — 1st ed.
        p.    cm.
    Includes bibliographical references and index.
    ISBN 978-0-374-15121-8 (alk. paper)
    1.  Television broadcasting of news—United States.    2.  ABC News.    3.  Westin, David,
1952–    I.  Title.

PN4888.T4 W45 2012
070.92—dc23

                                                                                    2011048104


Designed by Abby Kagan

www.fsgbooks.com

10   9   8   7   6   5   4   3   2   1

To Sherrie, without whom some of this wouldn't have happened and none of it would've meant what it did

# Contents

Introduction    3

1 | My Sister, Peter Jennings, and Lady Diana    13

2 | In the Line of Fire: The Story of the Blue Dress    36

3 | "Planet Earth": My Leonardo DiCaprio Problem    58

4 | Gore Wins? Bush Wins? How the Networks Blew the 2000 Election—Twice    81

5 | Showing the Flag: Journalism and Patriotism After 9/11    104

6 | War and Bias: Portraits of the Fallen    135

7 | The Swift Boat Saga: Is Balance Overrated?    156

8 | Is Any News Report Worth Dying For? The Bob Woodruff Story    176

9 | Can We Afford the News? Why ABC News Lost a Quarter of Itself    200

Acknowledgments    227

Index    229

# Exit Interview

## | Introduction

I blush today, looking back on how much I didn't know when I was named president of ABC News on March 6, 1997. I'd worked closely with my colleagues in news for years—first as their lawyer and then as head of the network. But I wasn't a journalist. Seeing it from outside is not the same as seeing it close-up, from inside a news organization: how deadly serious journalists can be about their responsibility to the public; how deep the bonds are between journalists who have worked together over the years through difficulties and dangers; how important curiosity and an eagerness to share stories are to good journalism—and how those same traits often carry over into the newsroom and fill it with gossip; how frequently journalists come under attack from those who don't like what they're reporting and how that can make them sometimes come across as defensive. I had a lot to learn.

All of these were things that someone who'd grown up in journalism might have explained to me. And I might even have listened. But when I moved from my spacious office as president of the ABC Television Network next door to a much smaller office in the older, somewhat run-down building that housed ABC News, no journalist could have predicted how fundamentally all of television news would change over the next few years; no journalist could have known that even as we were trying to respond to these changes, we'd be called on to cover so many extraordinary, history-making events.

It wasn't supposed to be that way. The 1990s were supposed to be the time when, in the fateful words of Francis Fukuyama, history ended. With the end of the Cold War six years before I went to news, the United States had lost its only strategic adversary when the Soviet Union collapsed and the Berlin Wall came down. We had moved into the age of American dominance when Pax Americana would rule for years to come. All of those diplomatic standoffs and military conflicts that we'd lived with since World War II were going to be replaced by treaties and commercial agreements. In March 1997 it looked as if the news would pretty much be relegated to covering how much all those new Internet companies would be making for their young founders, mixed in with the occasional scandal— celebrity or otherwise.

And then history came back from the dead. The president had an illicit relationship with a young intern, leading to his impeachment, a full trial in the U.S. Senate, and an ultimate acquittal. There followed in short order a presidential election that took a month for the Supreme Court to resolve; the terrorist attacks of 9/11; the war in Afghanistan; the war in Iraq; the Southeast Asian tsunami; Katrina; the historic election of 2008; and the most severe worldwide economic crisis since the Great Depression.

There was another thing that even the most experienced journalist could never have told me: how much I would come to love it.

I hadn't given a single thought to journalism as a profession until I was in my mid-twenties, and then it came up in an offhand way. I was clerking for Justice Powell at the Supreme Court and working on a criminal case in which a newspaper reporter claimed a constitutional right to cover a pretrial court hearing in Rochester, New York. The case was a difficult one, with several different theories argued by both sides. After argument, when the Court met in conference and took a preliminary vote, it was a tentative 5–4 vote for the result, but there was no real agreement on the rationale for that result.

As I sat with Justice Powell in his office one day working on the separate opinion that he'd decided to file, he paused to step back and reflect for a few minutes on journalists and what they do. As he saw it, we had to have robust journalism for our democracy to work at all. There was no other way for the people to learn what they needed to know to decide on the right course for their town, their state, or ultimately their country. But without missing a beat, Justice Powell volunteered that as much as he thought of journalists in the abstract, he personally "could never do what journalists do." I asked him why. He looked at me thoughtfully and said in his gentle Virginia drawl: "Why, David. Journalists every day have to pry into people's private lives, asking questions that are really nobody's business. And, at least sometimes, they even misrepresent who they are."

No, this wasn't something that Justice Powell felt that he could ever do.

Until then, there'd been no reason for me to think about what journalism was all about. I was, after all, looking forward to a career practicing law. But, like so many other things Justice Powell said to me during that year I spent with him, it made a lasting impression. He was a decent, thoughtful, and wise man. He'd experienced things that few, if any, had experienced: working as a young colonel in the top secret Ultra Project that broke the German code in World War II; running a major Richmond law firm that bore his name; leading the Richmond School Board through the desegregation conflicts of the 1950s; working with John D. Rockefeller in restoring Colonial Williamsburg; and serving as president of the American Bar Association in the 1960s. You wanted to pay attention to whatever he had to say, even if it didn't seem all that relevant to you at the time.

I went on to join Wilmer, Cutler & Pickering, a leading Washington law firm where I worked both in Washington and in London, first as an associate and then as a partner. By the early 1990s, I was established and headed in the direction I had imagined my career would go when I spent my year with Justice Powell: Washington law, with hopes of some form of public service down the road. Then I was taken in an entirely different direction; I was asked to come to New York to be the general counsel for Capital Cities, the parent company of ABC. Now, being general counsel was certainly not the same as being a journalist. But as my staff and I advised ABC News on legal issues and defended the organization when it was challenged in court, I encountered for the first time the sorts of issues that journalists confront every day. I went on to become head of the ABC Television Network overall, and my exposure to journalism expanded, with ABC News reporting directly to me.

During these years, the legendary Roone Arledge was in charge of ABC News. Roone had taken over in 1977 at a time when some people sarcastically referred to ABC as the "fourth out of three" broadcast news divisions. Long before he'd gone to news, Roone had built ABC Sports into a powerhouse, creating *Monday Night Football* and *Wide World of Sports*. Although Roone Arledge didn't create the Olympics, he was the one who transformed coverage of the games into the extravaganza we know today. When Leonard Goldenson, the pioneering head of ABC, decided to make ABC News competitive, he turned to Roone and gave him what amounted to a blank check. Roone cashed that check (and then some) and used it to put together an amazing stable of top news talent and produce pathbreaking programs such as *Nightline*, *This Week with David Brinkley*, and *Primetime Live*.

Roone was legendary not only for his creativity but also for some eccentricities in his management style. When he was wooing talent, he was more charming than anyone in the business. He had a wonderful smile, an impish sense of humor, and a love of life as great as his talent. He was also notoriously elusive. For several years when he ran both ABC Sports and ABC News, he kept offices in both places, and his subordinates swore it was so that it would always appear he was in his "other" office. He simply would not return telephone calls—from outsiders, from his own stars, or even from his bosses. You could never reach Roone at home at night. He had an outside answering service that took a message it said it would pass along to Roone—but you just didn't hear back. It was only years later, after Roone passed away in 2002, that one of his longtime friends came up to me at his wake and offered an explanation. As he put it, "Roone always figured that if you were calling him, it was about your problem. Roone didn't want to hear about your problem; he wanted you to deal with his."

Roone was unique as a creator and a showman. He also came along at just the right time in history. Roone was made for expansion and big ideas without the need for recognizing limits of any sort—and most particularly not financial limits. The 1960s, '70s, and '80s gave him the environment he needed to demonstrate all of his talents—first in sports and then in news. Roone accomplished what Leonard Goldenson had asked: he built ABC into the biggest and proudest of the three network news divisions.

And then everything changed. In 1995, NBC News regained the lead in the morning with its *Today* show. The next year, its *Nightly News* took over first place in the evening news race from *World News Tonight with Peter Jennings*. The same year, 1996, David Brinkley retired and, with Tim Russert at the helm, NBC's *Meet the Press* began to beat ABC on Sunday morning as well.

At the time, all this seemed cataclysmic. But for those at ABC News it partially masked a much more profound, long-term shift: the rise of cable news. CNN had made a name for itself in 1991 during the Gulf War. That was one thing. CNN had some success in its own universe but through the early 1990s it wasn't really seen as much of a competitor to the traditional broadcast network news divisions. Then, in 1996, the television news world changed forever with the start of MSNBC (backed by NBC and Microsoft) and Fox News (backed by Rupert Murdoch and News Corporation). And all of a sudden, whether we fully realized it at the time or not, we were on our way from a world dominated by three television news organizations to one with an almost unlimited number of news providers. And with that transformation would come some prominent news providers who regularly mix opinion with their news reporting and overtly embrace partisan positions. The world of television news had truly and fundamentally changed.

In the midst of all this, Roone's contract was drawing to an end. His long-term deal had him stepping aside as early as 1997 and no later than mid-1998 and moving over to be a consultant to the company. I was Roone's immediate boss; Bob Iger was president of the company (which the Walt Disney Company had bought the year before) and my boss. Bob and I knew that we had to find a successor to Roone, someone who would keep the best of what Roone had created but also fundamentally transform ABC News to deal with the changing needs and possibilities of the new media world. I spent months looking within the news division and outside the company, but I couldn't find the person we thought was right for the job.

So I volunteered. Bob may not have thought we'd end up here when we first started looking for Roone's successor, but neither had I. We'd both known that things were shakier behind the scenes at ABC News than the outside world knew. It wasn't only that running a news organization had never been on my list of things that I aspired to do; following a legend didn't seem like a wise career move. But I cared deeply about news and had enjoyed the time I'd spent working with the journalists at ABC. I knew I'd be a known quantity to many at ABC News, including to Roone. I thought I might at least oversee an orderly transition, get us over some of the challenges I knew were ahead, and pass it off to someone else. And so, on March 6, 1997, Bob Iger appointed me president of ABC News.

That first day on the job, I began with the editorial meeting that we held every morning throughout my time at ABC News. Back then, the meeting was held at 9:45 in an interior conference room near Roone's office with muted lights, gray fabric on the walls, and a long mahogany table that had been the ABC board table before Capital Cities had bought the network. At every editorial meeting, there was a recap from the various bureaus of what we knew had happened overnight or was happening that day, followed by descriptions of what the various programs were planning. As I recall, that March morning in 1997 there wasn't really much news to report. The biggest pending issue was President Clinton's ban on cloning research imposed the week before. In the absence of major news, a good part of the meeting was devoted to two things: Roone's introducing me to the troops and his berating *World News Tonight* for slipping so far in the ratings that it was being seriously threatened by the third-place *CBS Evening News*. And with that, we were off and running.

It hadn't been the plan, but I was about to have the most rewarding experience of my professional life. For just short of fourteen years, I got to work with exceptionally intelligent, curious, and dedicated people. We were paid to find things out that no one else knew but that everyone wanted to know. Then we took our reporting and used every bit of creativity and intelligence we could muster to present it to our audiences in ways that made it understandable, compelling, and something they could take with them and apply to improve their lives. And on our good days, when things were going just right, we had the chance to make the world a bit better. What could beat that?

It's fashionable these days to criticize the press. Politicians do it, men and women on the street do it, media commentators do it, and members of my own family do it. And there's plenty to be critical of. But when I read or heard much of the criticism during the time I was running ABC News, I often thought it would be better if those doing the judging had had some of the same experiences I had—if they had been able to come into an organization like ABC News and live with it, learning how it really works, discovering its strengths and its weaknesses, and getting some sense of the quality and dedication of the people who make up a great news organization. I don't pretend that this would eliminate the criticism. But if we are going to hope for improvements in our news media, a good starting point is gaining a deeper understanding of how major news organizations actually work, as seen from the inside.

We changed a lot of things while I was at ABC News. One of the smaller, but important, changes was to have the human resources department interview people who were leaving the company, so-called exit interviews, which have become routine in many companies. The theory is that when employees walk out the door, it's a good time to get a more honest assessment from them about the company, the people, and what could be improved. I didn't have the illusion that even about-to-be ex-employees would be completely honest. Who among us can ever say with certainty that we're being "completely honest," even with ourselves? But at least there's a chance of being more honest than we can be while we're in the job.

And that's what this book is. My own exit interview. Like most such assessments, it's a mixture of stories and lessons learned.

It's been more than thirty years now since that discussion with Justice Powell, and I suppose in my own way I'm still seeking to answer his questions—about what journalists really do and about whether they can do their jobs well and do the right thing at the same time. It's ironic that part of my answer lies in what the justice ultimately decided to do in *Gannett v. DePasquale*, that case from Rochester where the newspaper reporter wanted to be let in to cover a pretrial hearing and the judge was keeping her out.

As he did in other areas of the law, Justice Powell rejected the extremes of saying that reporters always had the right to attend pretrial proceedings or that they never did. Powell preferred to lay out general principles and leave it to the lower courts to do rough justice in individual cases. With time, I came to see the wisdom of leaving some play in the joints of justice to accommodate the imperfections of humans and the institutions they create. So, in the *DePasquale* case, Justice Powell agreed with the majority that in this particular case the court was right to keep the reporter out, but he wrote separately to say that there were principles underlying the First Amendment that might mean, in some future case with different facts, that the court would have to let a reporter in to cover a pretrial hearing. This just didn't happen to be, for him, that case.

Journalists are people, and news organizations are human institutions. They suffer from the imperfections that Justice Powell sought to provide for in the judgments that he rendered. But part of what I'd say to the justice today is an important thing that I took away from my time at

ABC News: There are people, many people, working in the major news organizations who come to work every day devoted to the mission of trying to get it right, trying to find out as much of the truth as they can about things that matter to people, and trying to find it out when others would rather it be kept secret.

Do some journalists sometimes go too far? You bet. Do some journalists sometimes misrepresent themselves when they ought not? Sadly, yes. Is it impossible really to get at the "whole truth" on any given story, on any given day? Surely. But it's a mistake and it's wrong to take the missteps of a few and make them the norm for the many. I got to see many journalists do wonderful work—original, important work. And even if they sometimes fall short, these dedicated men and women strive every day to overcome their challenges and imperfections. They talk at length, and sometimes heatedly, in the newsroom about difficult questions like the line between news and entertainment, and the dangers of letting bias seep into their work, and the proper role of journalism in reporting during times of war. They struggle to come up with answers to such questions— not answers in the pure, idealized form of the academic, but answers that inform the minute-to-minute reporting that is today's journalism.

I'd also tell the justice about how the obstacles to doing truly good work have grown for journalists in recent years. Strong journalism requires money, and money has gotten harder to come by as audiences have splintered. This is something I dealt with throughout my time at ABC News. Even the great news organizations simply don't have the same resources that they had a decade or two ago. They've had to make difficult decisions about how to deploy those resources to make sure that the best of what they do is preserved; they've had to choose between the essential and the merely desirable. Nobody likes it, but anyone who truly cares about the value of sound news reporting for our country has to address the economics without flinching. And that's often not pretty.

Finally, I'd tell Justice Powell that he was entirely right about how important good journalism is for our democracy, but that the quality of that journalism doesn't depend only on the journalists doing the work. It also depends on the people they're doing the work for. I came to understand that the public in the end will get the journalism it asks for—that it demands. Even the most serious journalists pay attention to whether they are holding people's attention. If people want more substantive journalism and less coverage of celebrity scandal, then the answer isn't to bemoan the state of journalism today, but to seek out the great, substantive work being done and turn off the latest juicy tabloid tidbit.

The world of journalism I came to know is a broad and diverse one. It has many examples of wonderful, uplifting work, and more than a few things that can make you cringe or even get angry. You have to be very careful about generalizing about the state of journalism today. But most people agree that, whatever they think of journalism overall, they'd like it to get stronger and more credible. We have it within our collective power to improve the news reporting we're getting by demanding it and rewarding it. We're a country of media critics voting every day for the journalism we want—voting by deciding what journalism will receive our time and attention. If we're going to have an informed country of voters, then we need an informed country of media critics to help us get there.

# 1 | My Sister, Peter Jennings, and Lady Diana

PETER JENNINGS: When you first heard the news today, did you think it was going to be as big a story as it's turned out to be all over the world?
DIANE SAWYER: Yes.
BARBARA WALTERS: Oh, yes.
—ABC News special, Diana, Princess of Wales: The Royal Tragedy, August 31, 1997

It was just after 11:00 on a Saturday night, and Peter Jennings was on the phone. I took the call in the middle of the ABC newsroom while we were broadcasting a special report live to the full network. I was off camera twenty feet from the anchor who was reporting the story, so I had to keep my voice down.

Peter got right to the point. "David," he said, "I've caught up with the coverage, and I understand Princess Diana has died."

I confirmed this was true.

"I also hear that you're thinking about airing a prime-time program on Diana tomorrow night, which is your call."

I confirmed that I had, indeed, ordered up such a special.

"As I said, that's your call, but I have to tell you that if you go ahead, you will never be taken seriously as the president of ABC News. This woman was not important enough for an hour in prime time."

Peter could be *very* emphatic. He didn't raise his voice, but you had no doubt about how strongly he felt or how certain he was that he was right. What he said stopped me cold. Here was our principal anchor, a man with decades of experience and a reputation for journalistic excellence, a man I deeply respected, telling me that I was categorically wrong in my first big news call.

I took a deep breath and paused. Peter was drawing on his wealth of experience in covering major news stories. At that point, I didn't have anything to compare. I'd lived a life outside journalism, and so I quickly searched for something, anything from my own experience that might help me respond. The stakes were high—for the network and for me personally. My mind went immediately to my sister Rebecca.

"Peter," I said, "you're right that Diana was not a head of state; she didn't command armies. But I have a sister in Ann Arbor, Michigan, who never reads the tabloids, but she's followed every detail of Diana's life from the moment she became engaged to Prince Charles. I think there are a lot of people around the country who feel the same."

Peter's response was immediate and not at all subtle: "I said that it's your call to make, and it is. But don't ask me to have anything to do with the special." With that, the conversation was over.

It was just over five months since I'd stepped in as ABC News president, and this was my baptism into the world of breaking news coverage. It began, as it typically does, with a call from out of the blue. It was Saturday afternoon of Labor Day weekend, the end of the summer of 1997. I was at home with my family. No special plans; just errands and chores and playing in the yard. A line connecting directly with the office had been installed on my home phone, so when we saw that line lit up, we all knew it was work.

The weekend-duty person on the news desk was on the other end of the line. There were reports, the desk said, that Princess Diana had been in some sort of car accident in Paris. There weren't many specifics at that point, but they thought I ought to know. Our weekend anchor, Kevin Newman, was about to interrupt network programming with a special report.

I turned on the TV to watch Kevin, then began switching back and forth between CNN and ABC to glean whatever facts I could. The first reports were all over the map, as they usually are when news is breaking: the princess was not injured, but her companion Dodi Fayed was; the princess was injured after all, but it wasn't serious; Dodi Fayed's injuries were serious; Diana's injuries might be to the head.

For years nearly everyone in the media had been following Diana's activities, most recently her charitable work and her new romance. Dodi Fayed was a very interesting figure in his own right. He was the son of the Egyptian billionaire who owned the Harrods department store in London and the Hotel Ritz in Paris. His mother was the sister of the international arms dealer Adnan Khashoggi. Born in Egypt, Dodi had attended Sandhurst military academy in England and had produced *Chariots of Fire* and *Hook*, among other films. Still, it was his romance with Diana in the summer of 1997 that put him on the map for most of us.

After about an hour, the story was that Fayed had died in the accident and Diana had suffered an injury to her thigh. That struck me as oddly specific and yet not informative. That's when I told my wife, Sherrie, I had a hunch that Diana was dead but that officials were holding the information. Sadly, one of the first lessons I learned about covering breaking news is that what you hear from the official spokespeople often cannot be trusted—either because they don't really know what's happening or because their job is to try to shape your coverage to their benefit. I got into my car and drove the thirty minutes to the newsroom.

By the time I reached ABC News headquarters on the Upper West Side of Manhattan, it was early evening. I went straight to the newsroom, which was combined with TV-3, the studio where Peter Jennings broadcast *World News Tonight* every weekday. But this wasn't a weekday, and both Peter and Roone Arledge, now the chairman of ABC News, were out of town, enjoying the holiday.

Already, the reduced weekend crew on the desk had been beefed up. Colleagues were on their computers and working the telephones on both the foreign and the domestic desks gathering whatever tidbits of news they could and lining up correspondents in the field and people to interview on the air. Whatever they got they fed to Kevin for his periodic special reports to the network.

The first thing I did was ask for a briefing on who we had in Paris and London. Our normal staff in London numbered about a hundred people, but we had only a handful of people assigned to Paris. And it was, after all, the middle of Saturday night in Europe. The first people we could get on the air were our ABC News Radio producer in Paris, Barbara Giudice, and our veteran correspondent Mike Lee in London. They were doing a fine job working with Kevin for his special reports, but we needed to move as many people into position as quickly as we could. We also had

Robert Krulwich, Bill Redeker, and Beth Nissen at headquarters in New York to do more reporting, relying in part on the video we had of Diana in our archives.

We still didn't have definitive word on Diana's condition. By 7:30, we were reporting that Dodi Fayed and the chauffeur had both been killed in the crash and that Diana was "in serious condition." Guided by Barbara Giudice's reporting from Paris, we were also focusing on the possible role of the paparazzi pursuing Diana and Dodi's car that night.

Beyond planning the basic news coverage, I knew I needed to get Phyllis McGrady on board. Phyllis was as talented and experienced a producer as we had at ABC News. She'd begun her career producing a daily news and political talk show in Washington, D.C., in the mid-1970s. In 1977, when she was still in her twenties, she came to produce for *Good Morning America* in New York. After a short tour at NBC News, she returned to ABC to produce for *World News Tonight* in Chicago and then came back to *GMA* in New York. She took over *GMA* as executive producer when she was just thirty-four. From there, she went on to produce Barbara Walters's specials and to create prime-time news programs such as *Primetime Live* and *Turning Point*, in addition to many prizewinning documentaries. In short, Phyllis knew "long-form" news programming (typically prime-time programs at least an hour long) better than anyone. I called and asked Phyllis to come in and start putting together a prime-time special that we'd air the next night if it turned out that Princess Diana was dead.

At 7:45, Kevin was back on the air reporting that Diana was "said to be in intensive care at the Salpêtrière Hospital in Paris. We don't know precisely her condition at this hour. We have had reports from French press agencies that she has a concussion, at least, a broken arm, serious injuries."

We included in Kevin's report a live two-way conversation with Mike Lee in London, as well as some video of Princess Diana talking about how aggressively the press had been pursuing her and her two sons wherever they went.

It wasn't until 9:45 that evening that we received official word Diana had indeed passed away, the result of injuries sustained in a traffic accident in the Pont de l'Alma tunnel on the northern bank of the Seine. The announcement came from the French minister of the interior, not from the palace. Kevin Newman went on air immediately to tell our audience, and we stayed on continuously, without commercial interruption, for several hours after that.

As with our prior reports, we relied on Barbara Giudice in Paris, Mike Lee in London, and video we had in our archives of Princess Diana. But we also had Barbara Walters on the telephone from Southampton, where she was vacationing. As happened so many times during my tenure, when there was breaking news, Barbara was one of the first people on the telephone to the newsroom offering to report—from wherever she was at the time. Barbara had spent time with Diana on many occasions and brought to the story a more intimate feel the way she does so well.

That night we also relied heavily on our longtime partner, the BBC, taking substantial portions of its live coverage. We had reports from Robert Krulwich on the paparazzi, from Beth Nissen on the life of Diana, from Bill Redeker about the circumstances surrounding the crash, and from John Donvan, our White House correspondent, who was on Martha's Vineyard with a vacationing president Clinton.

And so, from a standing start, we put together several hours of nonstop television reporting, using whatever and whoever was available to us. Kevin did a strong job weaving together what could have been a lot of unconnected pieces into a narrative that began to make sense out of a story that came out of the blue. Our reporters in the field did first-rate work. But we'd need more support to sustain what we all knew would be extended coverage over the next few days. We quickly inventoried the possibilities and decided to send Aaron Brown to Paris and Bill Ritter to London and to keep John Donvan, Bill Redeker, and Kevin Newman in the States to report from here. And of course we were spending every bit as much time getting further details about the story—about the crash, about the medical treatment, and about the royal family's reaction.

This was it. My first big breaking news story, and I was in the middle of it. I felt that adrenaline rush you get when the story is big, you're on the air, you don't know where it's going, and you're holding on for dear life just trying to get it right. Until I was responsible for the decisions, I'd had no idea how difficult, exhilarating, and satisfying breaking news could be. I thought we'd done well to that point. Looking forward, we had a lot of material in our archives from the extensive reporting on Diana we'd done over the years, we had our partnership with the BBC, we had our own people like Barbara Walters and Diane Sawyer who'd known the princess personally, and we were deploying all the assets of ABC News to report on how everyone was reacting. We were on our way to producing a prime-time special drawing on all that reporting and video. It may have been my first time, but I felt as though we'd gotten off to a pretty strong start.

And that's when the call came in from Peter.

He hadn't seen our coverage, but he was sure that we weren't off to a good start at all if we were planning on doing a prime-time special on the life and death of Princess Diana. Whether right or wrong, he had an important point to make, and I appreciated it at the time, even if I didn't love hearing it. The evening hours (between 8:00 and 11:00 p.m. on the East and West Coasts, 7:00 and 10:00 in the central time zone) have historically been reserved by the networks for entertainment shows. This is when the largest audiences are watching; it's when most of the money is made. It's the land of sitcoms, dramas, and what's called "reality."

There are, of course, a handful of news programs produced regularly for prime time. Programs such as *20/20* and *60 Minutes*. But these are there in large part to support the network prime-time schedule by bringing in audiences and revenue, just like the entertainment shows.

True news specials in prime time are different from any other news program. At their best, they're a blend of factual reporting and powerful narrative married to great visuals. They're "news" and therefore have to meet the highest standards of vetting. But they also have to be every bit as compelling as a drama or a film. They need to have great video, great editing, great writing, and most of all great storytelling. To pull all this together in a single day is a huge effort. That's why I asked Phyllis to assemble her team and start work even before we knew for sure that Princess Diana had died. We needed to bring in our most talented long-form news producers and editors, and we needed immediately to start gathering the reporting and the video we would need to tell the story.

During my tenure, we mainly did prime-time breaking news specials for natural disasters or man-made catastrophes. Years after the death of Princess Diana, we did prime-time specials when President Reagan and Pope John Paul II passed away. But, as Peter pointed out forcefully that night, the princess was not a head of state or a pope. Until that August night in 1997, the closest thing to the death of a universally popular British former princess had been the death of "the King," Elvis Presley, twenty years earlier—long before I came to ABC News.

The night Elvis died, ABC and NBC led their evening broadcasts with the news. CBS didn't. It gave the Elvis story seventy seconds following a long piece on the Panama Canal. And it drew the smallest audience for the *CBS Evening News* in years. Both ABC and NBC also ran thirty-minute special programs in late night after the local news. But even with a story as big as the death of Elvis, the networks didn't do prime-time specials the day of the event.

Peter's intense reaction to my decision had to do not only with the role of network news in prime time but also with Peter's role at ABC News and, frankly, his doubts about me. I'd been there less than six months. I'd come from outside the news division—even outside journalism altogether. I hadn't practiced law for years, but people still referred to me as a corporate lawyer. And they didn't mean it as a compliment. In their eyes, being a lawyer clearly meant that I lacked creativity or courage—or both. They thought that coming from "the corporation" must mean that I cared more about making a profit than about journalism. And that drive for profit meant that I'd push for more entertainment and less news coming out of ABC News.

This tension between profit and journalism was something I heard about and struggled with often at ABC News. Veteran TV journalists love to look back on a "golden age," when news divisions weren't expected to make a profit. This meant, they say, that people working in news divisions didn't need to be concerned with things such as ratings and costs and revenue. They usually overlook, however, that the networks' original investing to build news divisions was motivated by what was good for the network business, not what was good for journalism. From the beginning, television networks have been a mix—sometimes an uneasy mix—of entertainment and news. In the early days of TV, Washington in effect required that the networks broadcast news because the federal government periodically reviewed the worthiness of companies as licensees of the airwaves. An important part of that demonstration of good citizenship was showing a commitment to news coverage. By being good citizens and investing in news programs that aired in limited time periods, the networks were left free to make a good deal of money from all those entertainment programs.

But time and the move to deregulate in the 1980s wore away the public service obligations imposed on television licensees. News divisions have had to find other ways to prove their value to the companies that own them. They do this by contributing to the positive reputation of the companies overall and, yes, by providing some reasonable return on investment to shareholders. In other words, by making some money for the company.

As I was to learn fairly quickly, an important part of my job was to explain to my fellow journalists that we were after all a business—and therefore responsible for the costs we incurred and the revenues we brought in. If we truly cared about the journalism, then we had to make sure we had the resources to do the work—to deploy our reporters around the world and to invest in their spending extended periods of time digging out the facts. Addressing the economics was an essential part of doing the reporting.

Every bit as important, my job was to remind the corporation from time to time that we were much more than a business, that we owed it to the people we served to cover the news even when it was not, at least in the short term, maximizing profit. It's not an easy balance to strike.

Peter Jennings, though, was not about striking a balance. He was a journalist through and through. He was a leader of ABC News. He'd come from Canada when he was only twenty-six years old and by the time he was twenty-seven was the anchor of the ABC evening news. Critics at the time took issue with his lack of experience; he was, after all, competing with Walter Cronkite on CBS and Chet Huntley and David Brinkley on NBC. When he left the anchor chair after three years, he decided to do something about that lack of experience. He became a foreign correspondent and moved to Beirut, where he founded ABC's Middle East bureau. He immersed himself in the rich and complicated stories he found in that part of the world and distinguished himself with powerful reporting, including unparalleled coverage of the terror attacks that killed eleven Israeli athletes at the 1972 Munich Olympics. By the time he returned to co-anchor the evening news for ABC (with Frank Reynolds and Max Robinson) in 1978, Peter had covered pretty much every major international event for ten years. When I got there, he had been the sole anchor of *World News Tonight* for fourteen years. It's no wonder that he thought his judgment would be better than mine about the importance of a story about a British princess and a prominent Egyptian who'd lost their lives in a tunnel in Paris.

From the moment we announced that I would be taking over ABC News, Peter tested my bona fides. He was always direct with me. We had lunch soon after my appointment in one of the private executive dining rooms on the twenty-second floor of the Capital Cities/ABC headquarters on West 66th Street. After a few pleasantries, Peter got to the point. As he put it, "People at ABC News wonder whether you're really committed to what we do. Do you really want to make ABC News better, or are you just 'playing through' on the way to a higher corporate job?"

I tried my best to assure him that I was fully committed to ABC News. That I had no thought of moving up in the corporate hierarchy. Actually, I'd had a higher position (at least in the org chart) when I was the head of the network. I'd chosen to take a step down rather than up. But both of us knew that the real question wasn't about what I said; it was about what I was going to do. Peter was making it plain that I would have to prove myself—to him and to others.

Peter tested me for several years. Sometimes it showed up in a disagreement over a particular correspondent's assignment, sometimes over what we covered, and sometimes over how we covered major stories. But over time, as I gained experience in journalism and Peter and I gained experience working with each other, we came to understand each other well and to respect one another deeply. By the time his tragic illness struck, we had become close. As Peter often said, we agreed on all the big things, even if we still disagreed from time to time on some of the small ones.

But on this night in August 1997, Peter and I were just at the very beginning of our relationship. I was still the doubted and untested newcomer dealing with my first truly big news story—the death of a wildly popular princess. And I had Peter Jennings, one of the all-time greats in television journalism, telling me that I was making a terrible mistake—one that would literally put in jeopardy whatever career I might have thought I could enjoy at ABC News. I was clearly, in Peter's eyes, failing my first big test.

And I hadn't been able to reach Roone Arledge, so I really had no one to consult about the call I was making. Bob Iger and I had agreed that there should be some suitable transition period with Roone—we thought about three months. But Roone wasn't ready to step aside that quickly, and so three months turned into fifteen months, during which Roone was the chairman and I was the president, reporting to him. During this time, I knew that the health of ABC News depended on everyone's having a single boss. Roone was that boss. If we had disagreements, they were always in private. Roone deserved no less. I had great respect for him and for his remarkable career, and I owed it to him and to the troops to demonstrate that respect as his retirement approached.

As with Peter, my relationship with Roone would change with time. After he stepped down, he remained a consultant to ABC. I made a point of having a weekly lunch with Roone, partly out of respect and partly because I knew I could benefit from his wisdom and experience. We started these at his regular table buried in the back of Café des Artistes across West 67th Street from ABC News headquarters. As Roone became more ill with the bone cancer that would eventually take his life, we moved to restaurants that had no stairs so that it would be easier for him to get in and out. And eventually, the lunches moved to his apartment, where he would greet me in his wheelchair.

I learned a good deal from those weekly lunches. I learned that in the early days of ABC Sports he'd bought yellow sports jackets for all the young men (and they were all men at that point) and insisted they wear them so that they would have a sense of pride that they were part of ABC Sports. I learned of the hostility Roone had felt from staff at ABC News when he first started there. He told me how he'd wooed Diane Sawyer to leave *60 Minutes* and come to ABC News to start *Primetime Live*, but also how he'd failed to get Dan Rather to come over from CBS to anchor the ABC evening news. We talked about the disastrous pairing of Barbara Walters and Harry Reasoner on the evening news that he'd inherited and how he'd changed the entire format of the program to help Barbara save face and move on to a greater career when she stepped down. And, ironically, Roone told me more than once that he didn't believe that as great as his time in news had been, he'd be able to run ABC News in the new time of limited resources that I'd inherited. Whether he could have done it or not, I knew that he wouldn't have enjoyed it nearly as much as he had the glory days of the 1980s.

All of this came later, which was too bad, because one of the things I learned from my lunches with Roone would have helped me with Peter that August night in 1997. The fact was that the prime-time special on Princess Diana I was planning was an extension of what Roone had started at ABC News some twenty years before. Shortly after he took over, Roone had caused a stir by including in the ABC evening newscast extensive coverage of the capture of Son of Sam, the notorious serial killer who had terrorized New York City in the summer of 1977. At the time, Roone's decision was very controversial. It was seen by some journalists as a tabloid story beneath the dignity normally associated with long reports on the evening news. According to Roone, some of those journalists doing the criticizing came from within ABC News itself. Here was a showman who'd made his name in sports taking the evening newscast "downmarket." But the way Roone saw it, he needed to send a strong signal to a lagging news division—and to the world—that ABC News wouldn't hesitate to cover a big story of interest to the audience no matter what more traditional journalists might say.

When Peter laid down his marker about the Princess Diana special that Saturday night, I wasn't thinking about precedent—about what Peter had done or what Roone had done in the past. I was thinking only about our audience and what I thought it would want. I knew I didn't have much time to make a decision. If we were going to get that special ready, we couldn't stop and take a few hours to debate whether to go ahead. So I made my decision despite the strong protest of our main anchor, the face of ABC News.

After I hung up with Peter, my first thought was about who would anchor the special the next night. I knew that to get it ready, people would be "crashing" through the night and whoever I chose needed to get up to speed right away. My thoughts turned immediately to two of our most prominent and accomplished anchors, both of whom knew the story extremely well: Barbara Walters and Diane Sawyer. Was there a part of me that also relished the idea of Peter, who'd left me high and dry, having to watch Barbara and Diane do a big special in prime time that he should have had? Probably. I'm human. And so I called Phyllis McGrady and explained the situation. We agreed it would be best to ask Barbara and Diane to anchor it together. Phyllis called them despite the late hour, and they quickly agreed.

A little later in what had become a long night, Roone called in. It was now well past midnight. I explained everything—that I'd ordered up a prime-time special for the next night, that our principal anchor was refusing on principle to participate, and that Diane and Barbara were set to step in. Roone was none too pleased with Peter's reaction. Go ahead with the special, he said. And then he added this for good measure: Under no circumstances let Peter participate.

I got home well after two in the morning, but just a few hours later my home office line was ringing again. It was Peter, this time calling from his car on the way into the city. He'd read all the coverage. He'd been wrong, he said. This was a more important story than he'd realized. He wanted to be on the prime-time special. I respected Peter all the more for straightforwardly admitting he'd thought better of his initial instincts. And I felt some relief—and maybe a twinge of vindication—that Peter was after all agreeing with the call I'd made the night before.

Of course, now I had a new problem: an eager anchorman and a chairman—Roone—who'd said unequivocally that Peter shouldn't be involved.

I told Peter that of course I'd like him to co-anchor the special. Refusing him a role would have been a major statement to all of ABC News and even to the outside world. People would want to know what had happened. People would wonder about the relationship developing between the new ABC News president and the veteran anchor. But at the same time, Peter's change of heart didn't raise an issue with Roone alone. I'd already recruited Barbara and Diane to anchor. Pulling them at that point would have been an insult. They would have been, as they say in the news business, big-footed. And no one big-foots Diane Sawyer or Barbara Walters.

Finding myself in the middle between Peter Jennings, on the one hand, and Roone Arledge, Diane Sawyer, and Barbara Walters, on the other, I followed a maxim we used at my old law firm: If you can't fix it, feature it. I told Peter that if he wanted to anchor the special, he'd have to do it with Barbara and Diane. And he agreed without a murmur of objection.

My next call was to Roone to tell him that despite his caveats, I had agreed to let Peter co-anchor. I explained that Peter had agreed to do it with Diane and Barbara and that it looked as if we'd have enough material to do more than a single hour. All of this would give the special even more prominence. Roone accepted this, but I had the feeling that he would have decided otherwise. Roone saw a situation like this as an opportunity to teach an anchor a lesson. That wasn't my nature, and to be frank, my job at that point was to build a relationship with Peter. Roone had created Peter's career; I was an outsider coming in at the peak of that career.

So, on Sunday evening, August 31, 1997, ABC News aired a two-hour prime-time special titled *Diana, Princess of Wales: The Royal Tragedy*, co-anchored by Barbara Walters, Diane Sawyer, and—yes—Peter Jennings. It was early in the broadcast that Peter turned to Diane and Barbara and asked if they'd known from the start how big the story would become.

"Yes," Diane said without hesitation.

"Oh, yes," said Barbara.

Before her death, Princess Diana had been on the cover of *People* magazine twenty-nine times, more than anyone else. The Pew Research Center annual study of which news stories commanded the most interest among the public for 1997 ranked the death of Diana first, with 85 percent of Americans saying that they followed it very closely or fairly closely. As the Pew Center put it:

In an era in which virtually all Americans share very few things, the story of Princess Diana's death captivated the nation. Nearly nine in ten Americans paid attention to news of the tragedy and more than half (54%) followed the tragedy very closely. No other story this year has come close.

Modern communications have spawned an ever increasing diversity of tastes and interests and decidedly smaller audiences for everything from news stories to sit-coms. Add to this growing public cynicism and distrust, and the consequence is that there are very few things to which everyone pays attention. In fact, recent monthly news interest surveys have documented waning interest in all current events. The death of Princess Diana was one of those rare stories to upend the trends.

At the same time, the public's interest in the story of Princess Diana was not evenly balanced. There was a big difference between how interested men were and how interested women were in the story. Maybe that was reflected in my late-night conversation with Peter, in which he gave his own reaction and I responded with how I thought my sister back in Michigan would react.

> Speculation that the story of Diana drew more women than men proved right. Nearly two thirds of female respondents (64%) paid very close attention compared to 43% among men. While women consistently pay more attention to big news events than men—with the notable exception of war stories—this 21 percentage point gender gap is huge. Of the top 20 most closely watched stories in the past decade, only Jessica McClure's fate [the toddler trapped in a Texas well] provoked a gender gap even close—16 percentage points.

The main thing I took away from my initial disagreement with Peter Jennings about the Princess Diana story wasn't about who was right or wrong. There would be plenty of times to come when Peter was right and I was wrong. At least one of these had consequences far greater than whether we were devoting too much coverage to the death of a princess. Peter was much more skeptical than I about claims that Saddam Hussein had weapons of mass destruction in 2003. I wish that I'd deferred to his call then.

The important point about my disagreement with Peter over the Diana coverage was that it went to the heart of the basic tension we see in much of news coverage today between "news" and "entertainment." Often the historical importance of a subject isn't the only thing that determines how much effort or ink or video is used to cover it. Diana had been in line to be wife of the king of England, but that alone wouldn't have warranted the treatment she received throughout the media. Nor did her work with those suffering from AIDS or her efforts to ban land mines. The truth is, people were drawn to Diana whatever her historical significance. She was beautiful and glamorous—things that count when it comes to the visual medium of television. Whenever she appeared on air, your eyes were drawn to the set. She was the storybook princess whose happily-ever-after ending had somehow gone wrong. Some stories just make better TV. During my time at ABC News, we worked hard to tell important stories that didn't always have great visuals (stories about the economy or education, for example). But I learned that it was foolish simply to ignore the fact that what we see in a story is at least one of the things that influences what goes on the air and what the audience will sit still to watch.

My dispute with Peter over the Diana coverage was the first time I'd really had to think seriously about how we should decide which stories deserve the attention of the audience and which do not. How much needs to be said—how much can be said—about a former star football player accused of killing his ex-wife? Or about the untimely death of the pop star with the largest-selling album of all time? On the other hand, what if the audience really wants more coverage of stories such as these? How much should we listen to our audiences or anticipate what we think they're asking for? In the end, is "news" simply what the people want to see and hear about? Or is "news" a matter of what's historically important whether people want to see and hear it or not? Do we want those in charge of covering the news to "lead" us or to "follow" us as they make editorial decisions on what (and how much) to report?

I found myself struggling with this balance—a balance between what people *want* to hear about and what journalists think they *ought* to hear about—almost every day I ran ABC News.

There were always those taking "pure" positions on either extreme. Plenty of people took very seriously the notion that what we were doing was writing the "first rough draft of history," in the oft-repeated words of Phil Graham, who'd published and co-owned *The Washington Post*. These voices said the only thing I should consider in making news judgments was the importance of the story—and that importance should be judged within the longer-term view of history, rather than from the immediate viewpoint of what audiences might find important or interesting right now. For these people, it was wrong even to pay attention to the ratings our programs were getting.

On the other hand were those people, within both ABC and the corporation more broadly, who saw our success solely in terms of the size of the audience we attracted. It was all fine and good to talk about "history," but we were part of a for-profit corporation that had a duty to return money on the investment people had entrusted to us.

I found myself taking both sides seriously, and even agreeing with both—to a degree. I certainly agreed with those arguing that there was a difference between news and entertainment. Providing every salacious detail of a celebrity's misdeeds may be interesting to some in the audience, but it doesn't inform. It doesn't convey any particular truth about the situation or about the human condition. It simply entertains. I hadn't come to ABC News to convert it into a fact-based arm of the entertainment division. I also came to doubt that it would work even I'd wanted to.

There was also the wonderful surprise we got from time to time when we did something because it was important even though we didn't expect a big audience and the American people came to us anyway. Several times this response came from documentaries that Peter or Diane simply insisted on doing. Not all of them worked in terms of ratings, but several did—to our delight.

Take, for example, Diane Sawyer's documentary on poverty in Appalachia. This one-hour documentary arose from a long-standing curiosity Diane had about some of the outcasts who live among us in the most affluent country in the world's history. Diane has done several documentaries on topics such as women in prison and prostitution in America. She was particularly interested in exploring poverty in places you'd never expect to find it. She began in 2007 with an hour on Camden, New Jersey, telling the stories of children growing up in the most difficult circumstances only a few miles away from wealthy Philadelphia suburbs.

Then came "A Hidden America: Children of the Mountains." Diane and her team spent two years going to Appalachia and reporting the stories of families struggling to live their lives, take care of their families, and educate themselves in one of the poorest areas in America. It probably wasn't an accident that Diane had a particular feel for this part of the country, having grown up in nearby Kentucky. We did this documentary because it was worthwhile and, as important, Diane really wanted to do it. When we aired it in February 2009, it drew an audience of 10.9 million, the biggest audience for *20/20* on Friday night that we'd had in nearly five years.

Getting 10.9 million people to sit still for an hour watching a program on poverty was a source of great pride. But in all honesty, things like Diane's special are the exception rather than the rule. Diane Sawyer is unique in her ability to attract and hold an audience for a subject that the audience doesn't otherwise know it's interested in. She herself went up into the Appalachian hills to spend time with the people in their houses and down into the coal mines where they worked and into the schools where children were struggling to improve their lives. Diane's special mixed strong reporting with great writing, beautiful visuals, outstanding editing, and a memorable soundtrack. And in part because the visuals and the music were so effective, and in part because she's Diane Sawyer, the special got especially extensive promotion from the network. In short, she and her team brought all the skills of their trade to bear, and it worked.

So, as I participated in the debate within ABC News about the right balance between substance and ratings, I saw that simply going for the ratings wasn't for us. But I also had real difficulties with those who insisted, on the other extreme, that ratings shouldn't matter. It might sound good, but I didn't find myself able to run a news division that way. And in fact, I came to doubt that the people taking such extreme positions really meant what they said.

Early in my tenure, I hosted a series of lunches with colleagues to talk about the business, what we were doing, and where we could improve. I did this in part to learn the organization in all of its many facets and to get a sense of what people thought about where we were and where we should be heading. I also did it to begin communicating with people throughout ABC News about what I was thinking, about what I valued, and about where I wanted to take the news division. We purposely included a wide range of people—diverse both in terms of what they did and in their seniority. Toward the end of one of these lunches, a senior anchor proudly announced to the group, "I just don't care about ratings, and I don't think you should either." I thought as he said it that this view would make him popular with a good portion of the newsroom. But I didn't think I could let him go unchallenged. So I responded, "I don't agree with you, and I don't even think you truly believe what you're saying. Anyone who doesn't care about how many people are hearing what you have to report isn't a journalist; he's just keeping a diary for himself." This didn't end the debate, but it was a position that I felt strongly about and that I felt I needed to express early and often.

As I've said, ABC News is indisputably a business. It's also more than a business, but it is a business. So is just about every other news organization of any size or significance in the country today. That means a certain number of dollars have to be coming in to sustain the journalism. That was my primary duty as president of ABC News: to sustain the journalism.

To that end, I had to be aware that ignoring the business reality over any extended period of time would literally put ABC News itself in danger. And if this were repeated throughout the news industry, it could ultimately stop big corporations from spending the hundreds of millions of dollars they spend today on reporters doing the work.

But it's more than the business reality that makes it ridiculous to say that journalists should ignore their audience. The very nature of journalism means that the size of the audience matters. People become journalists not only to tell others about things they care about but also to get people to listen to them. Whether they want to admit it or not, how many people pay attention to what they have to report matters. Believe me, when a program or story drew big numbers, just about the first people I heard from were our journalists. Few feelings are as good as knowing when everything has come together and you've done well *and* good at the same time.

My experience at ABC News taught me that it was just as wrong to let the size of the audience determine how much to cover a given story as it was to ignore the audience altogether. This leads to mixed judgments that don't always fall on one side or the other of a clear line. Some people find that in itself grounds for criticism. But if you look at most television news coverage, at least by the major networks, you see the sort of inevitable shifting of the balance.

Sometimes there's wide coverage based on the audience's interest—stories such as the death of Michael Jackson and the wedding of Prince William and Kate Middleton. Other times, you can explain the coverage only because of the importance of the story, such as the coverage of the Iraq War after the first two months or so, when the audience's interest fell off dramatically. The sad truth is that if ratings were the only thing that mattered, the networks would never cover a State of the Union address or a presidential press conference or much of a presidential election. Each of these is available to the audience on any number of outlets. None of them brings big audiences to any news outlet.

Why should network news cover stories if not for the ratings? Two reasons. First, the long-term success of any network news division depends on the audience believing that if there is something they need to know, they can learn it by watching that network's news programs. Any network that fails in that basic mission runs the risk of losing the loyalty of its audience.

Second, the people who work in the network news divisions retain a deep sense of the public trust they hold. I was struck from the day that I came to ABC News by how seriously journalists take what they do—and take their obligation to the people they serve. I've heard time and again the skepticism of some about the motives of large corporations such as Disney in owning news organizations. I've heard the speculation about ways they may be intervening in day-to-day news decisions to aid their corporate interests. But I know firsthand that at least at a company like Disney, the leadership shares with the journalists a respect for the public trust they hold. This sense of public duty may no longer have all the underpinnings it once had in federal regulation of the broadcast airwaves. But it persists to this day, and it's a mistake to try to understand what the news divisions do without taking it into account.

The mission that I came to understand and articulate for ABC News was to do the best journalism *and* get the most people to watch it. It's relatively easy to provide earnest, serious journalism to a small, niche audience; it's also not hard to go for a big audience and throw all notions of real journalism out the window. The challenge is to try to keep it right at the intersection of the two. This isn't to say that we always got the balance right. Throughout my time there, I could look at one of our programs and think to myself that we were being a little too titillating, a little too earnest, or just right.

Getting the balance right isn't just a matter of the journalists assessing the story and figuring out how popular it's likely to be. It's also up to the audience to decide what they want—what they will come to and spend time with. Ultimately, it's the people who decide what news will be covered and how it will be covered. News organizations owe it to the audience to give them choices. But these are choices and, once made, they will inevitably affect the coverage for good or for ill. For every Princess Diana (where we were right in anticipating the public's interest) or for every Appalachian special (where we got the audience to come to something it didn't know it was interested in) there was at least a story or two where we probably went overboard with the coverage.

Consider the summer of 2001. We were weeks away from 9/11, but in July and August none of us in the media knew an attack was being planned. What were we focused on? Sharks off the coast of Florida (even though an American was more likely to be hit by lightning than attacked by a shark) and the suspicious disappearance of a young Washington intern involved in an affair with the congressman for whom she worked. There was a fair amount of speculation at the time that Congressman Gary Condit either knew what had happened to Chandra Levy or at least knew more than he was telling.

Years later, it would turn out that Chandra Levy had been the victim of a predator lurking in Rock Creek Park as she jogged and that the congressman had had nothing to do with it. But at the time, we didn't know this. The biggest news quest of the summer of 2001 was, without a doubt, an interview with the congressman. After vigorous competition (both inside and outside ABC News), our own Connie Chung got the coveted interview. It was to be an hour in prime time, and the only condition was that it would have to be done "live to tape" with no editing.

With my colleagues I sat in the control room at ABC News' Times Square Studios as we watched the interview live from the California location near Congressman Condit's house where Connie did the interview. She started by going straight to the heart of the matter:

> CONNIE CHUNG: Congressman Condit, do you know what happened to Chandra Levy?
>
> REP. GARY CONDIT: No, I do not.
>
> CHUNG: Did you have anything to do with her disappearance?
>
> CONDIT: No, I didn't.
>
> CHUNG: Did you say anything or do anything that could have caused her to drop out of sight?
>
> CONDIT: You know, Chandra and I never had a cross word.
>
> CHUNG: Do you have any idea if there was anyone who wanted to harm her?
>
> CONDIT: No.
>
> CHUNG: Did you cause anyone to harm her?
>
> CONDIT: No.
>
> CHUNG: Did you kill Chandra Levy?
>
> CONDIT: I did not.

From then on, the interview went over in detail what Congressman Condit would and wouldn't say about his relationship with Ms. Levy, about his cooperation with the police investigation, about what he'd told his wife, and about whether what he'd said about President Clinton during the Monica Lewinsky story contradicted his refusal to go into details about his own relationship with an intern. Connie did a very good job. The special rated well. But we didn't learn anything about what happened to Ms. Levy. Looking back on it now, it's hard to imagine what so captivated our attention and our imagination. This was a terrible tragedy for the Levy family and a disaster for Congressman Condit's career. But did it have lasting repercussions for our republic? Did it tell us anything important or interesting about the human condition? I doubt it.

What's worse, you could fairly say that the whole furor was in large part a creation of the media itself. All of us covered it extensively that summer—every detail, every statement and counterstatement. The death of Princess Diana was going to be a big story no matter what anyone in the media decided about its coverage. No one had to tell my sister Rebecca that she should be interested; she wouldn't have listened if someone had told her not to be. I'm not sure, looking back, that the same can be said for the coverage of the Chandra Levy disappearance. Sometimes our judgment simply isn't good enough and our vision isn't clear enough to separate out what truly matters from what is simply provocative.

Judgments like these would be difficult to get right if you had all the time in the world. But you don't. When we got word about the car crash involving Princess Diana and when Peter called in to register his objections, I didn't have the luxury of stopping our coverage, making sure I'd talked with those whose advice I would have valued, and thinking about it for a while before making a decision. People around me were looking for answers and direction. If we didn't get people on planes right away, we couldn't do extensive coverage. If we didn't book satellite time, we couldn't transmit video in time. If we didn't start to pull the tape we had in the library, it would be too late to produce edited pieces. If we didn't start booking guests to talk about Diana, someone else would have booked them, and they'd have been lost to us.

I learned that's how important news judgments tend to be made—in real time and without all the information you wish you had. Sometimes you're right in those initial judgments, and sometimes you look back and wonder what you were thinking. This is something that the critics, with the luxury of time and distance, don't always appreciate.

A little over three years after Princess Diana's death, I tried to explain what I'd learned about breaking news judgments to a skeptical congressional committee investigating the networks' mistakes in the 2000 election. I'd been called before the House Commerce Committee to explain how ABC News—along with all the other networks, broadcast and cable—had blown the projections for the presidential election of 2000, not once, but *twice*. Toward the end of several long hours of questioning, I bluntly told the House committee that as much as I was going to do everything in my power not to let down our audience again the way we had on that election night, I couldn't guarantee we wouldn't make mistakes in the future. By that point, I'd learned the hard way that there is no such thing as news reporting without some risk of getting it wrong. As I put it at the time, "To manage for zero risk in journalism is not to be a journalist, it's to be a historian."

I would have plenty of opportunities to get the balance right—or not. But on that first important call about the prime-time special, I'd managed to get it right. And Peter had acknowledged as much. We went on to cover all the events surrounding Princess Diana's death for a solid week—the tussle within the royal family over its reaction, the newly minted prime minister Tony Blair's emergence as a leader when the public needed him, the first appearance of Prince Charles and Princes William and Harry, the queen's return to London from Balmoral, all leading up to the historic funeral and interment. Peter went to London to anchor our coverage of the funeral with Barbara Walters.

There was another death of importance that week. In one of the ironies of history, Mother Teresa passed from this life in Calcutta on September 5, 1997, five days after Princess Diana died. True to form, Peter Jennings came to me and asked if we could broadcast the funeral live from India. This time, Peter and I had no disagreement. There was no question in either of our minds about the importance of this woman who was also known around the world.*

And so, after anchoring the funeral of a princess in London on Satur-

*Some speculated at the time that we covered Mother Teresa's funeral because we'd covered Princess Diana's and were too embarrassed to do the latter without doing the former. But Tom Nagorski was Peter's foreign editor then, and he told me later that Peter had directed him to draw up plans for covering Mother Teresa's funeral over a year before she passed away.

day that week, Peter went on to Calcutta to anchor live coverage, beginning after midnight East Coast time, of the funeral of a saint. I'll admit that, secretly, I hoped we would distinguish ourselves by being the only ones to cover Mother Teresa and that everyone else would be covering Princess Diana alone. But CBS News and NBC News took the Mother Teresa funeral live as well. To their credit.

# 2 | In the Line of Fire: The Story of the Blue Dress

Lewinsky says she saved, apparently as a kind of souvenir, a navy blue dress with the president's semen stain on it.
                                    —Jackie Judd, on World News Tonight with Peter Jennings, January 23, 1998

I first heard Monica Lewinsky's name at dinner on a warm evening in Old Havana on January 21, 1998. Earlier that day, Pope John Paul II had become the first pope to visit Cuba since Fidel Castro came to power in 1959. I was there with the ABC News team to cover the pope's historic visit. I'd arrived in the early hours of the morning and had spent the day visiting Roberto Robaina, the Cuban foreign minister, and Ricardo Alarcón, the president of the National Assembly. Peter Jennings joined me toward the end of my meeting with Alarcón and stayed on to do an on-camera interview.

After that, my schedule was clear for the rest of the evening, so I took my time walking from the hotel to Old Havana, soaking in a bit of the city—the charming old buildings in various stages of decline or restoration, the waves crashing against the seawall along the Malecón, the 1950s American automobiles still in wide use. In Parque Central, I watched Peter broadcast World News Tonight live in front of several hundred people. He was clearly in his element, enjoying the setting and the story of the pope's visit.

After World News Tonight, I joined Cokie Roberts and some other colleagues at El Floridita, a grand old restaurant frequented by Ernest Hemingway when he lived in Cuba. We'd just ordered dinner when a call came on my cell phone, and I took the call outside so that I wouldn't disturb others in the restaurant. It was the news desk, calling to tell me some of our reporters were working on a story that could be as controversial as it was important. A young woman named Monica Lewinsky, who had worked as an intern in the White House, had supposedly confided to a close friend that she'd had an intimate relationship with the president of the United States. What's more, Michael Isikoff of *Newsweek* was either just ahead of us or just behind us on the story. He might break it at any time.

My first reaction was simple: This was crazy. How could the president of the United States have been involved with a young intern? And how could it be that we had this story when almost no one else did? I immediately turned devil's advocate, challenging the strength of the story we thought we had. I asked about the source and about the intern, and quickly concluded we didn't have nearly enough to go with. How did we know the friend was telling the truth? Did we know anything about the young woman? The lawyer in me classified this as hearsay pure and simple, not admissible in any court of law and, to my mind, not enough to report on the air. The standards for journalism weren't the same as those used in trials, but the way the story was first described to me, this wasn't a close call. We weren't going with it.

I returned to my dinner and told my companions about the call. A short time later my phone rang again. Back out on the street, I learned we had it from multiple reliable sources that Attorney General Janet Reno had formally given the Whitewater independent counsel, Ken Starr, permission to look into the young woman's claims. Now I was floored. How could it be that a young girl's conversation with her girlfriend about a supposed affair had suddenly become a legal issue deserving the attention of the attorney general and the independent counsel (who had himself been a senior official in the Reagan Justice Department and a U.S. Court of Appeals judge)? The answer was that someone was claiming that the president might have obstructed justice in an attempt to keep his relationship with Lewinsky a secret.

As I stood on that Havana street, my mind and my heart raced. Charges of a president's obstruction of justice echoed back to the articles of impeachment brought against Richard Nixon a quarter century before, something I'd followed closely during my college years. If Ken Starr had received permission to pursue this charge, then this was a serious news story that we would need to report as soon as we were sure we were right. Of course, reporting such a story would bring down the wrath of the administration, and any friends of President Clinton. Reporting the death of Princess Diana was important, but there we were one among many, doing our best to distinguish ourselves. Breaking a news story about possible wrongdoing—perhaps even criminal wrongdoing—at the highest levels of the government was something altogether different. What we reported could change the future course of government and even the course of history. And we would be out there pretty much all alone.

I made two calls from the street in Old Havana. First, I called Roone. Roone wasn't always easy to reach, but this time I got through to him quickly. I explained the situation, and he agreed that provided we were entirely confident of the sourcing, this was a story that needed to be reported. I also called Bob Iger in Los Angeles, not because I needed corporate approval, but to make sure that if we did report the story, the higher-ups didn't hear about it first from others. It wasn't just me or ABC News that might come under fire from the White House and its allies; the reputation of the Walt Disney Company could also be at stake. I owed it to Bob to make sure the company knew what might be coming; I also wanted to make sure I had his support. Like Roone, Bob recognized immediately how explosive the story could be. He was the first one I heard speculate that if true, this could shorten President Clinton's time in office. But like Roone, he supported going with the story if we were sure we were right.

I excused myself from the dinner and went back to the Hotel Habana Libre, where ABC News had taken over a suite of rooms to serve as our local headquarters. I spent the next three hours talking with my colleagues in Havana and on the phone with New York and Washington cross-examining our reporters. These were some of our most experienced, trustworthy professionals, led by the Emmy Award–winning correspondent Jackie Judd and her producer, Chris Vlasto. Unbeknownst to me, they'd been working on the story for some time but until then hadn't felt they had enough to recommend going with it. At one point, someone in New York asked whether I wanted to know the name of one of their principal sources. I quickly said, "No, there are at least two governments listening in on this conversation."

By 11:00 p.m., I was confident we had the story. The question then became how to break the news. ABC News had long followed a practice of breaking news on the "next program up," and *Nightline*, our late-night program, would be coming on the air in about thirty minutes. Roone thought we should put the story on *Nightline*, but Ted Koppel, *Nightline*'s anchor, and his producer, Tom Bettag, felt just as strongly that it was too rushed and that they should stay with the program they'd prepared all day. The *Nightline* team had worked hard on "Crossing the Divide—Eve of the Pope's Arrival in Cuba," and if we went with a live program to break the Lewinsky story, we'd have to throw out all the hard work they'd done. But of far greater concern was the fact that there just wasn't enough time to prepare a new half-hour program. If we went the live route, we'd have to rely principally on Ted's debriefing Jackie and talking with our other reporters.

Ted's reluctance was understandable: this whole thing had just come up out of nowhere, it wasn't his reporting, and it sounded like something you'd read on the cover of a tabloid at the supermarket checkout. It made me anxious, too, that the story seemed to have evolved in the short period since I'd heard about it. How might it evolve over the next hour or two? Even if it didn't fundamentally change, we needed to make sure we had carefully vetted exactly how it was reported; the wording had to be just right and had to be fully justified by what we'd been able to confirm.

Roone was still chairman of ABC (for another six months), and he would have been well within his rights to overrule Ted and Tom and order them to do the live program. But unlike Roone, I was on the scene, and at that point in his career Roone didn't like direct conflict. He might complain about what Peter was doing on *World News Tonight* or Ted was doing on *Nightline*, but he very rarely outright ordered them to change. So Roone deferred to me. I decided we would leave *Nightline* as it was and instead wait to break the news on ABC News Radio and our brand-new website, ABCNews.com, which would give us a bit more time to work on the story. I didn't want to rush our report to air and possibly make a mistake, particularly with all the difficulties of doing this from three remote locations, Havana, Washington, and New York.

As I look back on it now, Roone was probably right. The *Nightline* half hour was a well-produced feature piece that set up later coverage of the news of the pope's visit, but the Lewinsky story was real news. I learned that a good rule of thumb was, when in doubt, go with news over features. It's not that often that you have a true exclusive, and the last thing you want to do is bury it. Once we knew we had the story, we should have gone big with it, and that meant putting it on *Nightline*.

In the end neither ABC News nor *Newsweek* broke the big story we'd been competing over. It broke just after midnight in an early edition of *The Washington Post*, followed by ABC News Radio and ABCNews.com only a minute or so later. The story really took off the next morning, when we included a full report on *Good Morning America*. Sam Donaldson and George Stephanopoulos came on to talk about what we knew and what it could mean. They were the first to mention on the air impeachment as a possibility.

If anyone was ultimately responsible for getting this story going, it was probably Michael Isikoff. We'd been chasing the same sources as he was, but I had the sense that if anything, he was a bit ahead of us. Poor Michael's first story didn't appear until some time later on *Newsweek*'s AOL website.

What followed was one of the oddest and quickest turnarounds I ever saw from a group of journalists. Months had gone into preparing to cover the pope's historic visit, but with the breaking of the Lewinsky story, most of the staff of all the news organizations jettisoned their plans, packed up all their gear, and headed right home. From that point on, the pope became a secondary story. Monica Lewinsky would be the lead for the foreseeable future.

Early the next morning, Ted and Tom and I flew back on the first plane we could get, which turned out to be an empty private charter that had just dropped off two American archbishops flying in to Havana to see the pope. The three of us spent the flight trying to come to terms with the story and talking about how best to cover it. From the beginning I think all of us had the sense that this was both one of the most tawdry and one of the most potentially important stories to come along in quite some time. It raised all the questions that we'd debated at length through the years about whether a president's personal life was relevant to the public he served. Did people truly care about a man's sexual behavior? Should they? What was our responsibility when it came to reporting on things like extramarital affairs?

By the time I landed in New York, the story had moved on at a breakneck pace. Clinton had met with his cabinet, and several cabinet officers emerged from the meeting to report that the president had told them, in the words of Secretary of State Madeleine Albright, "The allegations are untrue." She was joined by Secretary of Education Richard Riley, Secretary of Commerce William Daley, and Secretary of Health and Human Services Donna Shalala, all of whom "seconded" or "thirded" what Secretary Albright had said. There was little doubt that the first line of defense for the White House was that it just hadn't happened. Period.

But while the White House was denying the allegations, Matt Drudge was reporting on his website that Lewinsky had kept a piece of clothing that she had worn during one of her encounters with the president and that it was stained with his DNA.

As soon as I got back to my office from the airport late in the afternoon of January 22, our Washington bureau chief, Robin Sproul, called. One of our colleagues had confirmed through a confidential source that Lewinsky had kept a blue dress that she believed had the president's semen on it. I was dumbfounded. This was about as distasteful a claim as I could imagine involving a public official. If we reported this and it proved wrong, we would have unfairly sullied a president and damaged our own credibility in a way that almost nothing else could. We would be reporting something that my mother wouldn't want me even talking about, much less putting on national news. But given where the story was at that point, it also had the potential of being decisive. This had quickly turned into a "he said, she said" contest between the president of the United States and a young intern. Either it had happened as she was describing it to Ken Starr's office, or she was lying and putting at risk the effectiveness of an entire administration. There didn't seem to be any middle ground.

I called the colleague who had been dealing with the source to cross-examine him about the report. I did my best to test both why the source was in a position to know about the dress and whether the source might have reason to mislead us—or even out and out lie. How much did we know about the dress—where it came from, where it was now, and why it hadn't been cleaned? Who was the person telling us this? How could he or she have known about the dress? Had he or she had access to it? Perhaps most important, why was the person coming forward? Was there some agenda here that might mean we weren't being told the truth (or at least not the whole truth)?

I talked with Robin about what she knew, I talked with our investigative team, and of course I talked with Peter. By midday on January 23, less than forty-eight hours after I'd first heard Lewinsky's name, I was satisfied that we had a second important and controversial part of the story to report. I knew we'd be opening ourselves up to a good deal of criticism, but I didn't really hesitate once I became convinced we were right. And this time I made sure we featured the news prominently.

On the January 23 edition of *World News*, in addition to carrying the president's vicarious denials through his cabinet secretaries, we reported for the first time the existence of what would become the infamous "blue dress." As I've said, we weren't the first to report the story; Matt Drudge posted it on the Internet first. But we were undeniably the first major news organization to report that there was a blue dress that could well prove who was telling the truth, the president or the intern.

Those closest to the president continued to deny that he had had any inappropriate relationship with Lewinsky. It was clear that even in private meetings Clinton wasn't hedging. As his close adviser James Carville put it on *Meet the Press* that weekend: "He's denied it to his staff, he's denied it to the news media, he's denied it to the American people and denied it to his cabinet, and denied it to his friends. Can't be any more emphatic about that."

Five days after the Lewinsky story broke and three days after we'd reported on the blue dress, the president went before cameras to declaim, with a force that could easily be taken for anger, that he "did not have sexual relations with that woman—Miss Lewinsky."

I remember standing in the control room watching him on our live special report and thinking to myself, "You better be telling the truth, because if you're not, you're digging yourself into a deep hole."

The same day that Clinton was denying a sexual relationship with Lewinsky, anonymous "acquaintances" were raising questions about her credibility. An article in *The Washington Post* on January 28 quoted some of her former friends describing her "as having a pattern of twisting facts, especially to enhance her version of her own self-image." The next day, the *Post* reported that "acquaintances paint an image of a young woman who spoke freely of her fantasies with a variety of older men in positions of influence, who read sexual meaning into the merest chance encounter."

Then members of the press began turning a critical eye on us. On January 29, *The Christian Science Monitor* asked: "Are media standards drooping? In the rush to investigate Monica Lewinsky's allegations, critics say rumor is presented as fact." In the article, Jackie Judd defended our reporting, arguing that the blue dress "could provide physical evidence of what really happened," and the ABC News senior vice president for standards, Richard Wald, said, "We have not put anything on the air that we did not verify to make sure we didn't rely on any of the interested parties." But *The Christian Science Monitor* also quoted "several media analysts" as saying that our standards had slipped. Robert Giles, the executive director of the Freedom Forum Media Studies Center in New York, a joint venture of the Gannett Foundation and Columbia, chastised us for "a lot more liberal use of unidentified sources" and complained to the paper "it was such a fast-moving story that information was put on the air without judicious checking."

A day later, CBS News directly contradicted our story. CBS reported that the FBI had tested a dress and "no DNA evidence or stains have been found on a dress that belongs to Lewinsky." And two days after that, on February 1, *The Baltimore Sun* wrote that "the stained-dress story, with its promise of DNA certainty, survived for days, included in hundreds of news accounts qualified only by the inevitable shorthand 'reportedly' . . . [By] mid-week Lewinsky's lawyer, William H. Ginsburg, was challenging the story, expressing doubt that any stained dress existed. By week's end, the stain was fading. CBS News, citing sources, reported late Thursday that FBI tests on dresses taken from Lewinsky's apartment found no semen."

Exclusives in news are the gold standard. When you're telling people important things that no one else knows, you feel you're making a difference and, yes, getting credit for it. This is the way reputations are made—for news organizations as well as for reporters. The story of the blue dress taught me a funny thing about exclusives and it is this: They start to make you nervous when they remain exclusive for very long. When we reported on Lewinsky's blue dress, I fully expected others would match the story within days, if not hours. But that's not what happened. Other news organizations talked about the dress, but usually based on our reporting or what they said Ken Starr was investigating. They didn't claim to have verified our story independently.

For six months—from the end of January through most of July—no one either advanced or confirmed the story of the blue dress. But that didn't stop what seemed to be an endless stream of people from going on cable news channels to speculate about it—whether it existed, what it might show, and what the whole story said about the sad state of American journalism today. As Geraldo Rivera proclaimed on *Rivera Live* on July 8, "There is, ladies and gentlemen, absolutely no possibility that a so-called semen-stained dress exists."

The next month, Steven Brill, the founder of CourtTV and *The American Lawyer*, launched his new magazine, *Brill's Content*. The cover story for the August issue was "Pressgate," an article by Brill himself going through the early reporting on Lewinsky and excoriating the press—print and television—for what he saw as a shocking failure to do its job. Whether it was relying on Ken Starr's prosecutor's office, falling for an elaborate plan by a conservative book agent to get an anti-Clinton book written, or just generally resorting to unsubstantiated innuendo, Brill characterized "the media's performance" as "a true scandal, a true example of an institution being corrupted to its core."

None of this was helped by the fact that on June 7, CNN had aired an extremely controversial report on an entirely unrelated subject that was now raising other questions about the trustworthiness of television news. Dubbed Operation Tailwind, the report claimed that U.S. forces had used sarin nerve gas on enemy troops in Laos in 1970. The report had been based on various U.S. military sources, and it came after eight months of work. The problem was that it turned out to be wrong. The U.S. government—and particularly the military—immediately condemned the report, which triggered an investigation by CNN of its own reporting. As a result, it issued a complete and extensive retraction on July 17.

All in all, the spring and summer of 1998 were not good times for TV news. If Watergate was a presidential scandal that brought respect and prestige for the press, Lewinsky was a presidential scandal that was making us all look bad—and Operation Tailwind just made things that much worse. And it was an increasingly uncomfortable time for me, the relatively new president of ABC News. I'd made a call based on the best information I had. I had great confidence in our reporting team, despite their coming under severe scrutiny and criticism. I'd done my best to be sure of our sourcing. The White House was furious with us. They made that clear every day as we dealt with them through our Washington bureau. Some of our friends were openly critical of what we'd done or simply avoided discussing it with me, leaving me little doubt about how they felt. The fact remained that we were largely alone, and there was always the chance that there'd been something that I'd missed.

This was the backdrop for my first appearance as president of ABC News at the semiannual "press tour" in Pasadena, California, held by the Television Critics Association. Every summer and fall, print reporters from around the country come together in Los Angeles to meet with representatives of the entertainment and news operations of the broadcast and cable networks. Each network has a day or two to make presentations, hold question-and-answer sessions, and have informal, face-to-face talks with well over a hundred of the reporters who cover the media.

It was July 24. Roone Arledge had formally stepped aside at the beginning of the month, and I was there to talk about where I saw ABC News heading. I took reporters' questions for the better part of an hour. Midway through the session, the questioning turned to Jackie Judd's reporting on the now-famous blue dress. The questioner referred to Steven Brill's criticisms, noting that other reporters had "not been able to substantiate" Jackie's report, and asked whether I was changing our reporting rules because of the "Lewinsky/Clinton situation." I responded that I knew Jackie and her team, I'd been over the sourcing carefully, and I stood by our report and by her reporting. The reporters weren't satisfied with this and asked for more proof that we were right even though no one had matched our story for so long. I said that unfortunately I couldn't offer chapter and verse on the sourcing because we'd promised to keep our source's identity confidential.

Not satisfied with my answers, several reporters followed me into the foyer outside the meeting. I spent another twenty minutes answering the same questions with the same answers. One of the things I was pressed on in both the general session and the rump version later was whether I was confident that the dress would eventually be discovered. I had to say honestly that I couldn't promise that. I was confident that the dress had existed and had been as we'd described at the time we reported it; but there was no way I could be certain that it hadn't been destroyed in the meantime. That was my secret fear.

I had no way of knowing that four days later, on July 28, Lewinsky's lawyers would turn the dress over to Ken Starr's office for DNA testing. Or that the confirmed existence of the dress would lead the president to give a DNA sample and appear for videotaped testimony to be provided to the grand jury—testimony in which he would admit for the first time that he had had an intimate relationship with Lewinsky.

Vindication was one thing we felt at ABC News that day. We'd stuck to our story, and our reporting—reporting for which we'd taken a fair amount of heat—had proved right. But along with the vindication, I felt a strong sense of relief. No matter how much confidence I'd had in our reporting, it was always possible that something we didn't know had set us in the wrong direction.

Now that we all know how the story played out—the impeachment of the president, his acquittal in the Senate, and his successful completion of a second term in office—what can we say about the job the journalists did during this difficult period? I hear most often—and to this day—two basic criticisms of what we did.

First, some say that this was simply a tawdry story about a man's personal life that was beneath us to pursue as aggressively as we did. Past presidents, good presidents, may have had their personal peccadilloes, and the press didn't even try to find out about them. And if they did, they kept their discoveries quiet. What was different here, these critics say, is that there was a more or less coordinated effort on the part of President Clinton's political foes—what Hillary Clinton famously called a "vast right-wing conspiracy"—to stir up the media to pursue this story for political gain. We were used, plain and simple.

There's a lot to be said for this point of view—and pretty much all of it was said within the ABC newsroom starting with those first discussions we had about our reporting that night in Havana in late January. From the very beginning, I think everyone who worked on this story, at least at ABC News, had a deep uneasiness about what we were reporting. Talking on television about the sorts of details that ultimately came out wasn't going to cover any reporter in glory. This wasn't war reporting or the Pentagon Papers. Unlike Watergate, the alleged offenses here didn't go to the very structure of our constitutional form of government.

Still, on balance, we concluded that this was an important story that the American people should know about. The Justice Department had authorized on official investigation into whether the president had obstructed justice. In the end, the obstruction-of-justice charge disappeared, but we had no way of knowing this in those early days of 1998. It wasn't until Ken Starr's report and the proceedings in Congress months later that the story took a decisive turn in a different direction.

We may have had an obligation to report the Lewinsky story fully, but one criticism of what we did is, I think, largely fair. Whatever the motivations of individual reporters—whether a genuine belief in the importance of the story or some reporters' frustration with what they saw as a White House that was always spinning stories—when news of the scandal broke, some members of the press jumped on the story with unseemly relish. Much of the press corps spent thirteen months thinking that they were ahead of the American people and trying hard to get the people to catch up. They acted as if they needed to report just a bit more or come at it from a different direction or say it a bit louder, and then the American people would understand how serious the matter was and respond accordingly. Looking back, I think the American people actually understood the story pretty well within a very few days of its breaking. And having understood it, they made up their minds.

Did he do it? You bet. Did people find it reprehensible on a personal level? Certainly. But did the American people overall want Bill Clinton to remain their president despite his personal failings? Without question. Whatever was going on in his personal life, he was (the people by and large concluded) doing a good job on behalf of the nation as a whole. And this is why, when all was said and done, the people thought the country was headed in a good direction overall at the end of President Clinton's term.

As it turned out, the problem with the press here was not that we were spending a lot of time on something that wasn't newsworthy. It was that many of us misconstrued the significance of what we were reporting. The media wrongly assumed that the American people would not be able to separate out the personal from the professional as they assessed their president. But when you're in the middle of covering a story and you don't know how it will end, it's awfully hard to make these longer-term judgments. For all you know, this may be another Watergate that ends in the resignation of a president; or maybe not. And so the tendency is to go all out and make sure you can't be criticized later for backing off an important story. In retrospect, those of us in the press should have been a little less worried about being too soft on the president and a little more open to the possibility that we were wrong—not about the facts, but about what it all meant.

The second overall criticism of the Lewinsky coverage is that we were careless—even reckless—in what we reported and how we reported it. Steven Brill in his article incorporated a fair amount of what others were saying at the time about the news media in general and ABC News in particular: we were not being careful in our sourcing, at least some of us were relying too heavily on leaks from Ken Starr's office, and we were simply parroting what prosecutors and members of the president's political opposition were feeding to us. Much, though by no means all, of this sort of criticism focused on the blue dress and our reporting on it.

We said at the time that we had one solid source for our reporting. The truth was that we had a second source, one in law enforcement, confirming what our primary source had told us. We didn't invoke the second source, because we could never be certain that he wasn't relying on our primary source, which would undercut the value of having multiple sources.

Tomes have been written and legal battles fought about sourcing and journalism. How many sources are enough? Is one source ever enough? Should journalists use confidential sources? If so, should there be limits on when and how they're used? Can journalists promise sources that their identity will remain confidential? If journalists refuse to disclose confidential sources, can they be punished (most often by being put in jail)?

To be honest, I really hadn't thought a great deal about these questions until the story of the blue dress came to us, but then I got a crash course in this part of journalism. I read what others said about multiple sourcing; I listened to the criticism about our own sourcing. But I never found any hard-and-fast rule that I could apply in all circumstances. I came to believe that the most important things to figure out were whether whoever was talking to you was in a position to know—and whether he or she was telling you the truth. Obviously, the more sources you have, the more confident you'll be about your reporting. But there are circumstances where many sources telling you the same thing does you no good because they're all equally wrong.

Consider, for example, the media's reporting on Saddam Hussein and his supposed weapons of mass destruction during the lead-up to the Iraq

War of 2003. All of us in the news media at the time had multiple confiden-tial sources in government intelligence agencies around the world telling us that Saddam had WMD. And then the United States and its allies went in, sacrificing thousands of lives and spending hundreds of billions of dollars, and proved that all of our confidential sources were wrong. We have been and should be criticized for not doing our job when it came to reporting on Iraqi WMD. But it wasn't because we didn't have enough sources.

On the other hand, sometimes a single source can be enough to justify a report. The extreme example journalists give is when Henry Kissinger was national security adviser and would travel with members of the press to whom he would confide "off the record" what he was thinking about a given policy issue. It would get reported as "sources say" that Kissinger thought one thing or another. It would be ridiculous to tell the reporter to whom Kissinger had spoken that he or she needed to go get a second source.

Now, most of the time we don't have cases as clear as that. But I saw some situations where a single source could be enough. After asking about it in as much detail as I could and thinking about it long and hard, I concluded that our reporting on the blue dress was such a case. Was I right? It came out all right in the end, because our report proved accurate. After the dress had been turned over, the tests had been done, and the president had given his testimony, the Committee of Concerned Journal-ists issued a report on the story of President Clinton and Monica Lewin-sky. In it, the committee concluded: "The press was largely on the mark in its reporting on the dress that quickly became central to the Clinton-Lewinsky story. ABC's early reporting turned out to be highly accurate. The stain did turn out to be the president's semen."

There's something righteous about sticking to your story in the face of criticism. And it would be great if journalism was filled only with those stories of news organizations standing up to unfair criticism when they report controversial things. But the story's more complicated than that. The truth is that others, given all the facts about the blue dress story that I had at the time, might have made a different decision. And they might have been proven right. One of the hardest things about the pursuit of good journalism is that you have to make very difficult judgment calls where the line between the truth and its opposite is very fine. Too often, you're not sure which side of that line you're on, and there's never a short-age of people telling you that you're wrong.

Unfortunately, we've seen some prominent cases in recent years where great news organizations have done their very best but have come up short. We saw it with *The New York Times* and Jayson Blair. Blair was the promising young reporter for the *Times* who, from October 2002 to May 2003, committed what the paper ultimately concluded were "frequent acts of journalistic fraud," constituting "a low point in the 152-year history of the newspaper." Blair had moved up rapidly at the *Times* from an internship to covering major national stories. He wrote movingly of the wounded soldiers returning from Afghanistan and Iraq, and he told vivid stories about the life and family of Private First Class Jessica Lynch, who had been caught in an ambush during the invasion of Iraq, captured, and ultimately rescued by U.S. forces. He was assigned to cover the story of the sniper who terrorized Washington, D.C., for several months in 2002.

Blair's stories were great. The problem was that many of them were riddled with inaccuracies and misrepresentations; several were borrowed from reports in other papers.

To its credit, *The New York Times* did a thorough review of what had gone wrong and wrote about it all in a detailed report published in the newspaper. In hindsight, of course, it was obvious what could and should have been done to avoid the debacle. In hindsight it always is. But the simple and uncomfortable truth is that any news organization can be sullied by a single individual who is bent on cheating. News reporting requires too much independence, too much confidentiality, for there ever to be enough checks and balances—no matter how hard people try.

Two years after the Jayson Blair scandal, another great news organization went through its own torment. In September 2004, two months before the presidential election, Dan Rather had an investigative report on CBS's *60 Minutes II* documenting the alleged truancy of George W. Bush when he was in the Air National Guard. I watched the report with envy. It was another big scoop coming only four months after CBS's exclusive reports on the abuses at the Abu Ghraib prison in Iraq.

But early the next morning the story began to unravel. I read the *Drudge Report* as it started linking to blogs questioning some of the documentation that CBS had relied upon—particularly a typed letter supposedly from Bush's commanding officer at the time. You can't always believe what you read on the blogs, and this story clearly fed into a lot of political agendas. So that afternoon, I went to Chris Vlasto (the investigative producer at the center of our Lewinsky reporting) and asked him what he knew. Was the CBS report right? He said he thought the letter might well be a forgery. What's more, he said he suspected that the source of the letter was a man named Bill Burkett (a retired lieutenant colonel from the Texas Army National Guard). As Chris told me that afternoon, "If that's their source, then they're in real trouble" (his precise language was more colorful).

It went downhill from there. Dan went on the *CBS Evening News* to defend his reporting, the criticism grew, and ultimately CBS brought in two independent experts, the former Republican governor of Pennsylvania Dick Thornburgh and the retired longtime head of the Associated Press Lou Boccardi, to conduct a complete review of what had happened. Their report found substantial fault with what CBS News had done, particularly in relying on the letter. Several able, senior executives at CBS News lost their jobs, and Dan Rather was gone within a year.

I watched all of this with more than a little sadness and apprehension. I knew that if CBS News was dragged through the mud, it wouldn't help ABC News. Most people would tend to lump us together; the only difference in their minds would be that CBS got caught. And I had real empathy for the problems CBS News had faced in trying to authenticate an important document from long ago. We'd had our own close call when I first came to ABC News. Before I arrived, ABC News had paid a fair amount of money to the acclaimed investigative reporter Seymour Hersh for his help in putting together a documentary on the Kennedys—Jack and Bobby. Hersh was about to publish a book called *The Dark Side of Camelot*, and Peter Jennings was set to anchor our special. Roone urged me to get involved, saying that Hersh had uncovered some explosive material definitively linking the Kennedys to Marilyn Monroe.

When I sat with Peter and Mark Obenhaus, the producer, they showed me a facsimile copy of a document that looked as if it was a deed of trust. I quickly read through it, which didn't take long, as it was only a handful of typewritten pages. In it, the sum of $600,000 was put in trust for the benefit of Mrs. Gladys Baker—the mother of Marilyn Monroe. The document purported to be signed by John Fitzgerald Kennedy and witnessed by Robert Kennedy. It was dated 1960, the year of John Kennedy's campaign that would make him president and his brother Bobby the attorney general of the United States.

Roone was right that this could be explosive. But in law school we learned that "no document speaks for itself." For it to be considered credible evidence, there had to be something outside the document that told us that it truly was what it purported to be. Typically, that would mean a person who was there when the document was produced. Here, of course, all of the people named in the document were long dead.

Mark told me that they'd taken the document to some of the best handwriting experts in the country. They were unanimous in their opinion that the signatures of the Kennedy brothers were "consistent with" their real signatures. "Consistent with?" I asked. "What do you mean 'consistent with'? That's not the same as saying they're genuine." Mark explained that "no handwriting expert can ever tell you for certain that a signature is authentic. People's handwriting varies too much. They can tell you that something is a forgery, but not that it's real."

This clearly wasn't good enough. We agreed that Mark and his team had to continue pursuing other ways of determining whether the trust document was real or not. And, lo and behold, a few days later Mark called to say that the supposed deed of trust I'd reviewed was forged. It was not only a fake but not a very good fake. Given what I'd learned about handwriting analysis, how could we have gotten so definitive an answer so quickly? Because it had been typed on an IBM Selectric II typewriter. On the original of the document, you could see where typos had been corrected with the lift-off tape that came with the Selectric II. But the Selectric II didn't even go on sale until the early 1970s—more than a decade after the date on the document.

Suddenly what Sy Hersh had was important in ways no one had anticipated. The document he'd obtained didn't say anything about the Kennedys, but it did raise some powerful questions about who was forging documents with the former president's signature on them and why. It turned out that a New York lawyer, Lawrence Cusack, had represented several prominent people in the 1950s and '60s, including Mrs. Baker and the Archdiocese of New York. When Mr. Cusack died in 1985, his son (Lawrence Cusack III, known as Lex) inherited boxes of documents bearing the authentic signatures of famous people either his father had represented or who had corresponded with his clients, such as the archdiocese. The enterprising son taught himself to forge these signatures and embarked on a lucrative career of creating rare documents, which he sold to collectors. This fake deed of trust was one of those forged documents.

Peter Jennings sat down to interview the forger on camera and confronted him with the incontrovertible evidence that at least some of the documents he'd sold couldn't be real. He had no explanation. As a result of Mark's investigation and Peter's interview, the man was indicted, tried, and convicted. A federal court sentenced him in 1999 to serve ten years in prison and pay $7 million in restitution.

All this came back to me when I watched seven years later as questions were raised about the authenticity of the letter George W. Bush's commanding officer had supposedly written. Some of the questions sounded an awful lot like what we encountered in the Cusack case—especially questions about what type of machine had been used to produce the letter. I knew how easy it could be to make a mistake in this tricky area.

I would love to be able to say that it was only other news organizations that got it wrong in deciding when to press forward and when to back off a story. But we at ABC News made our mistakes as well. In the midst of the Iraq War, our investigative unit reported "exclusively" that a senior Iraqi official, Ali Hassan al-Majid, had been killed in southeastern Baghdad by a U.S. military strike. Al-Majid had been nicknamed Chemical Ali because of his central role in Saddam Hussein's use of chemical weapons on his own people, in clear violation of international law. His reported death was a big story so early in the war.

But soon after our story went on the air, I took a call from an irate CIA public affairs officer who vigorously denied the report. When the CIA is telling you that the international criminal they're after isn't really dead, there's good reason to listen. They aren't always right, but they're in a position to have information we don't, and they have little incentive to downplay the success of the U.S. military. So I promised to get into it immediately. It turned out that although we had multiple sources for our report, we hadn't bothered to check with the CIA itself (or anyone else in the U.S. government for that matter) before going public with our version of the events. It was a major mistake. We had to admit on the air that our reporting had been premature, at best.

We weren't the only ones overly eager to report Chemical Ali's demise. A few days later, on April 7, CNN.com reported that this time he'd *really* been found dead. The British military spokesman in Baghdad confirmed this, although the British defense secretary in London would go no further than to say there were "indications that this is the case." The U.S. defense secretary, Donald Rumsfeld, declared that "the reign of terror of Chemical Ali has come to an end." But it turned out that Chemical Ali was still very much alive.

Five months later Chemical Ali was finally captured. He was subsequently tried and executed by hanging on January 25, 2010.

Although we were not alone, I was embarrassed that we'd gotten the reporting wrong about Chemical Ali. So I made sure we had a rule in place that we would never report on events with national security implications without first running them by representatives from the responsible government agencies—both to give them an opportunity to confirm or deny and to hear from them any concerns they might have about our reporting accurate information that could compromise national security interests.

If our experience in reporting on Lewinsky's blue dress showed the value of standing up to criticism over a story, the *60 Minutes II* debacle—and my own experience with the forged Kennedy documents and Chemical Ali—showed the potential risks in pressing forward with controversial reporting. No matter how careful you are, you can always be wrong. How can you distinguish the reporting you need to stand behind (and ignore the criticism) from the reporting that you need to pull back on (because the criticism is justified)?

That you're facing vigorous criticism doesn't really help all that much. You're criticized just about every time you report anything important or controversial. Subjects of unpleasant reports have every reason to attack, hoping they can get you to back down, and I learned the hard way that public officials and corporate officers are always unhappy with any reporting that seeks to hold them accountable. They particularly don't like leaks, and they want to do everything they can to stop them. They often see the same facts in very different ways from what reporters are writing.

If they complained only about mistakes, it would make things easier. But it isn't just the flawed reports that get the criticism; often it's the truth that hurts the subject of a report the most.

Report on a defect in an automobile that has led to several deaths? The automobile maker (who also happens to be a major advertiser) will present a tome on why the claim is utterly without any basis in fact—until the Consumer Product Safety Commission announces an investigation and the manufacturer undertakes a major recall.

Report on fundamental weaknesses in the security of our ports by importing depleted uranium—undetected—in a wooden chest? The U.S. Customs Service will threaten prosecution for filing misleading customs forms—until members of Congress publicly take the service to task.

Report on the several credible studies finding no link between vaccinations and autism? The parents of autistic children and public advocates will attack, claiming that you're influenced by the drug companies that manufactured the serum (and are also your advertisers, suggesting an inherent conflict of interest). And then it turns out that the researcher who had first said the vaccinations caused autism was making it up.

I knew how aggressively subjects of critical reports would come after ABC News from my time as general counsel of the company and then as the head of ABC. Several times I'd been called upon to answer the critics, whether in defending against threatened legal action or in answering to public officials or advertisers. Being in the trenches with your team of reporters when they're under fire leads to a natural instinct to defend them. It feels good to stare down your critics when they come after you and your reporters. You feel noble.

But you can't simply reject all criticism any more than you can simply accept it and back down. It isn't the criticism that makes sticking with a story hard. It's knowing that you could be wrong. No one is right 100 percent of the time. Any of us who have been the subject of press reports ourselves know this all too well. And that's why that noble feeling of backing your colleagues can lead to disaster in some cases. Sadly, some of the worst infractions in journalism in recent years have resulted, in part, from those in charge sticking by journalists without considering the possibility that the critics may just be right.

My experience taught me to do two things when deciding whether to go forward with controversial reporting (or defend it after it had aired). First, I always had a fresh set of eyes review the work. No matter how good the reporters, it's just asking too much of them to require that they set aside their investment and belief in their work and objectively decide whether they may have made a mistake. And I didn't want whoever was doing the review to also have responsibility for the success of the programs or outlets on which the reports would air. I made sure that I had reporting directly to me a senior executive who was charged with all independent review. Over time, I increased her staff with others who had experience reporting, supervising reporting, and reviewing standards. This approach sometimes led to conflicts within the newsroom, but they were healthy conflicts that I knew improved the quality of the work. This executive and her team went over all controversial reports before they aired. I knew about the issues from the beginning and could decide whether to go forward. Not infrequently, subjects of possible reports would contact me directly to ask about pending reports or to complain when they thought things were not being handled right. I turned all of these over to my "editorial quality" executive for her to review and take into account.

Second, as important as the independent internal review was the attitude we brought to that review of criticism. When reporting is challenged, you have to resist that strong temptation to circle the wagons, defending your journalists and their reporting against all attacks. There has to be a balance between the need to stand strong on controversial reporting you believe in and an openness to consider the possibility you might be wrong. Part of this involves vetting the critics in ways similar to how you vet a source. Are they in a position to know what they're talking about? Do they have an agenda that may color what they have to say? Do they have specifics that can be checked and that can help validate (or undermine) their criticism?

Then, once you've included independent, experienced colleagues in the review and you've done your best to consider the criticism with an open mind, you have to make a decision. Do you have the story solidly or not? Are you treating the people and institutions you're holding up to the light fairly or not? Have you represented their point of view? If the answers to these questions are yes, then you go forward. Not perhaps without reservations, but without hesitation. You owe it to your viewers and listeners to tell them what you believe to be the truth, no matter how controversial and no matter how uncomfortable. You do it because it's right, not because you hope to win a popularity contest. We certainly weren't popular with our reporting on Monica Lewinsky's dress. But looking back on it now, I have no doubt that we were right.

# 3 | "Planet Earth": My Leonardo DiCaprio Problem

I just want to say this to David Westin. You know, I've been in a lot of tough spots. Don't let this get you down. You may not be America's news leader, but you're the king of the world! [Laughter]
— President Clinton, Radio and Television Correspondents' Dinner, April 16, 2000

Maureen Dowd of *The New York Times* put it best: "You've got to hand it to David Westin. The president of ABC News has achieved the impossible: he gave the Clinton White House the moral high ground." I was hurt and more than a little angry when I read those words—not least because they were true.

The seeds for my embarrassment were sown in December 1997, before I'd even heard of Monica Lewinsky. That was the month *Titanic* premiered, the blockbuster film directed by James Cameron. *Titanic* earned $1.8 billion at the box office—making it the biggest-grossing movie ever, until Cameron beat his own record with *Avatar* in 2010. In March 1998, while a grand jury was hearing testimony in the Lewinsky case in Washington, *Titanic* won eleven Academy Awards on the opposite coast in Los Angeles. Leonardo DiCaprio was one of the brightest stars in Hollywood. Two years later, he would be sitting down at the White House with President Clinton for an interview to be included in an ABC News special. By that time, the president had put his scandal behind him, but DiCaprio's interview would create its own small scandal for me.

The possibility that Leonardo DiCaprio would work with us on an ABC News special first came up in the fall of 1999 and, frankly, seemed far-fetched at the time. Walking the halls of 147 Columbus Avenue where the newsmagazines were housed, I poked my head into the office of Phyllis McGrady, then our executive producer for special programming. We talked about several projects, and in the course of our talk Phyllis asked whether I'd be interested in an hour-long prime-time special on the environment around the time of Earth Day the following spring. When the idea first came to Phyllis, she'd rejected it because Peter Jennings had recently done an environmental special that hadn't registered with the audience. DiCaprio was going to be the honorary chairman of the Earth Day festivities, however, and Chris Cuomo, then a correspondent for *20/20 Downtown*, knew him personally. Phyllis suggested that if we could get the star of *Titanic* on the special, we might be able to attract a bigger, younger audience for a serious ABC News documentary on climate and environmental issues.

At first blush, it seemed unlikely but a good idea. What could go wrong with combining some serious environmental reporting with the drawing power of a megastar?

After that, I didn't hear much about the special for several months. It was a busy time for ABC News. In November and December, we were immersed in producing *ABC 2000*, a twenty-four-hour live program showing the dawning of the new millennium from around the world. Our millennium program was only one of many ideas people pursued throughout the media in the year leading up to January 1, 2000. But as the time drew closer, most of the grand plans we heard about fell by the wayside. Ours was born partly out of practicality. Months before, a consortium of international broadcasters approached our colleague Jeff Gralnick and asked us to join them. For a relatively modest fee, we would have live access to their feeds around the world that night; we, in turn, would give them access to whatever we were airing.

Once we joined this consortium, the question became how best to use all this video. I thought we should use it to structure our entire program. We would have the sights and sounds of midnight celebrations in every time zone over a period of twenty-four hours. Why not stay on the air for the entire time, showing the first moments of the new millennium as it came to every corner of the world? Some people, including Roone Arledge, weren't so enthusiastic. But Peter Jennings was. He saw the program's potential right away and insisted on anchoring it himself, going for twenty-four hours straight. And that's what he did.

It was a triumph; 175 million people watched at least some of the broadcast, and it won the praise of the critics. We stretched the capacity of ABC News to the limit, sending people to every corner of the globe and enlisting just about every single person on the staff, as well as an army of freelancers.

As we got into the New Year, I turned my attention to covering the presidential election—my first as ABC News president. We were also preparing for Diane Sawyer's exclusive interview in Miami with Elián González, the six-year-old Cuban boy who had been plucked from the water off the Florida coast after his mother died trying to flee with him to the United States. Elián was the subject of a bitter dispute between his Cuban father, who wanted him back in Cuba, and his Miami relatives, who fought for political asylum for him. It was very controversial at the time because the boy was so young and there was so much political heat surrounding him. Despite various objections, we went ahead with the interview, a month before federal marshals seized the boy and returned him to his father in Cuba.

The day after the last of Diane's interview aired, I took a break to drive over to Pennsylvania and visit my daughter at college. As I was driving west on Interstate 80, I got a call on my cell phone. My colleagues back in New York wanted to give me a heads-up that DiCaprio would be going to the White House to interview President Clinton later that morning for the prime-time special.

I was stunned. Leonardo DiCaprio interviewing the president of the United States? On behalf of ABC News? How had our prime-time special turned into this? I'd thought DiCaprio was simply going to make an appearance on the special, perhaps with Chris Cuomo talking with him about his interest in the environment and his role in Earth Day—not interview the president.

I was quickly assured that it wasn't going to be an interview in the conventional sense. It was really only a walk around the White House with the president so that we could see the various steps the First Family had taken to be more environmentally responsible. Things like double glazing the windows and replacing traditional lightbulbs to save energy. This was still very different from what at least I'd envisioned when we first talked about DiCaprio being on the special. But given the circumstances (including the fact that the White House was expecting our crew in a matter of moments), I supposed it would be all right. And having President Clinton on our special might well help us with our overall goal of drawing a bigger, younger audience to a program about the environment. Once again, I thought the matter was settled.

After visiting my daughter, I drove back to New York and was out to dinner with my wife, Sherrie, at a local restaurant. My pager went off, and I called the news desk from the public telephone just outside the restrooms. Things had changed again. Instead of a casual walk through the White House to chat about things done to make the place more eco-friendly, DiCaprio had sat down for a formal interview with President Clinton. To make matters even worse, reporters had been told at the afternoon White House press briefing that the president had spent part of his day being interviewed by DiCaprio on behalf of ABC News. The Washington press corps was already having a field day at our expense.

How, I asked, could this have happened? When I'd first learned of DiCaprio's going to the White House only a few hours before, my instinct had been that this was a bad idea. But I'd been assured that it wouldn't be a real interview. How had the ground rules changed so fundamentally and so quickly? This time I was told that it had all been the White House's idea. We'd pitched only a casual walk-and-talk, but when DiCaprio and our crew showed up, the White House had insisted on a formal sit-down interview. How could one refuse the president of the United States? It was all their idea. Or so I was told.

The next day was Saturday, April Fools' Day, and the criticism began in earnest with a Howard Kurtz piece in *The Washington Post*. Kurtz described our choice to use DiCaprio as a "decision of Titanic proportions." As he put it, "The news division of Peter Jennings and Ted Koppel decided that the heartthrob was the ideal person to chat up Bill Clinton for an hour-long special on the environment."

I spent that morning on the telephone, hearing how upset everyone was in our Washington bureau. Any number of other press outlets were intently pursuing the story, talking with various ABC News employees in Washington who were only too eager to share their dismay over DiCaprio's interview.

We had a real problem on our hands. But I comforted myself with the thought that we still had the better of the argument. Sure, we'd enlisted DiCaprio for our special, but he was the chairman of Earth Day, he was knowledgeable about the environment, and he could bring people to our special who otherwise wouldn't be bothered. Sure, we sent him in to talk to the president, but it wasn't as if we'd planned a real interview. We'd meant it to be just a walk-and-talk, and it was the White House that had changed the rules at the last minute, right?

I dashed off an e-mail, hoping to reassure my Washington colleagues that things weren't as bad as they were being told by their friends in the Washington media. I addressed it to the most prominent people in the Washington bureau, about ten in all. People like Ted Koppel and Sam Donaldson and Cokie Roberts, as well as our Washington bureau chief and the executive producers of *Nightline* and *This Week*. I included Peter Jennings for good measure—not because I thought he was likely to stir the pot, but because he was such an important part of the editorial heart and soul of the institution. I wanted him to know what was really going on. Or at least what I believed was going on.

My e-mail was nothing if not colorful. At least for me. I said flatly that "we did not send [DiCaprio] to interview the President. No one is that stupid." I emphasized that there had never been an interview planned, but only a "walk-through." I asserted that someone such as Leonardo DiCaprio could play a role in an ABC News special, "but the role must be that of a sincere, informed celebrity—not a journalist. All roles of journalists must be played by journalists (duh!)." (And yes, that "duh" was mine.)

Not surprisingly, this e-mail was leaked almost immediately. After the fact, someone claimed that I'd asked that the e-mail be leaked. There wouldn't have been anything wrong with this; it was my e-mail, and I believed everything I'd said in it. But none of the leaks came from me. The person at ABC News dealing with the press at the time did come to me that weekend to say that Bill Carter of *The New York Times* was considering writing something on the story. I told her that she could give Bill a copy of the e-mail. Carter didn't end up writing, and so we never gave him the e-mail. But it quickly showed up in news reports nonetheless.

The much bigger problem was that the White House was going to town on the substance of what I'd written. White House staffers immediately took me to task, saying that ABC News had put in a request as early as February for Leonardo DiCaprio to interview President Clinton for the environmental special. We stuck to our guns. I still believed that the White House was simply trying to spin its way out of a jam.

The next week brought reports from various news organizations of the DiCaprio interview and our battle with the White House over how it came to pass. The Associated Press reported that "at ABC News, there was discontent when staffers heard that a movie star had been given this plum of a newsgathering assignment." The *Philadelphia Inquirer* called it a "titanic uproar at ABC News" and reported that "several high-profile correspondents made their displeasure known" to me. The *Washington Post* continued its coverage, repeating my claim that the walk around with DiCaprio had become a sit-down interview with the president at the last-minute insistence of the White House—and then gave details of the White House rebuttal, including that we'd put the first request in for a presidential interview back in February through the Council on Environmental Quality. *Salon* reported on the clash over the facts, asking whether I was "lying? Incompetent? Both?" *Salon* came up with a third possibility. Perhaps this had all been part of an elaborate plan to get as much attention as possible for DiCaprio's upcoming movie *Gangs of New York*, which was being produced by Miramax, a Disney affiliate (something I don't think I even knew about at the time and certainly was the furthest thing from my mind).

At one point, a newspaper reporter confided to me that he'd never seen the White House go after a news organization with such enthusiasm. Members of the Press Office seemed positively gleeful as they called reporters to volunteer information showing that ABC News had sought and planned a DiCaprio interview with the president from the very beginning—even going so far as to share internal White House e-mails.

As if this weren't enough, DiCaprio himself told the media that he'd been prepared for an interview—prepared in part by ABC News producers. It became obvious that the White House was right, and I was wrong. Clearly, I hadn't known all the facts. But that hadn't stopped me from publicly asserting unequivocally that what I'd been told by our producers was the truth.

The criticism built to a fever pitch in time for the annual Radio and Television Correspondents' Dinner in Washington the following Thursday, April 6. This dinner is an annual event for print, radio, and television reporters who cover Congress, and draws about a thousand people in black tie at the Washington Hilton, a sort of parallel event to the White House Correspondents' Dinner also held in the spring. The crowd is a mix of reporters, executives, celebrities, and other prominent Washingtonians, including the president and First Lady, the vice president, members of the cabinet, senators and congressmen, senior military officers, and pillars of Washington society. It tends to be a long affair, with a stream of remarks and awards and a performance by a prominent comedian. The centerpiece of the evening comes when the president gives his remarks, which are typically humorous and usually come at the expense of himself and the media represented in the room. The major media organizations all pay for tables at the dinner that they populate with their most prominent anchors and correspondents, notables from government, and other celebrities. Many also hold receptions before the dinner in one of the smaller meeting rooms scattered around the hotel.

As I left the ABC News reception that evening to walk into the dinner, I was escorted by a camera crew from *Entertainment Tonight*, trying to interview me about what had now been dubbed Leogate. This is not the sort of situation you want to be in as a news division president. But this was just the beginning. Entering the hall, all of us were offered "Free Leo" buttons courtesy of the White House chief of staff, John Podesta. As one of the larger contributors to the event, we had a table right down in front, just below the dais on which President Clinton was seated.

When the time came for the president's remarks, the sounds of Celine Dion singing "My Heart Will Go On" from *Titanic* filled the room, and the president stood with his hand over his heart. Smiling, he walked to the podium bearing the presidential seal and asked: "Haunting, isn't it?" The joke wasn't lost on anyone in the room. It went downhill from there. Here's how President Clinton began his remarks that evening:

> You know, usually I go for Hail to the Chief. But this week, I can't seem to get that song out of my head.
>
> Good evening, President Nolan [of the RTCA], Senator McCain, members of Congress, members of the Radio and Television Correspondents Association, distinguished journalists . . . and Mr. DiCaprio. [*Laughter*]
>
> Now, ABC doesn't know whether Leo and I had an interview, a walk-through, or a drive-by. [*More laughter*] But I don't know if all their dam-

age control is worth the effort. I mean, it's a little like rearranging the deck chairs on "This Week with Sam [Donaldson] and Cokie [Roberts]." [*Groans and laughter*] Don't you news people ever learn? It isn't the mistake that kills you. It's the cover-up. [*Laughter and applause*]

Look, I want to say right now I have nothing against ABC. I like ABC just as much as I like all the other networks. [*Laughter*] Just the other day, for example, Diane Sawyer came to the White House for an interview. Actually, she called it a "visit." [*Laughter*] And everything was fine until she asked me to do some crayon pictures in the Oval Office [a reference to Diane's interview with Elián González]. That was weird. [*Laughter*]

But, I just want to say this to David Westin. You know, I've been in a lot of tough spots. Don't let this get you down. You may not be America's news leader, but you're the king of the world!

The last line, as you can imagine, was delivered by the president of the United States with his arms outstretched, imitating Leonardo DiCaprio's character on the prow of the *Titanic* in the hit movie.

For at least part of the president's remarks, I had a C-SPAN camera trained on me for my reaction. I remember trying to keep a smile on my face, but on the video there's only one shot of me, and I look more grim than entertained. It's fair to say that President Clinton and our competitors in the room that night had a better time than I did.

The president's performance at the dinner prompted a new round of criticism of ABC News and of me. This is when Maureen Dowd wrote her column ridiculing me. Fox News righteously asked whether ABC News was "making a mockery of journalism." One of the things that Fox has always excelled at is making what it has to say on particular stories fit within an overall narrative for its audience. This time, they tied the DiCaprio interview together with the mainstream media's desire to "brainwash young kids that the combustion engine is [the] greatest threat to mankind" and the apparently unrelated but huge mistake they saw in my letting William Kristol go from the roundtable on *This Week* on Sundays. The story even got coverage halfway around the world in *The Times of India*, which came at it from the other direction, saying that ABC News was "kow-towing to its influential but insecure journalists."

Despite the furor, we had yet to put anything on the air—neither the planned special nor any part of the Clinton-DiCaprio interview. In my

April 1 e-mail, I'd written that I would decide whether and to what extent we would include the interview after I'd seen the edited hour and could view it in context. I wanted to see whether the interview added to the special or not. If it did, then I thought we should include it; if not, we'd leave it out—just as we did with other interviews and segments that did or did not make air depending on what they added. Although, in all honesty, I don't think there's ever been a time that ABC News bothered the president of the United States for an interview and then decided not to air it.

My waiting to screen the entire special became the subject of additional debate and speculation. Some thought that the best and quickest way to put all this behind us was simply to leave the interview (and perhaps the entire special) on the cutting room floor and move on.

The afternoon before that correspondents dinner, Sam Donaldson came to my office in our Washington bureau to give me his advice. Sam was a veteran of the Washington wars. If he hadn't seen it all, he'd seen a good deal of it. His simple plan had more than a little wisdom in it. The way Sam saw it, three of the most useful words in Washington were: "Mistakes were made." The use of the passive voice—something I'd always been taught to avoid—could be immensely helpful. I didn't have to own up to the mistake; I didn't have to assign the blame to anyone else. Sam's strong, direct advice was to admit that "mistakes were made" and retreat. Don't air the hour. Let it go.

Sam had a good point. If I'd followed his advice, we might have gotten through the whole ordeal faster than we did. But there were others, including those working on the special, who warned that not airing the DiCaprio interview would only fuel the fire. Then it would become the presidential interview that "ABC News doesn't want you to see." Interest would be aroused further than it already was. Maybe there was something in the interview, something so bad that we didn't want anyone to see it ever. By simply broadcasting the completed special, including DiCaprio's interview, we could show the world that there was nothing objectionable in it.

When we finally had a version of the hour put together, I saw that the interview was completely straightforward. It wouldn't make major news (most presidential interviews, in my experience, don't), but neither would it detract from the substance of the special. Most important, if I killed the hour, I'd be conceding there was something wrong in our addressing some serious environmental issues and getting people to pay attention—something I still believed in. We'd go ahead as planned.

And so, on Saturday, April 22, we aired *Planet Earth 2000*, which included three minutes of DiCaprio's interview with the president. In the end, the world of journalism did not go spinning off its axis; nor did a large audience come to the program despite the star's presence and all the publicity. Our Earth Day special attracted only about 1.5 percent of all adults between the ages of twenty-five and fifty-four that night; it drew an even lower percentage of the younger audience. To give you a sense, it was way behind what the network was otherwise airing on Saturday nights at the time—reruns of movies such as *Tin Cup*, *Air Force One*, and Kevin Costner's legendary flop, *Waterworld*.

The fallout in the press from the DiCaprio interview continued for a while after the special had aired. No one really took issue with what DiCaprio had done—only that he was the one doing it. But *Salon* said I would lose my job, predicting that I wouldn't last as long as President Clinton (whose second term was to expire in nine months). And Jane Mayer wrote a decidedly unflattering profile of me in *The New Yorker* based in part on unnamed sources within ABC News who she said had "serious questions" about my "judgment and credibility." Mayer emphasized my lack of news experience and cast me as a strange combination of a cynical, calculating corporate operative and a callow, starry-eyed bumpkin from the Midwest. In one of those little ironies, a couple of years later Jane and I were both at a New York party, and Barbara Walters, having forgotten all about the profile, introduced us, saying, "Jane, you should do a profile on David." Jane quickly said she didn't think I'd want that, and I just as quickly said she'd already done one, and that was more than enough.

None of this was much fun at the time. But looking back on it now, some people can't quite grasp why it was such a big deal. Was it just one of those moments the media obsesses over for a while and then forgets as we all pass on to the next public spectacle? Have our expectations about news changed so much that today the DiCaprio fracas would pass unnoticed? Or are there deeper lessons for me to learn from the whole fiasco?

Having a movie star interview a president went straight to the heart of something many journalists are sensitive about. Given that sensitivity, it was hard for people to believe that I wasn't trying to make a major statement by having DiCaprio interview the president for our special—a statement, not about the importance of the environment, but about the importance of journalists. It was hard for some to believe the simple truth that at the time my attention was directed elsewhere. I'd been absorbed in the millennium program, coverage of the presidential election, and Diane's interview with Elián González. And this came on top of running an organization putting on more than thirty hours of original television programs each week, staying on the air around the clock on radio, and running a 24/7 digital operation. Not an excuse, but a fact. I really hadn't given much more thought to the environmental special than that we were trying something innovative to get some people to watch an hour on a serious subject who otherwise might not. I missed the larger DiCaprio issue until it blew up in my face.

It wasn't only me who was distracted. The senior people overseeing the special were deeply involved in a much more ambitious and innovative set of news programs scheduled to air that summer, the pathbreaking *Hopkins 24/7* series showing for the first time a documentary-style behind-the-scenes look at a great American hospital. Producers were shooting and editing hundreds of hours of video and so relied on freelancers for the environmental special more than they would have done otherwise.

When I finally focused on the special featuring DiCaprio, I made a bad situation worse by making two mistakes. I didn't get command of the facts before responding to the press, and I didn't go on the offensive, challenging our critics to explain exactly what it was that we'd done wrong.

I'd done internal corporate investigations when I practiced law, and I knew that first accounts are almost always wrong (or at best incomplete). What's worse, the people who usually know the most about what happened are also the ones with the most to gain or lose from the outcome of the investigation. This means that you can't necessarily trust what you're being told. Despite this, when I heard that DiCaprio had sat down with the president, my first reaction was to rush to our public defense based on what I was told without doing enough checking to make sure. A rookie mistake if ever there was one.

There were those at the time who called on me to fire the people directly involved—not for having DiCaprio do the interview, but for misleading me about what led up to it. I asked the executive responsible for enforcing our standards to do a review and tell me what had happened. She concluded that we'd pressed the White House for both a walk around *and* an interview. What the White House did at the last minute was eliminate the walk around (probably because of time constraints)—it didn't add the interview. But who exactly misled whom along the chain of command was never clear. I couldn't look anyone in the eye and be certain that he or she had lied to me. I always suspected that someone down the line had pursued the interview aggressively and not fully informed their bosses, who, like me, had been focused on other things. When those bosses responded to my alarm, they didn't have the full story, and so they led me in the wrong direction. In the end, I decided to give the two people overseeing the project a formal reprimand and move forward.

Lacking a complete knowledge of the facts, I was too willing to accept without questioning the underlying premise of our critics. Implicit in all that gleeful commentary about how foolish we'd been was that it would have been a horrible act of journalistic malfeasance if we *had* arranged for DiCaprio to interview the president on the subject of the environment. Journalists I respected and who had been doing their jobs much longer than I had were writing that I'd done something terrible. In the heat of the moment, and maybe because I still was very much aware that I hadn't come to my post with a traditional news background, I deferred to their judgment.

Henry Grunwald, the legendary editor of *Time* magazine, tried to point this out to me at the time. He called me in the middle of the press coverage of the DiCaprio interview to say he thought the entire matter was nonsense, that what we'd done was no different from *Time* having a celebrity guest editor for an issue—something he'd done often. Of course, when newsmagazines like *Time* do this, they make it clear that the guest editor's role is not the same as that of the regular editor, and by this point Henry was long gone from *Time*. His successors crowned me "Loser of the Week" when the DiCaprio story broke.

I watched over the years with grudging admiration as some in the media effectively pursued a very different strategy from what I did with DiCaprio. When attacked, they typically struck back—hard and fast. Roger Ailes at Fox News has been particularly effective in doing this. Maybe if, instead of getting defensive, I'd challenged the public critics to tell their audience exactly what was so evil in having a famous person talk with the president about the environment, things might have turned out better. Maybe. But it wouldn't have addressed my internal critics, seasoned journalists who still weren't sure about me and so understandably jumped to the conclusion that I'd brought in DiCaprio to do their job because I didn't really appreciate what they did for a living. If I hadn't taken this criticism from inside my own organization so personally, I might have dealt with the problem with more detachment and sure-footedness.

Whether I'd meant to or not, with Leonardo DiCaprio's interview of the president I'd raised real questions about who is and who is not a journalist. As with my decision about the coverage of Princess Diana, this touched on the line between news and entertainment, but in a very different way. With the death of Diana, we deployed some of our best and most experienced journalists to cover a story that some may have thought lacked the substance of a major news story. With our environmental special, there was no question that we were justified in doing a prime-time special on an important subject. The issues raised were about who was doing the reporting, not whether we were covering a major news story. Throughout, I focused on the substance of what we were doing—even as our host of critics focused on DeCaprio.

It's understandable that journalists are particularly sensitive about who should—and who should not—be considered a "journalist." Journalism may be a profession, but it's a profession that differs from others in one important respect. There's no official way of knowing who is in the profession and who is not. Lawyers take standardized exams and are "called to the bar." Doctors take board exams. Accountants, dentists, veterinarians, and investment advisers all have state (and sometimes federal) tests that they have to pass. They all are subject to some form of government certification and government rules and regulations. Having been admitted through a formal process, they can be suspended or even banned from practicing their profession—officially and finally.

None of this applies to journalists. No state agency gives you a card that says you are a journalist. There's no journalism exam that you take and have to pass. Anyone can claim to be a journalist, and many do.

Walter Lippmann discussed this very issue back in 1920: "What are the qualifications for being a surgeon? A certain minimum of special training. What are the qualifications for operating daily on the brain and heart of a nation? None."

Lippmann went on in the same essay to warn that although the regulation of journalists "is a subtle and elusive matter," if journalists did not somehow find a way to deal with the quality-control problems within their profession, "some day Congress, in a fit of temper, egged on by an outraged public opinion, will operate on the press with an ax."

This hasn't happened. But in the century since Lippmann wrote, who is—and who is not—a "journalist" has become even more ambiguous and confused.

Long before DiCaprio went in to interview President Clinton, presidents and presidential candidates were figuring out ways to sidestep traditional, trained journalists in order to get their messages to the American people. At least as early as 1992, presidential candidates began turning up on daytime talk shows, in late-night arenas, and on cable programs to speak to the American people—all without the intermediary of an interviewer who is trained as a journalist. Remember presidential candidate Bill Clinton playing the saxophone on *Arsenio Hall* and talking about underwear on MTV?

And times have continued to change since then. It's not unusual to find sitting presidents chatting with the women of *The View* in the morning and Jon Stewart on *The Daily Show* at night.

Meanwhile, the airwaves are regularly given over to celebrities reporting on important subjects that once would have been reserved strictly for professional journalists. We have Bono telling us about problems in sub-Saharan Africa. Actually, we have Bono traveling to Africa with the secretary of the treasury to talk about such matters—and all the major news organizations cover it. We have Angelina Jolie traveling to Kenya with the economist Jeffrey Sachs for a half-hour cable program on the United Nations Millennium Project. We have George Clooney doing a prime-time special for NBC News with its anchor Ann Curry about the southern Sudan. If Bono or George Clooney were to sit down with President Obama today to talk about what the United States should do in Africa, I don't think anyone would find it objectionable—or even remarkable. To the contrary. We now have the distinguished journalist Nick Kristof writing in *The New York Times* that celebrities like Angelina Jolie and Mia Farrow and

Sean Penn "have shown a more sustained commitment" to covering stories such as Haiti, Darfur, and Bosnia "than most news organizations."

If we did our environmental special with Leonardo DiCaprio today, any objections would likely come from cable news commentators charging that liberals in the "mainstream media" were at it again, trying to sell the "myth of climate change." They wouldn't be about the journalism of an actor interviewing a president.

Further clouding the issue has been the dramatic expansion of cable news and the blogosphere. Virtually anyone with access to the Internet can hold forth on the issues of our day and reach thousands—or even millions—of people in a way that, in Lippmann's time, only newspaper reporters and columnists could. When we had DiCaprio interview President Clinton in April 2000, we were just on the cusp of the era of blogging and social networking. But even then we were seeing the cable news channels populated with a mix of experienced, able journalists, novices, and mere performers. And we could certainly feel the tsunami of information sources coming our way through the Internet. The question of who was a "journalist" was very much on people's minds—and particularly on the minds of those who made their living as journalists.

Journalists may be in a more vulnerable position than other professionals, but it's not clear that there's anything to be done about it. We can't make journalists into regulated professionals the way that lawyers and doctors and dentists are regulated. The First Amendment wouldn't permit it. It's no accident that the only profession explicitly protected by our Constitution is the press.

Not only would it be unconstitutional; it would be wrong. Back in law school I learned that the First Amendment made it possible for the press in this country to serve an essential "checking function" when it comes to the government (in the words of my constitutional law professor, Vince Blasi). I saw this checking function demonstrated time and again at ABC News over the years. By its very nature, government has great power, power that can overwhelm individual people and smaller institutions. At its best, the press can help restrain the government's exercise of this power—not by legislation or regulation or armed force, but simply by disclosing what the government is up to. As Thomas Jefferson put it: "No government ought to be without censors; and where the press is free no one ever will."

In modern history, we have seen any number of instances where our government argued strongly that the press should not publish information. We saw it with President Kennedy's anger over press reports about the Bay of Pigs invasion; we saw it when the Nixon administration went all the way to the Supreme Court to prevent the *Times* from printing the Pentagon Papers; and we've seen it in any number of less publicized cases right up to the present involving the war on terror and our efforts in Iraq and Afghanistan. If our government had the power to regulate the press in this country, can there be any doubt that it would use that power to stop the publication of reports it found objectionable?

So, for the most part, the press in this country is immune from state regulation. But this immunity comes with a price. It makes journalists less secure in some ways. And it even makes it harder for journalists to seek protection from the government.

I saw this tension firsthand in the lobbying journalists and news organizations have done for a so-called federal shield law. In recent years, prosecutors, private litigants, and some courts have grown more willing to compel journalists to give evidence in court—even when the evidence reveals a source to whom the journalist has promised confidentiality. If journalists were regulated professionals like lawyers or doctors, communications with them might well be protected in the way that we protect doctor-patient relationships, or conversations between lawyers and clients. But historically there hasn't been a comparable journalist-source privilege.

Almost all of the states have taken care of this by providing at least some form of protection for journalists seeking to keep their sources confidential. There isn't any such protection, however, at the federal level. So journalists have been arguing for years for Congress to enact a federal law to "shield" them from having to disclose their sources at least in some circumstances.

I did my part to support this sensible piece of legislation. I testified before the Senate Judiciary Committee, and I walked the halls of Congress talking with representatives and senators who served on the relevant committees. But I remember being pressed pretty hard by one senator about who should be considered a "journalist" in this day and age. The senator's concern didn't stop at just making sure that "real" journalists got to assert the protection. This particular senator had had personal experience with well-recognized journalists from established newspapers getting things wrong (or at least wrong in the senator's view) and attributing their reporting to anonymous sources. What was to prevent some journalist from simply making up a source and a story? How could we make sure that there really were confidential sources out there who had been given promises that their identities wouldn't come to light?

I tried to assure the senator that in my experience, established news organizations took the vetting of confidential sources very seriously and that there were mechanisms in place to guard against the dangers described. But I'm not sure I persuaded the senator that day. And the basic question I was being asked was fair: How could Congress step in to help "journalists" without defining who they are—and then making sure they weren't abusing the protection they were being offered by the government?

If government regulation isn't the way for journalists to feel more secure in their profession, what about self-regulation? Not the way that lawyers regulate themselves with the ultimate sanction of the government to enforce their decisions, but more in the nature of peer review and criticism. In Great Britain, for example, the Press Complaints Commission regulates newspapers and magazines. Putting aside the problems laid bare by the *News of the World* scandal (in which the commission failed to uncover the illegal activities of newspaper reporters intercepting private cell phone messages), it seems that the commission is relatively successful. But the Press Complaints Commission doesn't even apply to television and radio, and it's based on a threat of the government to regulate the newspapers directly—something that couldn't happen in the United States.

There may be no formal, legal definition of what makes someone a "journalist" in our country, but there is a true difference between people who have trained and devoted their lives to learning a craft and those who have not. I thought I knew this before going to ABC News, but I'm not sure I appreciated it fully even after I'd been there three years and the DiCaprio spectacle was dropped on my doorstep.

The public got a glimpse of how much skill, talent, and plain hard work go into truly good television news interviews in the film *Frost/Nixon*. We see David Frost, who hasn't been a professional news interviewer, struggling to prepare for long sessions interviewing former president Nixon on camera. *Frost/Nixon* may be a bit dramatic, but it shows a basic truth about how hard it is to conduct a good television interview. Most people don't get to see this side of the craft.

During my time at ABC News, I saw anchors prepare for interviews with an array of heads of state and other important news makers. In the fall of 2002, for example, I traveled with Barbara Walters and her producers to Havana for her second interview with Fidel Castro. The first Walters-Castro interview had come some twenty-five years before and had included her traveling with "El Presidente" across the Bay of Pigs in a small motorboat. Back then, President Castro was in his early fifties and in his prime. Now, after much negotiation and preparation, Barbara was going back to interview him again at a very different point in his career.

Barbara followed her normal routine for doing interviews. Long before we headed down to Cuba, she gathered possible questions from as many of her colleagues as she could, adding them to the dozens of questions she wrote herself. Then she spent hours with a small team of her most trusted producers culling, combining, refining, and changing the order again and again until she had firmly fixed what she wanted to ask, how she wanted to ask it, and the flow the interview should take. This process continued all the way down on the plane and for the two days we waited at the Hotel Nacional for our audience with Castro. By the time we got the call late at night to come set up at the Palace of the Revolution for the interview, Barbara had it all in her head. Because she was prepared so thoroughly, she could listen to the answers and follow the interview where it took her, always knowing the points she wanted to make sure she covered. What may look like a relaxed, natural conversation in a Barbara Walters interview has behind it extensive thought and work—and experience.

Over and above the curiosity, preparation, and skill of a great television interviewer is a strong competitive spirit. When Fidel Castro first came in the room for the interview and Barbara introduced me, he started the conversation by pulling Barbara's chain. "Barbara," he said, "I'm looking forward to our talk. And, of course, Andrea Mitchell [from NBC News] will be coming for a talk later in the week." We'd heard that Andrea was also coming down for an interview with Castro. We were first, but Andrea had access to a twenty-four-hour cable channel in MSNBC, and NBC's

*Dateline* was scheduled to air that week before Barbara's special. So if we weren't careful, NBC could end up airing a Castro interview before we did. I never knew whether this was a serious possibility or whether Castro just enjoyed getting a rise out of Barbara. I certainly thought I saw a twinkle in his eye. But get a rise it did.

Back at the hotel in the wee hours of the morning, Barbara turned to me and asked me to talk with the foreign minister (whom we both knew) to urge that they make sure her interview aired before any others. It made sense for me to do the asking, both because Barbara needed to meet again with Castro first thing the next morning and because it would be easier for me to explain how important Barbara's interview was than for her to be praising her own work.

So the next morning, while Barbara and her team were headed to a high school to meet Castro for a walk around and some further conversation, I arranged to meet the Cuban foreign minister, Felipe Pérez Roque, in his office. There, in the presence of his exotic tropical birds on their perches behind him, I made my pitch. He was sympathetic, but he said that only Castro himself could make the commitment that I asked for. So we climbed into his aged Lada automobile and went to join Castro, Barbara, and a couple thousand schoolkids. Barbara asked whether I'd achieved my mission, and I told her I had to talk with Castro himself. So, as we were walking from one classroom to another, I told the Cuban leader I needed a few minutes of his time. I got what I took to be a noncommittal response. For the next hour or so, we wandered around the school; everywhere we went, the students cheered for their leader. Finally, just as we were about to leave, Castro gestured to me to come into a small room just off the corridor. We were joined by Barbara, an interpreter, and Chuck Lustig, the head of our foreign desk.

I sat on the sofa with Castro. He leaned over and placed an arm behind my back. It was my job to pitch the longtime dictator of Cuba, a man who had dealt with John F. Kennedy and Nikita Khrushchev, on why he should give us an ABC News exclusive.

"Thank you, Mr. President, for your time and your candor, both in the interview with Barbara last night and in your time with us in the school today. I believe that you have said some interesting and important things about your country, about yourself, and about your attitude toward the

United States. Things that are important for the American people to hear for themselves.

"And now, I have to apologize for involving you in the mechanics of how American television works. This is something I deal with every day, but not something you would normally have to think about. But the truth is that the way TV works in America, for you to reach as many people as possible, it's important that Barbara's interview be the first one to air in the United States. If you give another interview to someone else that airs around the same time, it will dilute the force of what you are saying, and neither of us would want that."

Fidel Castro paused, smiled, and then said, through his interpreter, that he agreed, that he would not do the interview with Andrea Mitchell. And then he turned to me with that twinkle I thought I'd seen the night before and asked, "How long have you had your job?" I told him about five years. "You will do well," he said.

Barbara Walters is one of several exceptionally skilled interviewers whose experience and disciplined work ethic I watched lead to powerful television interviews. I saw Diane Sawyer as she prepared for her interview with the Clinton independent counsel, Ken Starr. Ted Koppel once took me to an interview he was doing with Shimon Peres in a room with only the Israeli foreign minister (which he was at the time), Ted, and the cameraman present. George Stephanopoulos dazzled all of us with his discipline and the depth of his preparation for his first presidential debate.

I got to see firsthand what makes a true journalist, and I came away without any doubt that there is a set of skills, a craft, that sets the professional journalist apart. But ultimately, it doesn't matter what I learned about the special qualifications for journalists. In the absence of any formal regulatory system, it's up to the people to decide for themselves who is and who is not a journalist, just as it's ultimately for the public, not the government, to reward or punish journalists for what they do.

We saw this at ABC News, for example, in the public support we received when some in the government went after us for something we reported in the aftermath of 9/11. One of the ongoing issues of real importance after the terrorist attacks was the extent to which our government had taken action to protect us in the future. Soon after 9/11, we saw this increased protection most obviously in the new forms of security at our airports. This was dramatic, visible, and substantial. But from the beginning, we reported along with others that one of the areas of greatest vulnerability was not seen by millions of Americans regularly: our nation's ports. There were particular concerns about the possibility of a weapon of mass destruction being brought to our shores in the massive containerized shipping that passed through cities such as New York and Los Angeles.

To illustrate the point, on the first anniversary of 9/11, Brian Ross and our investigative unit took some depleted uranium from Austria, hid it in a wooden chest, transported it undetected to Turkey, and from there shipped it into the United States through the port of New York. The depleted uranium in itself was not a danger, but its footprint on a scanner would have been similar to a low-grade nuclear weapon encased in the appropriate shielded container. We chose Turkey in particular as a plausible location from which a terrorist might be sending a nuclear device, given its proximity to the former Soviet republics where there was a good deal of fissile material. People had expressed concern that some of this material could become available on the black market.

As we had expected, we encountered no difficulties in bringing the uranium into New York and taking delivery. Needless to say, the U.S. Customs Service was none too pleased when we aired our report on the first anniversary of 9/11. It responded by "attack[ing] . . . the report and defend[ing] . . . the agency's record of detecting radioactive materials and the arsenal of gadgets at their disposal."

If Customs was angry with us for what we did in New York in 2002, it was furious when we did it again in 2003 for the second anniversary of 9/11. Once again we used depleted uranium hidden in household goods. But this time, we shipped it from Indonesia, a well-known operations center for al-Qaeda, and the destination was Los Angeles. This time Customs claimed that it knew about the uranium all along and allowed us to pick it up only so that its agents could follow us—a claim for which I never saw any evidence. We brought the depleted uranium from Los Angeles to New York, called Customs, and voluntarily turned it over. This time, the government decided to go after us, saying it had opened a formal investigation into whether we had committed an offense by filing a customs form that failed to specify that the "household goods" we were bringing into the country included some depleted uranium in a suitcase.

Things came to a head when one afternoon our senior vice president for editorial quality, Kerry Smith, who had vetted the Ross report, told me that there might be a warrant executed by the FBI to search our New York offices. Reportedly, Customs wanted to get its hands on whatever evidence we might have that would support its pursuit of a criminal prosecution. I responded by arranging to have cameras rolling, recording any federal agents who made a thorough search of our newsroom and editorial offices.

In the end, all of this went nowhere. There was no search, and there was no criminal complaint. I'm sure this was because it became public. Jon Stewart did a hilarious send-up of the entire fiasco based on the obvious point that if we were relying for our security on terrorists filing accurate and complete customs forms, then we were truly in deep trouble. Members of Congress stepped into the fracas. Senator Chuck Schumer said the federal investigation of ABC News "is not only against the American ethos, but will hurt our safety." Senator Dianne Feinstein said she thought "this is a case in point which established the soft underbelly of national security and homeland defense in the United States." Senator Charles Grassley wrote to Attorney General John Ashcroft, "If my neighbor told me my barn was on fire, my first instinct would be to thank my neighbor and get some water for the fire. I worry that the government's first instinct is to pour cold water on the neighbor."

What does all this have to do with Leonardo DiCaprio interviewing the president? Experiences such as these taught me that the court of public opinion is ultimately the place where both journalists and their critics are best judged. I've seen public disclosure and public reaction both protect journalism and police it. The power to reveal is great. It can be used for real good, as in the case of our uranium imports, or it can be abused. But the most effective check on such abuse is the same as it is for abuse by those in the government. It is not the government or some regulatory body that corrects the press; it is the people whom those in the news media serve. If journalists overstep their boundaries, their colleagues at other news organizations, bloggers, and citizen journalists will relish pointing it out to the public. And if the public objects, reporters feel it when their audience begins to turn away. Ultimately, this is the most threatening discipline that can be imposed, for audiences are the media's lifeblood.

It's not up to any official or ombudsman or guild to tell us who can practice journalism. It's up to the public to award individuals the title of journalist by paying attention to what they have to report. If we consistently report things that the public finds valuable and reliable, then our audience is likely to come back for more. If not, they will go elsewhere to get their news. No one tuning in to see Leonardo DiCaprio interview President Clinton about the environment mistook him for Ted Koppel or Diane Sawyer. Viewers knew what they were getting—and what they were not getting. It was up to them to decide whether it was worth their time and attention. Judging from our modest ratings, it appears that the public agreed with my critics. They loved Leonardo DiCaprio as an actor; they weren't as taken with him as an interviewer of presidents.

# 4 | Gore Wins? Bush Wins? How the Networks Blew the 2000 Election—Twice

Stop please, Gary. Stop. Stop. Gary, I apologize. We're going to make a projection now. ABC News is now going to project that Florida goes to Mr. Bush. Just stop and absorb that for a second . . . Take a look at it. That takes Mr. Bush, by our projections, to 271.

Unless there is a terrible calamity, George W. Bush by our projections is going to be the next president of the United States . . . and I feel obliged to add, at the moment, if this result holds. [ABC News political director] Mark Halperin nods in his usual way when I say something like, "if this vote holds."

—Peter Jennings, ABC News live coverage, 2:20 a.m., November 8, 2000

We called it "Vote 2000" at ABC News, and it was my first opportunity to lead the coverage of a presidential election. It promised to be an exciting one. President Clinton had been in office eight years, the first Democrat to serve two full terms as president since Franklin Roosevelt. Conventional wisdom was that the only way for a Democrat to win was if the American people wanted what amounted to a third Clinton term.

There was no doubt that President Clinton had been hurt by the Lewinsky scandal. A full 60 percent of Americans polled at the end of his term said that the country was on the wrong track morally. But in sharp contrast, two-thirds of the people thought we were headed in the right direction overall. This wasn't surprising. The country was at peace, inflation was low, and remarkably, given where we are today, the nation was actually running a budget surplus. All of this led the American people to appreciate what Bill Clinton had done as president even as they disapproved of some of what he'd done as a man.

Into this complicated situation stepped two men. One, Al Gore, had been the vice president under Clinton. He was intelligent and diligent but a bit stiff and not particularly charismatic—and in this way the opposite of Bill Clinton. On the other side was Governor George W. Bush of Texas. He was part of the Bush dynasty, the son of a former president, the grandson of a senator from Connecticut, and the brother of the governor of Florida. Mr. Bush was inexperienced in international affairs and sometimes appeared to be disengaged or uninterested. But he was likable and had a good record as a pragmatic Texas governor. He'd also raised a formidable war chest early. He was not to be underestimated (although many in the media tried their best).

At ABC News, we began our preparations well over a year before the election when, in the summer of 1999, we selected our "off-air" reporters. These highly sought-after jobs give relatively junior journalists the opportunity to start traveling with candidates months before any scheduled caucuses or primaries—and, for that matter, well before most of the rest of the press showed up on the campaign trail. It was our way of getting to know the candidates before they were surrounded by handlers and consultants and Secret Service.

Following a tradition, ABC News invited all of the candidates in for informal, off-the-record conversations in the summer and fall of 1999—another opportunity to get to know them a bit before the primary season started. All of the candidates, including the vice president, accepted our invitation—all but one. Mr. Bush's people said that the governor would receive us in Austin, Texas, but he would not travel to New York.

So, on November 16, a small group of us, including Peter Jennings and Sam Donaldson, flew to Austin to meet with Governor Bush and members of his campaign staff. After lunch with Karen Hughes at a local Tex-Mex restaurant and short meetings with Karl Rove and Joe Allbaugh (Bush's campaign manager), we went to the Governor's Mansion for a fifty-minute session with Bush himself. We were joined by Condoleezza Rice, then an official at Stanford University and a senior foreign policy adviser to the governor. (Rice years before had been a consultant to ABC News on foreign policy issues, working directly with Peter Jennings. Peter liked to joke that he was the one who had discovered Condoleezza Rice.)

All of us were struck that day by how likable Bush was. He had a relaxed, friendly demeanor and seemed completely at ease. He answered all of our questions without hesitation or a hint of self-doubt. In talking about an upcoming foreign policy address that he was working on with Dr. Rice, he went into some detail about U.S. relations with Russia. When I asked whether we would be spending as much time talking about Russia if it didn't have nuclear weapons, Bush thought for a moment and then admitted that, no, we probably wouldn't. It was a refreshing and honest answer. I glanced across the room at Rice. If I read her reaction right, she wasn't sure that her candidate should be quite that refreshing and honest with us.

I spent a couple of days on the campaign trail just before the New Hampshire primary at the end of January 2000. Our political director, Mark Halperin, and I joined Senator John McCain on his "Straight Talk Express" bus for a ride to a rally in Portsmouth, watched Vice President Gore awkwardly go into a local shop in Keene to buy a pastry, and stood in the frigid cold of Dublin sipping hot apple cider around a wood fire blazing in an oil drum as Senator Bill Bradley did his best to rally the troops, joined by his former NBA competitor Bill Russell. This was retail politics, one-on-one, as intimate as it gets.

After watching *World News* from our work space in the Holiday Inn back in Manchester, we went to a rally at a local club where Governor Bush was to speak at the Lincoln Dinner. The atmosphere surrounding Bush was altogether different from the scene around Senator McCain or Senator Bradley or even Vice President Gore. There was no question of actually getting to talk with the governor. He wheeled up in a luxury bus, surrounded by security and staff (and our own off-air reporter, John Berman). We were kept a healthy distance away. It felt as though he were president already.

Well before the time of the conventions in the summer, the battle lines were pretty clearly drawn. It would be Governor Bush against Vice President Gore. Bush promised to "restore dignity to the office of the presidency"—a none too subtle reminder of Monica Lewinsky under the desk in the Oval Office. On the other side, Gore emphasized the peace and prosperity that the administration he'd served had brought to the country. At that point, the United States was running a healthy budget surplus of over $200 billion a year; there'd been thirty-three consecutive quarters of job growth, with the jobless rate below 4 percent; and the stock market had grown by more than 225 percent over the prior eight years.

But as strong as this record was, and as high as President Clinton's job approval ratings were, Gore didn't embrace his boss wholeheartedly. I watched the vice president's acceptance speech sitting in our work space in the Staples Center in Los Angeles with George Stephanopoulos. It seemed to me that Gore was making a mistake in not simply saying he'd keep doing what President Clinton had done. But George, who knows much more about American politics than I do, strongly disagreed. In his estimation, too many voters would turn against Gore if he were tainted in any way with the moral lapses of President Clinton. George thought the vice president simply couldn't take that risk.

And so the race played out through the summer and fall of 2000 with Bush and Gore going back and forth in the polls, never separated by more than a few points. By the time of the election, most polls had Bush ahead, but there were reports that Gore was closing in on Bush, and he might be closing fast.

On November 7, 2000, the nation went to the polls to elect a new president. Surprisingly little happens in a network newsroom the morning and early afternoon of Election Day. There are the standard stories about polls opening around the eastern United States, with the traditional first balloting in Dixville Notch, New Hampshire. On this day Dixville Notch went for Bush by a vote of 21–5. We had reporters scattered around the country to report on voter turnout, and we checked in regularly with election officials to keep tabs on any irregularities. But we all knew that none of this had much to do with the ultimate question of who would be our next president.

ABC News for many years has had a two-part system for analyzing voting data. It's part of a consortium called the Voter News Service (VNS) that includes CBS, NBC, CNN, Fox, and the Associated Press. Collectively, the members of the consortium pay more than $20 million every four years to fund a staff of experts that develops sophisticated computer models to analyze the various data coming in on election night and provide statistical analyses showing the probability of various outcomes.

The cornerstone of this huge effort is the exit poll, something that everyone—the candidates, the political pundits, the networks, and the public at large—loves to hate. Designed first and foremost to offer an early read on who's winning and who's losing, they also provide valuable clues to why voters are making the decisions they're making, and they can identify voting trends across the country. Everybody criticizes exit polls, but nobody can get enough of them. Or get them soon enough.

What I didn't know, but was about to find out, was how imperfect exit polls could be. Back in 2000, we paid the VNS consortium to send workers to polling places around the country and hand out questionnaires to people coming out of polling places. We tried to make this a representative sample by choosing certain polling places. But local laws and regulations restrict how close the people handing out surveys can be to the polls; no one is required to fill out the questionnaires, so there can be some self-selection; the surveys are completed by the voters, rather than having someone ask them the questions; and—what's become an increasing problem and factored largely in the 2000 election—the exit polls don't cover absentee ballots. We tried to compensate with telephone polls, but the fact remained that a large and growing part of the electorate couldn't be surveyed at the polls because they never went there.

Over and above the millions spent on exit polls, the consortium pays millions more to the Associated Press for providing actual vote count as it comes in from the counties around the country. The networks take the exit poll results, the actual vote count from the AP, and precinct tallies from the states and put them all into the computer models to make projections.

To run all this, ABC News employed a group of experts collectively known as the Decision Desk. The Decision Desk was charged with looking at the computer models and data provided by the consortium, applying its own computer models and its own expertise, and advising when it was safe to project winners. All of this—the exit polls, the early, partial vote counts, the computer models, and the Decision Desk—was part of a complicated and very expensive system designed for one thing: to tell viewers who won without their having to wait until all the votes were counted. Through the years there has developed an unbelievably ferocious competition to be the first to project a winner.

In this competition, ABC News believed it had an advantage. Long before I arrived, I knew of the Decision Desk's reputation for uncanny accuracy. It was a basic tenet throughout the entire company that the ABC News Decision Desk was better than all the rest. It got it first, and it got it right. It was a combination of the ability and experience of the people and the special computer models they had constructed. The rest of us frankly didn't understand how the Decision Desk worked. For the most part, we were a group of liberal arts majors who'd never taken statistics and didn't really understand the discipline. But we were confident. We had a policy of not projecting any race unless we had a statistical certainty of 99.5 percent. How more sure could we be?

The first inkling most of us had that the 2000 election might not work according to plan came in the early afternoon of Election Day itself, when the first of the three waves of exit polls came in. About 3:00, a large group of us packed into a fifth-floor conference room at 47 West 66th Street a few feet outside my office. The entire election team was either in the room or on the speakerphone—including Peter Jennings, George Stephanopoulos, Cokie Roberts, Mark Halperin, other members of our political unit, people from our special events team, an array of producers, and executives and others who were just plain curious. The briefing was led, as usual, by the head of the ABC News Decision Desk. We also were joined by the head of our Polling Unit, who was there to help interpret larger trends we were seeing in the exit poll surveys—things like how men were voting versus women and what issues were figuring most prominently in why people said they were voting one way or another.

You could never really rely on the first wave of exit polls, because it was just that—the first wave. Everyone knew two more waves were coming, so anything you learned was supported by only one-third of the data. But the first wave of exit poll data in 2000 was particularly unhelpful. If things kept up this way, it looked as if we wouldn't know all that much for several hours, when polls around the country began to close. Looking back on it now, waiting for actual vote data seems only reasonable. The election teams at the networks were spoiled, however. For several prior presidential elections, the various data and projections had pointed pretty decidedly in one direction or the other by the afternoon. Those behind the scenes at the networks felt that they were always just about the first to "know" who was going to win.

In 2000, things weren't going that way. In fact, early indications were that we might not be able to tell anything in nearly half the states—

twenty-three to be precise—at poll closing. In state after state, we were told things were "too close to call." No one could remember the last time we'd had this much uncertainty at this point on Election Day. What was worse, there were problems in the numbers, problems that indicated we should be relying on the early exit polls even less than we normally would. For example, the first wave of exit polls had a very heavy concentration of female voters—heavier than what we had seen at this point in any previous presidential elections. Where were all the men? It was possible that this year for some reason all the women had decided to vote early and the men were waiting until later in the day, but we had no way of knowing whether this was true or whether there was something wrong with the exit polling itself.

You might think, given all these conflicting and incomplete reports, that we could at least be confident that in the end the election would be very close. But our experts warned us that they couldn't even predict that. The early data suggested that Vice President Gore might be doing better than expected in many places—far better. We just didn't know much of anything.

Not long after we digested the first wave of exit poll information, we began to hear about leaks—to the campaigns and on the Internet. Rumors swirled that after all the suspense, things were pointing decidedly in the direction of Vice President Gore. I had no way of knowing who was doing the leaking, but it was clearly coming from someone inside the networks. And what I knew told me that what was being leaked was completely unreliable. Never mind that we steadfastly refused to confirm any of the rumors; never mind that the science of statistics, as explained to us by our own experts, said that at that point we had no real basis for thinking either side had an advantage; never mind that there were particular reasons for us to question the reliability of the early exit polls more than we normally did. Some people with access to the first wave of exit poll results evidently had decided they were saying something important. And some of these people had chosen to leak to the campaigns (and ultimately to other members of the press) that early returns favored Gore.

I never learned who leaked the early exit poll returns—or even whether the leaks had come from us, from our competitors, or all of the above. There's a symbiotic relationship between political reporters and the campaigns. For this symbiosis to work, the reporters feel they have to share what they know (or think they know). This wasn't something new in 2000. I'm told that information about early exit poll results had been traded back and forth among a small group of reporters and political operatives for years. But this time was different. By 2000, the Internet and e-mail had come into their own. An e-mail sent by one person inside a network to one campaign worker could quickly spread to a much larger audience not familiar with the many flaws in early poll results. The genie was out of the bottle.

We may have gotten off to a rocky start, but through all the excitement and confusion of the afternoon and evening of November 7, we remained steadfastly confident in the ability of our Decision Desk to sort it all out. They'd never let us down before, and we were sure they wouldn't let us down this time.

ABC News was scheduled to air its regular East Coast version of *World News Tonight* at 6:30 and then immediately come back on the air with our special report that would air to the entire network until we had a new president. That broadcast was expected to last at least until 11:00 p.m. eastern time. The second wave of exit poll results came in just before *World News Tonight*. It didn't help much. Many, too many, states remained very much up in the air. This included key states such as Ohio, Pennsylvania, and Florida—although, in fairness, the exit polls through the second wave were largely in line with the consensus of the preelection polling for these states. Both Florida and Pennsylvania were expected to be too close to call at poll closing; Ohio was showing pretty much the advantage for Bush that preelection polling had predicted, but the difference to that point still made it a reasonably close race. Many more votes would have to be counted and many more numbers crunched before we could make projections with the certainty our system required.

After listening to the second wave exit poll results, I went back to my office on the fifth floor of 47 West 66th Street, one floor directly above the control room. Peter Jennings and the rest of our on-air team were twenty-two blocks south in our Times Square studio ordinarily used by *Good Morning America*, where we'd built a special, elaborate set for election night. In my earlier days at ABC News, I'd gone to the control room for special events, sitting on a stool right behind the producer and director. But I'd learned from experience that when I did that, I shut myself off from much of the world. It was too easy to get caught up in the drama within the control room and lose perspective. By the time of the 2000 election, I preferred to remain for the most part in my office, watching our coverage much as someone would at home. That way, I could follow what others were reporting and communicate more easily with the Decision Desk and others inside and outside ABC News. Throughout the evening, I'd take the short walk down to the control room to see how things were going and whether we needed to make any adjustments.

On this particular night, I'd asked a few of my colleagues to watch all the networks' coverage in the common area just outside my office. There was too much going on for me to catch it all, and I wanted to keep track of what everyone was reporting and when. I also asked for their ongoing critique of our reporting.

As *World News Tonight* was airing, our Decision Desk was hard at work determining which states, if any, we would be able to project as polls began to close on the East Coast at 7:00. They were watching Florida closely, where the exit polls had Gore with a lead of 7 percent. It was still not enough to make a projection, but it was a lead, and it seemed to be holding up as more data came in. We would have to wait until we had some actual vote counts in Florida to be able to make a final projection. And so, when Peter came on the air to begin our special election coverage that night at 7:00, he said that Florida at that point was "too close to call," even though 90 percent of the Florida polls had closed (the other 10 percent being in the Panhandle, which is on central time).

By 7:40, VNS had provided us with actual vote tallies in eight of the sample precincts in Florida we typically looked to for a barometer of how things were likely to come out. These actual votes reinforced what the models were already showing. If anything, the actual votes suggested that the exit polls had understated the Gore advantage. All this raised the confidence level of our statistical models above that 99.5 percent mark. I got a call from the Decision Desk saying we'd be ready to make projections in several states by 8:00, including the important state of Florida.

I'd been following Gore's slim lead in our data for Florida, but I was still surprised when I got that call from the Decision Desk. We already knew Florida would be critical to this election. We'd said it again and again in the days leading up to November 7. And we'd all thought it would be a close race. We hadn't had enough to call the race when the majority of the polls closed at 7:00, but here we were less than an hour later—and before the last 10 percent of the Florida polls had closed—saying we were sure enough to project the winner in Florida.

I asked how sure we were, exactly. I was told that the computer models we'd used successfully for so many years fully justified the projection. By this time, it was a few minutes before 8:00, and both CBS and CNN had already projected that Gore would win Florida. Our format through the night was to give about ten minutes to the local stations for their own political coverage before the top of each hour. Peter wasn't actually on the air at the time. The question was whether we should take the extraordinary step of preempting local programming with a special report to the full network (something that some stations might decide not to take) or wait the few minutes until 8:00. I decided we should wait but that we could go ahead and make our projection on ABC News Radio, which was broadcasting nationally throughout the evening, and on ABCNews.com.

And so, at 7:55 eastern time, ABC News Radio and ABCNews.com projected that Vice President Gore would carry the state of Florida. Just after 8:00, when Peter Jennings came back on for continuing election coverage, he made the projection on the full ABC Television Network. Almost immediately, Governor Bush and his top political adviser, Karl Rove, began challenging the networks' projection of a Gore win in Florida. In retrospect, Karl's eagerness to challenge us on the record should have given me pause. But at the time, I chalked it up to partisan advocacy and went on.

My attention quickly turned from Florida to our overall coverage. It felt as though we were behind on just about every projection. We'd get to the same projection sooner or later, but we were almost always a few minutes (or more) behind our direct competitors. I could see it watching the television screens in my office; my colleagues were coming in to make sure I was seeing what they were seeing. I became increasingly frustrated. We'd been planning for this night for over a year. We'd invested tens of millions of dollars. It was one of the most important stories that any national news organization covers. And here we were, coming in second. Or third. Or worse. You might ask what difference it made; being first was only one of the things that defined excellence in election coverage. And with so many outlets making projections of one sort or another, it's one of the least important things. But in the heat of the moment, it's the one thing you can measure for sure. It just wasn't realistic to ask competitive newspeople not to pay attention to who's getting the story first.

I knew that night that we were being more conservative than our competitors, but I couldn't tell whether that was because we were showing the caution that the situation required or because we weren't pressing hard enough. I checked with my colleagues at the Decision Desk but was told that too many races were simply too close. We couldn't be any more aggressive. So I stuck with the system that had never let us down, and I made a mental note to come back and do a postmortem on exactly why we seemed to be consistently behind the others.

While I was focused on our competitive disadvantage, the basis for our Florida projection for Gore was shifting. At 8:10 and 8:40, our models continued to show a solid lead for the vice president in Florida. Even at 9:10, with 36 percent of the county vote tallies recorded, our projection for Gore appeared solid. But about this time the first indication of trouble appeared. We got vote tallies both by county and by precinct. They fed into different statistical models, which we compared with each other. By 9:10 the two started showing different numbers on computer screens. Both models continued to tell us that Vice President Gore would win in Florida, but the precinct numbers were starting to weaken. At 9:40, VNS sent a message to us and the other members that questioned the reliability of the projection all of us (including VNS itself) had made for Florida. As our experts went over the numbers coming in, it became clear that if we'd known at 8:00 what we knew an hour and a half later, we never would have made the projection that Florida would go for Gore.

Shortly before 10:00, the Decision Desk called to tell me something had gone wrong and that we would have to pull back our projection in Florida and return the state to the "undecided" column. The AP had already retracted its projection; CBS and CNN were doing the same.

I was shocked. In over thirty years of election coverage, ABC News had never had to retract a projection in a presidential election. What could have gone wrong? But by this point it was far too late for me to open up the black box that was our Decision Desk and sort out what was broken. And even if I had, it would take me weeks just to understand how the system worked, much less figure out what we could do to fix it—or even who should do the fixing.

And so, once again, I decided we had no choice but to rely on our Decision Desk to pull us through the night. The serious review that was obviously needed would have to wait until after the dust had cleared. We were still on the air live, competing as best we could, and we had a presidential election to cover, not to mention 435 House races and 34 Senate races.

At shortly after 10:00 that evening, Peter Jennings went back on the air to retract our projection that Florida would go for Gore and to put the state and its twenty-five electoral votes back in the "undecided" column.

The evening dragged on into the early morning hours, with various state returns putting electoral votes in one column or the other. But Florida's critical twenty-five electoral votes remained up for grabs. We now realized that whichever way Florida went would almost certainly determine who the next president of the United States would be.

About 2:15 in the morning, I was watching as Peter Jennings interviewed the managing editor of *The Miami Herald*, Larry Olmstead. In his questioning, Peter pointed out that "we're looking at minuscule numbers in terms of exit poll percentages," and the editor noted that exceedingly close races were going on in Florida, not only for president, but also for Senate and Congress and the state attorney in Miami-Dade County. In the middle of this exchange, I saw Fox News on another monitor make its projection that Florida would go for George W. Bush and declare that he would therefore become the forty-third president of the United States. Fox went straight to its prepared, elaborate graphics package with all the pomp and circumstance that attend these announcements on network television. Ironically, at about this point Peter was saying to Olmstead that "no one has made the 1948 mistake yet," referring to the infamous *Chicago Tribune* banner headline that had mistakenly proclaimed: "Dewey Defeats Truman."

Almost immediately, NBC News made the same projection—both on the NBC Television Network and on MSNBC. After well over a year of intensive preparation, we now had been beaten by not one but two competitors.

I quickly went down to the control room. No, it's fair to say that I ran down the stairs about as fast as I could. As I went into the room, I looked up at the monitors in the corner that showed what our competitors were doing. By this point, I could see that CBS News had joined Fox and NBC in proclaiming George W. Bush our next president. Peter was still interviewing Olmstead about other Florida races and how his newspaper would be covering the election in the morning edition. I asked the executive in charge of our political coverage, Paul Friedman, if he realized that others were making a projection in Florida while we were talking with a newspaper editor about local coverage of races in his state. In my mind, I was being very restrained and calm; I'm not sure that a video of how I was actually coming across would reflect that restraint and calm.

Of course, Paul and everyone else in the control room knew about the other projections. How could they have missed them? They were watching all the monitors just as I'd been. They weren't any happier than I was with our being beaten. As we talked, CNN became the fourth television news organization to project the Florida race would go for Bush. Now it was official; we were dead last.

Paul was on the telephone with the head of our Decision Desk. He relayed to me that they still weren't confident in projecting a Bush win in Florida. But it did look as if it would go that way. Paul asked, "Do you want to overrule them and go with the projection?" I said no. As embarrassing as it was, I felt we should stick with the game plan, rely on our people and our models, and take our lumps. By this time, Peter had moved on from the *Miami Herald* editor to begin asking our polling director, Gary Langer, about votes for Ralph Nader in Florida and how they might (or might not affect) the outcome. And all the time our competitors continued to celebrate the election of a new president.

A short time later, the control room telephone rang. It was our Decision Desk, saying that they were now comfortable making the projection. Marc Burstein, the executive producer, immediately told Peter through his earpiece; Peter broke off his discussion of Nader with Gary—"Stop please, Gary. Stop. Gary, I apologize. We're going to make a projection now"—and ABC News joined the others in projecting that George W. Bush would be our next president.

While it was happening, it seemed to take an eternity for us to get from that first Fox News projection to our own. But when we went back over it later, only five minutes had passed—Fox projected Florida for Bush at 2:15, NBC at 2:16, CBS and CNN at 2:18. Peter made our projection at 2:20. Late or not, our work was done.

Or so we thought.

Almost immediately, Peter and Mark Halperin started to ask questions on the air about whether this thing was truly over. Even as Peter was announcing that George W. Bush would be the next president, he wondered aloud on the air about how we could be sure about our projection: "I'd love to see the popular vote in Florida, because it's Florida we want to key on at this moment now, with 97 percent of the precincts reporting. That doesn't mean that the vote is completely called. That does not mean there will not be a challenge. That does not mean that the absentee ballots have yet to be considered, and I'm not quite sure how our polling unit actually considered them, but we may want to ask them in just a moment."

The way these things work, network anchors don't have the luxury of reviewing the basis for an election projection before they make it live on the air. They're even more dependent on the strength of their Decision Desk than I was. I'm not sure Peter realized how right he was to raise questions from the start, but certainly his instincts as a reporter over so many years and in so many uncertain circumstances taught him to be cautious, particularly when so much had already gone wrong that election night. Then word came from the Gore campaign that the vice president would be making a statement in about twenty minutes, which most people thought would be some form of concession. So maybe we could rest easy despite Peter's hesitation.

From then on, I stayed in the control room, watching our coverage but also monitoring the vote counts as they were reported to us. For the first half hour or so, our projection looked to be on even sounder footing than when we'd first made it. VNS numbers showed Governor Bush's lead growing to over fifty-five thousand votes with only an estimated sixty-eight thousand votes left to count. The chances of Vice President Gore's overcoming that lead by taking all of the remaining, uncounted votes were astronomically slim.

At 2:30, Vice President Gore called Governor Bush to concede defeat. Clutching at straws, I was frankly relieved. If the vice president conceded, then our projections must be right. It didn't occur to me at the time that Vice President Gore and his team were relying on our projections rather than looking at their own, independent analysis of the voting.

At 2:48 a.m., Bush's lead dropped dramatically. At the time, we didn't know why; weeks later we'd learn that someone working for the County of Volusia had made a clerical error, giving Bush credit for thousands of votes that he shouldn't have had. We'd relied in part on these erroneously reported votes when we made our projection. When the error was discovered and reversed, the Bush projection didn't look quite so solid any more. At 3:00 a.m., the remaining votes for Palm Beach County were reported, and Bush's lead dropped to only eleven thousand. At just this moment, the vice president's motorcade was heading for an outdoor rally at the War Memorial Plaza in Nashville to give his public concession speech. While Gore's car moved, we watched as Bush's minuscule lead got only tinier.

On the set at Times Square, Peter, George Stephanopoulos, and Mark Halperin, were watching the Florida secretary of state's website as it reported actual votes coming in. They could see for themselves how narrow the Bush lead had become. They debated on the air whether these numbers were really ahead of what the VNS was reporting or whether VNS was ahead of the secretary of state. Then word came that the vice president was having second thoughts. He had placed a second call to Governor Bush to withdraw his earlier concession. In the control room, my heart sank. Things had gone from bad to worse, with now two erroneous projections about the critical state of Florida.

Shortly after 4:00 a.m., Bill Daley, Gore's campaign manager, came out to address the crowd gathered in Nashville. Instead of conceding defeat, Daley said the race wasn't over.

By this time, it was clear to everyone—to Peter, to those of us in the control room, and to our audience—that our projection of Florida going for Bush wasn't supported by the facts. He might ultimately win, but we didn't have enough information to predict that with confidence. As Peter put it, "Let's get back to Florida because in the interest of sobriety, if nothing else, we are going to take Florida back into the too-close-to-call column. So we now have our second major switch of the night . . . this is astonishing."

We stayed on the air for almost two more hours, getting off at 6:00 a.m. There were still more results coming in. We went more than once to the two candidates' camps for reactions. We talked about the recount in Florida that was now inevitable. There was still an incredible story to report, even after eleven hours of nonstop coverage.

As we know now, that contest would continue until it was ultimately resolved by the Supreme Court some thirty-five days later, on December 12. Over the course of the month, the nation would learn about "hanging chads" and the "butterfly ballots" that caused some voters to confuse Pat Buchanan with Al Gore; they would know all about Florida's election laws and its secretary of state, Katherine Harris. But at that moment, as I got in my car to drive home to Bronxville, all I knew was that I was exhausted and embarrassed—and that we had a very big problem on our hands. After showering and changing, I was back in the office within an hour. We had blown it—big-time—and I needed to figure out what had gone so terribly wrong. In the words of our competitor Tom Brokaw, "We don't just have egg on our face, we've got omelet all over our suits."

The first thing I did when I got back to the office was talk with Kerry Smith, our senior vice president for editorial quality. Kerry had a team of people whose job it was to make sure we got our reporting right. They reviewed all investigative reports, all long-form pieces, and anything else that might be controversial. Working with our in-house lawyers, they asked questions about sources, reviewed underlying documents, and made changes where necessary. They maintained our extensive written standards and periodically went through the organization giving seminars on those standards and on journalistic ethics more generally.

Up to that point, Kerry and her team had never been involved in the work of the Decision Desk or election projections. For many years the Decision Desk had been kept separate from the rest of the News Division—separate from standards and practices, separate from our other political reporting, and separate from any sense of what other news organizations were projecting. This was meant to protect it from undue influence, but it also made it a black box removed from the real world. I understand, by the way, that this was largely how Decision Desks worked at the other networks.

That Kerry had not been involved in any of our projections made her the perfect person to figure out what had gone wrong. She was an experienced journalist who'd dealt with flawed reporting before. She wasn't involved, so she wouldn't feel any need to be defensive. I'd learned my lesson from the DiCaprio fiasco; I wasn't going to rely on those with the most at stake to tell me what had happened. I asked Kerry to enlist the in-house lawyers, interview anyone she needed to interview, review the necessary documents, and give me a complete analysis of what had gone wrong and what we needed to do to fix it.

Kerry and her team were still doing their interviews and reviewing the computer projections when Congress weighed in with vigor. A week after the election, on November 14, I watched the chairman of the House Commerce Committee, Billy Tauzin of Louisiana, hold a press conference. He thought the mistakes he'd seen us make on election night might be more sinister than just human error. As he put it, "In short, the evidence is mounting that there was some kind of bias in this system. Now, was it intentional bias or was it accidental bias? Was it a bias because of modeling? Or was it a bias because of personal bias or prejudice of persons working at the networks? I can't answer that. I don't know." And so he set a hearing of his committee at which the networks would be called to defend what we'd done.

I spent a good part of the next two months going through our process for projecting election results. It turned out that we could replicate all the computer screens from throughout the night as our Decision Desk had reviewed them at the time. I personally sat for hours with a colleague, Dan Merkle, going over these screens one by one. Dan was the best statistician we had on the team and (in my opinion) the best in the business when it came to how the networks made projections on election night. He patiently explained as best he could how our computer models worked. Together, we took apart what had happened—both where we'd gotten it right and where we'd gotten it wrong.

On February 14, 2001, I appeared with my counterparts from NBC, CBS, CNN, Fox, and the Associated Press for several hours as members of Congress questioned and criticized us. As I said at the time, those of us in the press are constitutionally protected from government oversight of our internal editorial processes. But we are fully accountable to the American people for the accuracy of what we report—particularly when it's on a subject as important as a presidential election. I saw the congressional committee as representing the people in asking understandably searching questions about what had gone wrong on election night.

The night of the 2000 election produced the worst-ever failure in the history of U.S. election coverage. The only possible comparison was the one that Peter had alluded to at about the time of the second Florida projection—the infamous "Dewey Defeats Truman" headline from more than fifty years earlier. But at least in 1948, President Truman hadn't been misled by the media to call and concede to Governor Dewey before the mistake was caught.

Our internal analysis showed that it wasn't just one thing that had gone wrong in Florida. And everything had gone wrong in the same direction, at more or less the same time. We had underestimated the number of absentee ballots being cast in Florida. Actual vote counts coming in early in the evening turned out to be unrepresentative of what would come in later. Our exit polls had overstated Vice President Gore's performance and understated Governor Bush's. Late in the night there was that mistake someone had made in counting the votes in Volusia County that overstated Bush's lead. And the VNS model had led us to believe fewer votes were left to be counted than in truth there were. Taken altogether, it was a mess.

We might have recovered from any one of these errors. For example, actual vote counts as they began to come in should have shown us whether the particular exit polls taken in Florida that day had some statistical bias—that the data for some reason were overstating one candidate's support. But instead of pointing us in the right direction, the actual vote tallies through much of the night suggested that if the exit polls had been off, it was in *underestimating* Vice President Gore's likely victory margin. This time, early actual vote counting led us further from the truth rather than toward it.

About the only consolation we could take from the autopsy of our coverage was that in the end our reporting had no intentional bias. To his credit, Representative Tauzin, having first raised this possibility a week after the election, came back later to admit in public that upon further examination, he had found no reason to believe we had done anything intentionally wrong.

Similarly, suggestions by some that Fox News had triggered a stampede to project Florida for Governor Bush in the early hours of the morning were never supported by fact. It was true enough that John Ellis, the governor's first cousin, was running Fox's Decision Desk that night and that he reportedly had been in contact through the night with his cousin's campaign. It may not have been the smartest thing to have someone tied so directly to one of the campaigns making the projections; certainly we wouldn't have allowed it. And it probably didn't help some people's perception that John wasn't the only Bush relative involved that night. Jeb Bush was, after all, the governor of Florida. But all of us were looking at the same data that night, and at the time we made the projections, they were justified by the systems we had in place. Fox may have gone first, but not by much. And I have little doubt that if the numbers and computer models had not warranted our subsequent projections, we would not have made them when we did.

The lack of real evidence of any intentional wrongdoing or bias was cold comfort. All of us understood that we had some profound weaknesses in the way we projected election results, weaknesses we would need to address aggressively.

In the wake of the 2000 election debacle, ABC News took several steps to make sure we wouldn't repeat our mistakes ever again:

- We reviewed and rebuilt our computer models.
- We tightened our protocols to anticipate a wider range of human and other error.
- We put the entire election projection apparatus under the supervision of the editorial quality team.
- We changed the staffing of our Decision Desk.
- We increased our polling of voters who wouldn't normally be interviewed by traditional exit polls (by increasing phone polls of absentee and early voters and, especially, interviewing voters on cell phones as well as on landlines).
- We insulated our Decision Desk team from what the competition was doing as much as we could, but we also resolved that we would talk directly to the campaigns to get their thoughts and objections before making critical projections.

We took all of these steps on our own, without government direction or support and without consulting with any other news organizations. But one additional reform that could help avoid problems in the future would need government action: Congress could pass a law that all polls across the country have to close at the same time. One of the things we were criticized for in the aftermath of the 2000 election was our making the projection (at least on ABC News Radio and ABCNews.com) in

Florida a few minutes before the polls had closed in the Florida Panhandle, representing about 10 percent of the electorate. Some people claimed that our projection might have discouraged some Panhandle voters from going to polls. Whether this is true or not, it would make sense simply to decree that everyone has to get their votes in by the same time. That might mean East Coast polls closing later and West Coast earlier, but it would address at least some of the problems we saw in 2000. Given the networks' commitment not to project any race until all of the polls are closed, it would mean that everyone would have to wait until all the voting was done, which in my view could only improve the quality of the reporting of election results. Thus far Congress has not been willing to do this.

The reforms that the networks have already instituted make it less likely we'll have a repeat any time soon of the 2000 election problems. But there's also a larger, more important lesson that I took away from this unpleasant experience, something that applies to journalism far beyond an election night that comes around every four years. What really tripped us up was our own hubris combined with an excess of competitive drive to be first. We believed our past success at predicting presidential elections early and accurately meant we were too good to make major mistakes.

Our trusted system for projecting election results was not the precise, carefully tuned machine that all of us had come to believe in. It was riddled with problems. None of these problems mattered in the vast majority of elections simply because they weren't really that close in the end. But when the 2000 presidential election came along with razor-thin margins, the system collapsed, and all of its flaws were exposed for the whole world to see.

The 2000 election taught us a lesson in humility—one that we can hope will last at least for a while. We were overconfident. We were also overcompetitive. From the center of our reporting that night, I saw the animal spirits of competition (including my own) play a major—and ultimately destructive—role. All of us were disappointed that we weren't learning earlier than we had in years past who was going to win. All of us were dismayed with how much earlier some of our competitors were making projections. Rumors began to circulate that night that they had new, secret tools that gave them a better and earlier insight into races. Or maybe they were just willing to tolerate a higher level of risk. Whatever the cause, we knew we were being beaten. And on election night, we acted as if it were all about who had the results first, without really thinking through where this could lead us to.

When we look back on it now, it's both obvious and painful to see that we had it all wrong—wrong not only in the projections we were making, but in our understanding of what was at stake for us in television news. All of the indications throughout the day were that this would be an election like none we'd seen. None of the data fit the pattern we'd come to expect. We knew Florida (along with Ohio and Pennsylvania) would likely be critical to the result. But when the models and the statisticians told us it was okay as early as 8:00 in the evening to declare a winner in Florida, we didn't hesitate. We knew our competitors were projecting Florida; we wanted desperately to match their reporting. All that was required was the go-ahead from those on our Decision Desk, which it provided.

At ABC News, we had a unique opportunity to begin to reclaim some of our credibility in the early hours of that Wednesday morning. We'd made the wrong projection for Gore in Florida early in the evening, just like everybody else. But by the time 2:00 a.m. rolled around, it was clear that Florida would be decided by a razor-thin margin, whichever way it went. And when we got clearance to make our projection for Bush, we already were dead last. I should have put two things together—the fact that this was a historically close race and the fact that we were not going to distinguish ourselves by being first anyway—and just refused to make the projection. Let it play out until we were absolutely certain. Maybe even until all the votes were counted. But I didn't. And so we followed our competitors into folly for the second time that night.

After it was all over, it became clear that the real story of the 2000 election was that there was no projection we could have made with confidence that night—not for Bush and not for Gore. The election turned out to be a statistical tie. We could have counted all the ballots again and again, and each time the margin between the two candidates would have fallen within the margin of error. The only thing we could have reported accurately on election night was that we had nothing to report—that we'd all have to wait for the recount.

A decade later, television news was continuing to pay a price for the mistakes of the 2000 election. The price was far dearer than the embarrassment of being called before Congress and shown how fallible we were. We paid a price in our credibility with the American public. A month after the election Gallup conducted a poll in which almost two-thirds of Americans said they found that "news organizations' stories and reports are often inaccurate"; only one-third found that news organizations "get the facts straight." Nine years later, a Pew study similarly found less than 30 percent of Americans believed that news organizations got their facts straight, while 63 percent said that news stories were often inaccurate.

A host of factors contribute to such figures. It's not only the 2000 election that at least some news organizations have gotten wrong. We've seen a series of missteps that would raise questions in anyone's mind about what was going on at even some of our most prestigious news organizations. There's been an overall decline in Americans' respect for virtually all of our institutions. It isn't surprising that the press suffers from the same loss of confidence as everyone else.

It would be easy to leave it there. And that's where most media critics do leave it. We as journalists should always make our top priority getting it right. Who could possibly argue with that? If that's our creed, why do we see examples of mistakes, small and large, in journalism every day?

The problem is that it's not only about getting it right; it's also about getting it first if humanly possible. And the two are often at war with each other. If we wait too long, if we take too much time in checking and double-checking our sources—or in waiting until we can find additional sources—the time may have come and gone for our audiences to do anything about the information we are giving them. Journalists are often witnesses to history in the making. Often what they write or say will ultimately be the equivalent of first drafts for the history books.

But there's another sense in which journalism and history are very different pursuits with very different purposes. History involves learning about the past so that we can understand our origins and learn from what has come before. Much of journalism involves understanding our present in a way and at a time when we can do something about it. We can't do anything about the Norman invasion of England or the trade in African slaves in the American colonies. But we can do something about wars that our country is contemplating and our health-care system and our national debt.

We would not want to live in a country where *The Washington Post* didn't care whether it beat *The New York Times* or *The Wall Street Journal* on a story. That competitive spirit is an important spur to some of the best journalism that is done today. It's also one of the risks that people run in reporting the news. Journalists do everything they can, consistent with the need to make sure their reporting is timely, to get it right. But the disturbing truth is that if we never, ever made a mistake, we probably wouldn't be doing our jobs. The only partial antidote for this uncomfortable condition is for us to admit to mistakes when we make them—admit them promptly, completely, and without reservation. And then do all we can to make sure we don't make them again.

The election of 2000 gave journalists the opportunity to do both: admit an enormous mistake and take strong measures to make sure we don't repeat it.

# 5 | Showing the Flag: Journalism and Patriotism After 9/11

We do not very often make recommendations for people's behavior from this chair, but as [ABC News correspondent] Lisa [Stark] was talking, I checked in with my children and it—who are deeply distressed, as I think young people are across the United States. And so if you're a parent, you've got a kid in some other part of the country, call them up. Exchange observations.

—Peter Jennings, ABC News Special Report, September 11, 2001

September 9, 2001, was a perfect day for sailing on Long Island Sound, clear and sunny with just the right wind. My family and I spent the afternoon on the water with our friends and neighbors, the Isaacsons. Walter was the head of CNN, and his daughter, Betsy, had been to sailing camp that summer. She was impressing us with her hand at the tiller. We could see south all the way to Manhattan, including the landmark twin towers of the World Trade Center. Walter and I fell into talking shop—and in particular bemoaning the lack of real news. That summer had been dominated by stories of shark attacks on swimmers in Florida and the death of a young congressional intern, Chandra Levy. Later, my wife would say she wished we'd never complained about how quiet the news had been.

Less than forty-eight hours after our sail, the twin towers were gone and the Pentagon was on fire. September 11 was in some ways a day like November 22, 1963. President Kennedy's death separated the world that came before from the world that came after. Everyone old enough remembers exactly where they were and what they were doing when they got the news. Even the children sensed that what had come before was somehow safer and more serene than what came after.

I remember learning that President Kennedy had been shot as I sat at my desk in the sixth grade at Brownell Elementary School in Flint, Michigan. The voice of our principal came over the intercom, a small speaker mounted high on the wall of our classroom. Normally, the intercom was used only for morning announcements or to summon a student to the office. But this was the middle of the day, and the news came from far outside the walls of our small school. That first announcement told us that the president had been shot on a trip to Dallas and that his condition was unknown. Our teacher, Mrs. Thomsen, tried to reassure us as best she could with so little information. Then, a short time later, the principal came back on to announce that President Kennedy had died and that school was dismissed for the day. We were all sent home. I remember some of the girls in the class crying; Mrs. Thomsen cried as well. We all filed out of school and made our way home in near silence.

When you're eleven and you learn that your president has been assassinated, you don't really know what to make of it. You haven't lived enough of life to put it in any context. Is this a once-in-a-lifetime catastrophe, or is this something that grown-ups regularly have to deal with? Does it change our lives fundamentally, or is it just another passing story? I spent that weekend watching television. Watching reports about our new president, Lyndon Johnson (whom I don't think I'd paid two minutes of attention to until he became president). Reports about the hurried search for the assassin. Reports about some man named Lee Harvey Oswald being shot in a basement somewhere in Texas. Footage of a widow and her two young children, a caisson with a coffin, and a riderless horse. All in black and white, because you'd never seen a color TV at that point and black seemed to be the color of the time. And as you tried to make some sense of it all, you watched and cued off two things: the reaction of your parents and the reaction of the TV network anchors and correspondents. As best I recall, it was CBS News that we turned to back in November 1963.

When you're an adult and you're working in a news organization, such momentous events are completely different in some ways. Journalists are affected by national tragedies just as any citizen is, but they also have to cover them. You don't have time to reflect on what has happened or to talk it through with your co-workers, friends, and family members. You're too busy trying to gather the facts and assemble them into an understandable story so that the audience can begin to make some sense of it all. Journalists have to be the first to put it all together intellectually, but they may be among the last to make some emotional peace with what they've witnessed and reported.

There was one issue, though, that 9/11 put front and center for journalists, an issue that demanded immediate answers. Did the fact that our nation had been attacked change our role as reporters? Did our feelings of patriotism change how we would report or what we would report? Should they?

The morning of 9/11 was the Tuesday after our Sunday sail with the Isaacsons. I got into the office in time to watch *Good Morning America* as it began at 7:00 a.m. I remember it being that clear, brilliant day in early fall that so many people have talked about. Nothing unusual happened for the first hour and forty-five minutes of *GMA*. I spent time split between watching the program and answering e-mails. My main task that morning was trying to help Barbara Walters secure an interview with the Chinese leader Jiang Zemin.

Charlie Gibson and Diane Sawyer led *GMA* with two items in the news: the ongoing trial of Andrea Yates (the mother accused of killing her five young children) and reports that Michael Jordan would return to professional basketball with the Washington Wizards. Claire Shipman was doing the newscast that morning from Washington, substituting for Antonio Mora, and she had an interview with then secretary of commerce, Don Evans, about increasing concerns that the economy was headed into a recession. There was an update on the ongoing travails of Gary Condit, that congressman suspected (erroneously, it turned out) in the disappearance of his young intern, Chandra Levy. All in all, it was a typical day in morning news programs.

By 8:30, we'd moved on to Charlie interviewing Sarah, the Duchess of York, about her efforts with Weight Watchers to help residents of Milwaukee lose weight. The segment went long, and when we went to commercial at 8:48, we knew there wasn't much program time left before the local stations would take back over with their programming at 8:55.

I was watching all of this, at least out of the corner of my eye, from my office on West 66th Street. My routine was to have all of the morning programs on my office monitors so that I could check out the competition. While *GMA* was in commercial, I noticed on the television tuned to CNN that there was video of smoke coming out of the side of one of the World Trade Center towers. I switched on the audio for CNN. They weren't sure what had happened, but one of their employees said he had seen a large jet crash into one of the towers. There were reports the plane seemed to have had some trouble flying. Others reported that it may have been a small commuter plane.

A couple of minutes later, at 8:51, *GMA* came back from commercial, and by then Diane and Charlie knew something was going on. We had live video coming from the traffic helicopter of our local New York station, WABC-TV, showing one of the towers on fire. Diane said there were re-ports of "some sort of explosion" at the World Trade Center. In her words: "One report said—and we can't confirm any of this—that a plane may have hit one of the two towers of the World Trade Center. But again, you're seeing the live pictures here. We have no further details than that."

Charlie gave some background on the World Trade Center, including that it had been the site of "the explosion a couple of years ago brought about by terrorists." Like Diane, Charlie emphasized that at that point we knew nothing more than that there had been some sort of "major inci-dent there." And with that, we sent notice to our affiliated stations around the country that we would go to a special report so that Charlie and Diane's reporting would go live to everyone around the country watching ABC stations, instead of being seen on the East Coast alone.

From my office, I was as much at a loss as my anchor team. I called down to the news desk, but they were watching the same pictures I was. They didn't have any real information. In those first few minutes, there was just too wide a range of possibilities. It seemed bizarre that a plane would accidentally fly into the World Trade Center towers—particularly on a bright, clear September morning. I do remember that as we took in video that showed the scene more clearly, the gash across the building looked to me like something more than what a small, private aircraft could cause.

Early in the special report, we got our correspondent Don Dahler on the telephone. Don had an apartment four or five blocks north of the World Trade Center and had heard the roar of the plane. He said on the air that it had not sounded anything like a propeller plane. "It was perhaps a jet, but it could have been a missile as well," he said. And he confirmed that there was a "gigantic hole that encompasses a number of floors."

It was 9:03, and as Don was talking with Charlie and Diane on air, he suddenly broke off. "Oh my God," he said. Diane repeated, "Oh my God. Oh my God." All of us watched on live television as a large aircraft flashed across the screen and crashed into the second tower. Charlie Gibson registered the shock we all shared: "That looks like a second plane has just hit." Diane responded, "Terrible." Without missing more than a beat, Charlie started to pick up pieces of the story: "That second explosion, you could see the plane come in just from the right-hand side of the screen, so this looks like it is some sort of a concerted effort to attack the World Trade Center that is under way in downtown New York."

And so, in a moment, the range of possibilities narrowed. This couldn't be a coincidence. It couldn't be an accident. By now Jeffrey Schneider, our head of communications, had joined me in my office. I didn't have any special insight into what had happened. But we had done a fair amount of reporting on al-Qaeda and Osama bin Laden leading up to this point, and I told Jeffrey this could be bin Laden.

Back in May 1998, more than three years before, ABC's John Miller and the investigative producer Chris Isham had trekked into Afghanistan to conduct an interview in person with Osama bin Laden. This is something we'd been working on for some time as part of our overall reporting on international terrorism. We'd been following bin Laden for several years, and John's interview turned out to be the last one bin Laden would give to a Western journalist. Ironically, there was some doubt in our newsroom about how important the interview was, or even whether to air it at all. Some people thought this was a major terrorist figure; some wondered whether he was more of a show-off. We decided in the end to put it on the air because, on balance, we concluded that bin Laden was at least an important part of a growing terrorist threat. The interview appeared on *World News Tonight with Peter Jennings* on June 10, 1998.

In the interview, bin Laden repeated to John his call for Muslims to take up arms against America, and, prophetically, he drew no distinction between military and civilian targets. Bin Laden said, "We believe that the worst thieves in the world today and the worst terrorists are the Americans. Nothing could stop you except perhaps retaliation in kind. We do not have to differentiate between military or civilian. As far as we are concerned, they are all targets."

Two years after our Osama bin Laden interview, but still more than a year before 9/11, I was invited to join a few other journalists for a dinner meeting with the Joint Chiefs of Staff at the house of the commandant of the Marine Corps in Washington, General James L. Jones. The subject of the dinner wasn't Osama bin Laden; it wasn't even terrorism. The dinner was organized by Bob Woodward to discuss the growing difficulties that our military leadership was having explaining what they needed to Congress and to the media. One of the points the general staff officers made was that so few members of Congress had served in the military. What they didn't say, but what wasn't lost on any of us, was that the same could be said of most of the press corps covering both Congress and the military.

At the end of the dinner, conversation turned to a test that had just been done as part of an overall plan to build an antiballistic missile defense system. I got the impression that none of the officers there was particularly keen on the plan. They just didn't think that the biggest threat facing our country was a ballistic missile attack. So, I asked, what in their judgment was the biggest threat? To a man they said our biggest threat was an attack by terrorists on U.S. soil.

As unexpected as the 9/11 attack was, there had been plenty of warning signals for us all.

As the awful gravity of the attacks began to sink in, Charlie and Diane continued their coverage of the events from their position at Times Square. I ran downstairs to talk with Peter Jennings, who was following our coverage and tracking all the reporting coming in from an array of sources. We talked about when he should go on the air. Diane and Charlie were doing a great job piecing together the snippets of early reports. But they were down at our Times Square Studio, removed from the newsroom and the hub of most of our reporting, and Peter was our principal anchor. I told him that we needed him to take the lead sooner rather than later. Peter took the anchor chair in TV-3 just off the newsroom floor, and Charlie handed off to him shortly after 9:10 a.m.

I went to the control room and spent most of the rest of the day and night shuttling between there and the newsroom one floor below. Because Peter was on the air constantly, I would go onto the set and stand off to the side when we needed to talk, grabbing a few minutes with him when there was a taped piece on the air. In hurried conversations we talked about the reporting, but I also brought him up to speed on decisions I was making behind the scenes about our coverage, what was in the pipeline for him, and logistics I thought he should know about. By this point, Peter and I had worked together for more than four years. We'd done the millennium broadcast together. We'd come to know each other and trust one another. The time for testing was over. I don't remember a single disagreement with Peter over the next several days of breaking news coverage.

No one had the time for or luxury of shock or reflection that day. We needed to figure out everything we could about what was going on, and we needed to move people into position to report on the story. We still had Don Dahler on the telephone downtown near the towers, but we were having a very difficult time moving anyone else near the scene or getting a satellite truck down there. We were relying heavily on our New York station, WABC-TV, which fortunately was doing an outstanding job covering the story visually. At the same time, we were bringing in our Washington reporters, including John McWethy at the Pentagon, to report on any government response and, of course, John Miller, our resident bin Laden and terrorism expert, who joined Peter on the set.

My job was to figure out what we needed logistically and to do whatever I could to make sure we had it. I had to make sure we were coordinating among the various parts of the division. And I had to keep track of our overall coverage as best I could. Maybe most important, I needed to be in a position to decide what we would report and what we would not as we picked up various pieces of the story. Peter was on the air live, so he wasn't in a position to vet sources or weigh how certain we were of a given report. And in those early hours, so many reports were all over the place—of planes that might or might not have been hijacked and buildings that might or might not be additional targets. People in the newsroom were coming to me that first morning and afternoon with all sorts of wild possibilities they'd heard from one source or another. In another context, on another day, many would have been incredible; given what was happening, almost anything seemed possible.

We had plenty of solid information. John Miller, sitting next to Peter, was monitoring police and other first responders' communications and talking to his sources at the FBI and the New York Police Department.

John McWethy was on the air with Peter recounting the steps being taken by the Defense Department to respond to the crisis, including the activation of a counterterrorism cell within the Joint Chiefs of Staff. Our aviation expert, John Nance, was on the air explaining what was feasible (and not) in attempting an air rescue from the tops of the towers.

At 9:30, President Bush came before cameras to give his first remarks about the attacks. He was in Sarasota, Florida, visiting the Emma E. Booker Elementary school, where he had been reading to a class of second graders when he'd first received word of what was going on in New York. In his brief statement, the president said what had happened was a "national tragedy," confirmed that two planes had crashed into the World Trade Center, called it an act of terrorism, and reassured us that the full resources of the federal government would be directed toward helping the victims and their families and determining who was responsible. He asked for a moment of silence. He also said he'd be heading straight back to Washington.

Shortly after the president's remarks, we went to Claire Shipman, who reported that a large plume of smoke was coming from somewhere behind the White House. The White House itself had been evacuated in a rush. We saw video of staffers running from the West Wing of the White House. At first we thought there'd been an explosion somewhere in downtown Washington just west of the White House, which is where we saw the smoke. But then John McWethy called in to say that there was a fire at the Pentagon, and then the Associated Press reported that an aircraft had crashed near the Pentagon. As it turned out, of course, the plane did not just hit near the Pentagon but scored a direct hit on the southwest side of the building itself. That smoke we'd seen was visible all the way across the Potomac at our bureau near the White House.

At this point, it was only 9:37 a.m. eastern time, less than an hour after the first reports of a plane crashing into the World Trade Center's North Tower.

The rest of the day and night—and several days and nights after that—were consumed with questions and decisions. One of the first was something I'd never thought of and never dreamed would come up. Our reporters on the scene told us that they were seeing men and women jumping to their deaths from the upper stories of the towers. I was stunned by the thought that as we were feverishly working to cover the story, there were people a few miles south of me at that moment facing a horrific decision: would it be better to lose their lives relatively quickly in the fall or face the smoke and flames that were rapidly engulfing the buildings? The question put to me was, do we show it on the air? I didn't really hesitate. We would not. We could state it as a fact on the air; it was part of the story. But actually showing people taking their own lives was simply too grotesque.

If I'd had more time, I might have consulted with others—either my colleagues at ABC News or my counterparts at other networks. I'm sure I would have thought through and given a more developed set of reasons for my decision. I probably would have said that even with the urgency and importance of the overall story, we still needed to show some respect for the dignity of the thousands who were facing unimaginable horrors. But there was no time for consultation or reflection. We were either going to show the video—now—or not. In the moment I had to think about it, it didn't seem to me that showing the falling victims, rather than simply reporting the fact, was so valuable to our audience that it warranted this invasion of privacy. And then I didn't think about it again. Once I'd decided, I needed to move on to other things right away.

Other questions were more a matter of logistics. Where could we establish an operating base near the World Trade Center? We ended up renting an apartment in the upper floors of a building three or four blocks north and getting access to the roof to position our cameras.

One of the biggest problems we faced in those early hours was how we would manage to stay on the air. You might think that with all the news happening, it wouldn't be a problem to fill the time. But there was a danger of repeating the same things over and over—and also a danger that in trying to say something new, we could make a mistake. So in the course of that first day we set up a platoon system. Marc Burstein, our executive producer for special events, ran the control room with Roger Goodman, our longtime director. We were fortunate because Marc and Roger had been the core team who had put our millennium program on the air just eighteen months before. They'd distinguished themselves with that program and with a wide range of special, breaking news reports. They were never better than on 9/11 and the days following.

Under Marc and Roger, we assembled two teams of producers and other support staff, each of whom took one-hour shifts in the control room. While the first team was in the control room under the overall supervision of executive vice president Paul Friedman, a second team would go to work in a conference room just below the control room and adjoining the newsroom. This second team gathered the reporting and various elements—video and live interviews—and put them into a coherent one-hour block of news programming. When the first team left the control room after an hour, the second team would replace it to put on the hour they'd been working on. The first team then took over the conference room and started to prepare their next hour. And so the two teams leapfrogged each other through the day and night.

To support the production teams and help drive our reporting, we immediately combined all of our investigative resources from throughout the division. This became the ABC News Investigative Unit, which we built on after 9/11 and went on to become one of the strongest editorial operations at ABC. In addition to this, we drafted people from our news-magazines to produce pieces ordered up by the production teams.

People came pouring into work from all over, whether they were supposed to be on duty or not. Ted Koppel was overseas and couldn't get back to the United States because all air travel was halted. He volunteered to anchor *Nightline* from London. George Will was stuck in Minnesota. He bought a car so that he could drive himself back to Washington.

The only time I smiled that day came courtesy of Hal Bruno, the long-time ABC News political director. Hal had retired just over a year before, and we hadn't heard much from him recently. ABC News had a system that allowed anyone within the organization to go on a secure "320" line and report breaking news that would come over small speakers in our newsrooms and offices around the world. Needless to say, the 320 had been going off all morning long. In the midst of all the confusion and frenzy, I heard Hal Bruno come over the 320 line. In addition to being one of the most experienced political reporters in the country, Hal was a long-time volunteer fireman with strong ties to the community of firefighters, so when he heard about the fire at the Pentagon, he rushed there and started reporting as though he'd never retired.

Once Peter took his anchor chair that morning, he didn't really leave it for the next seventeen hours, taking breaks only to get something to eat or drink or to use the restroom. I was worried that he was pushing himself too hard. We had Charlie Gibson ready to come in and relieve him. But Peter insisted that he was fine and that he wanted to stay in the chair.

Another time, I might have thought that the anchor was staying on as a matter of guarding territory, not wanting to relinquish center stage to another anchor or correspondent. But that wasn't Peter that day. Through it all, Peter Jennings was the "anchor" for ABC News in all the meanings of that word, and I think he sensed that. From the time he took the chair just after 9:10 that morning until our final sign-off nearly a hundred hours later, whether he was physically in the anchor chair or someone was spelling him, Peter was the one reaching out for all of the resources we could give him, asking the right questions, and piecing together the story for our audience. He did a magnificent job sorting out the facts from the rumors at a time when there were far, far more of the latter than of the former.

Peter was perfectly prepared for the story: he knew New York, he knew Washington, he knew about terrorism, and he probably knew more about the Middle East than any news anchor in history. It had been Peter who guided the country through the horrific tragedy of the terrorists' attack on the Israeli Olympic team in 1972, reporting from the Olympic Village as Jim McKay anchored the coverage for ABC Sports. To my mind, there has never been anyone better at covering breaking news, live on national television, than Peter Jennings. And on 9/11 and the days that followed, he was as good as he'd ever been.

And if there was ever a time when the nation needed its anchors, this was it. All of us were stunned. None of us could get our bearings right away.

While the nation was reeling from what had happened and what might yet come, no one in the federal government was in a position to come on television to help us start sorting it all out. The president was on board Air Force One, headed not back to Washington as he'd first said, but to an undisclosed location. Vice President Cheney had been taken to a "secure location" that turned out to be a bunker somewhere underneath the White House. Congress was being evacuated. And as we learned afterward, those in the government in those first few hours really didn't know much more about what was happening than the rest of us. They were trying to sort it all out just as we were. But those of us in the news media didn't have the option of simply shutting down and telling the American people we'd get back to them. We were on the air, and the enormity of the story required that we remain on the air. We were fortunate to have people like Peter Jennings (and Tom Brokaw and Dan Rather) with experience and judgment to be our anchors as we all tried to sort out the truth from the rumor and begin to make sense of it all.

This is not to say that even Peter could immediately absorb the enormity of what was happening. When the South Tower came down just before 10:00 that morning, Peter was on the air with John Miller. John first referred to it as a "new large plume of smoke" coming from the building. Peter speculated that it might be that "something fell off the building." He then went to Don Dahler, who was on the street four blocks north of Ground Zero. Don explained that "the second building that was hit by the plane has just completely collapsed. The entire building has just collapsed, as if a demolition team set off—when you see the old demolitions of these old buildings."

Even with an eyewitness on the scene, Peter at first could not believe it. Don repeated that "it has completely collapsed." Peter asked, "The whole side has collapsed?" Don said it again: it was the entire building, not just a side. Peter asked one more time, to be sure, "The whole building has collapsed?" And once again, Don confirmed that it had. Peter pressed again: "That's the southern tower you're talking about." Don took us through what had happened again. Peter's reaction was human and genuine: "We are talking massive casualties here at the moment and we have—whoo—that is extraordinary."

A good amount of our early efforts to cover the story went into making sure we had teams at the local hospitals ready to report on the victims. As the day wore on into night, it became all too clear that this would be largely unnecessary. There simply weren't that many injured to be treated. Nearly all the victims were dead.

The first group to claim "credit" for the attacks was the Democratic Front for the Liberation of Palestine, which, as Peter pointed out, was one of the "most militant of the Palestinian organizations." But Peter went on to say, "We have to caution you in all the obvious ways, before the day is over, there may be any number of people who claim responsibility."

One of the many confusions that first morning centered on what turned out to be American Airlines Flight 93. We had reports by 9:30 that another commercial airliner had been hijacked and was being tracked somewhere northwest of Washington. I was in the control room when we heard conflicting reports about whether it was over Ohio or Pennsylvania and where it was headed. At one point I was told it had been shot down by U.S. military aircraft. We reported none of this at the time. Later we would learn the story of the passengers storming the cockpit and of the crash in the Pennsylvania field southeast of Pittsburgh. But that morning, so many conflicting reports were pouring in that we often did not know what was true and what was speculation.

As good as Peter was, we knew we couldn't keep up this pace, and we also knew that we would be on the air for some time to come. So we set up a system that we thought we could sustain over several days. Elizabeth Vargas took over as the anchor for our coverage at 2:00 a.m. on September 12. Diane and Charlie took over from Elizabeth at 5:00 a.m. and took it to 10:00 a.m., which gave Peter a break for some rest. Peter was back in the anchor chair at 10:00, continuing throughout the day and evening, with Charlie giving him a break for an hour or so in the early evening. Then Ted Koppel came on with a special edition of *Nightline* at 11:35, turning it back over to Elizabeth at 2:00.

That first night, after Elizabeth had taken over for Peter in the early hours of Wednesday morning, I decided I should try to get some rest as well. It would take too long to drive home to Bronxville, knowing I had to be back in the office in two or three hours. So I walked to the Essex House on Central Park South, a few blocks from ABC News headquarters, at about 3:00 a.m. There wasn't a single car on the street; all I saw was a military Humvee at Columbus Circle with a soldier manning a gun in the turret. A strange and sobering sight. The only sounds came from the occasional fighter flying patrol over the city.

I checked into my room, took off my clothes, took a shower, watched some of our coverage, and lay down to sleep. But my mind continued to go over the events of the day, and I kept hearing those jets above, and so after ten fitful minutes I put my clothes back on and went back into the office.

ABC News stayed on the air continuously until the early morning of Saturday, September 15. By the time we signed off, we'd been on for ninety-one straight hours under the most difficult circumstances imaginable. To end our marathon coverage, on Saturday morning Peter anchored an hour special addressing the questions of children. We included on the set a group of children and young adults and sprinkled among them experts on child psychology to help understand how children were thinking about what they were hearing and seeing. We meant this as a way to help the children, but those of us in the control room quickly realized that many of the questions and problems the children were wrestling with were exactly what we were thinking about ourselves.

One issue addressed on our children's special was the effect of all the networks' repetitive showing of the planes crashing into the towers and of the towers coming down. This was something we'd been talking about in the newsroom, and we'd already had some complaints from viewers. By the end of the week, the video had been shown hundreds of times on all of the broadcast and cable networks, as well as on local news programs. One of the child psychologists we had on the air with Peter on that Saturday morning, Dr. Kyle Pruett of Yale, explained that small children do not understand that this was an event in the past. Each time they saw it, they experienced it as something new. This hit me particularly hard because one evening that week my stepdaughter, Lily, who was six at the time, asked why they kept crashing planes into buildings.

We were unwittingly making our children even more afraid than the already horrific situation warranted. What's more, the constant rerunning of the video for all sorts of purposes—some outlets had taken to using the chilling video as bumpers or opens to programs—was already making the unthinkably tragic into something banal. We were potentially hurting the children while desensitizing the adults. And I thought back to my decision that first morning not to show the people jumping from the towers. What about the loved ones of those who were lost—or still missing? Were they thinking every time they saw the video of the towers crashing to earth that they might well be watching the moment their father or mother or child lost his or her life?

The question was whether there was a legitimate news reason to keep showing this video. I couldn't see one—or at least no reason that justified the damage we might be doing to some in our audience. Just about every adult in the country by that point had seen the towers crashing to earth, and most had seen it time after time. Anyone who'd seen it once was not likely to forget.

On the way home after the children's special, I called Kerry Smith, our head of standards, and we agreed that from then on we would not show the video of either the crashes or the collapses. We could show still photographs if necessary, but no more moving video.

I saw firsthand what journalists are made of on 9/11 and the days following. One of the things that struck me most powerfully was how much we expect of newspeople during times of national crisis. This was a time when all of us wanted desperately to be with our loved ones. And our loved ones needed us. But just when they needed us most, our duty was to remain at the office around the clock. Peter reflected this dilemma when he spoke emotionally that first day about his having quickly called his own two children, Lizzie and Chris, and encouraged those in the audience to reach out to their own children.

The role of the professional journalist feels different in times of real, important news. When there isn't anything momentous going on, when the stories are about celebrities or the back-and-forth of the markets or the politicians, let's be honest: the best, most experienced journalists don't need to bring all their skills and knowledge to bear. But when there's a crisis, people need to hear and see and read what the journalists who know their stuff have to say. It's at moments like this, moments as awful as 9/11, when those of us working in journalism are reminded powerfully of why we're in news in the first place. It's to cover the really important stories, the stories that change lives and the lives of nations. It's to make sure we get it right when it really matters that it's right. And, sadly, like the unanimity that 9/11 brought to us as a nation, I fear that powerful sense of purpose can fade just as quickly.

We were fortunate not to lose anyone in the attacks of 9/11. Our colleagues at Channel 7, the local ABC station, were not as fortunate. One of their engineers, Don DiFranco, was on the 110th floor of the World Trade Center North Tower when the first plane struck. He called from the roof to the station's control room that morning to warn that there might be a disruption in service because of the attack. He was one of the nearly twenty-eight hundred people who died.

Our national security correspondent, John McWethy, and his team were in the Pentagon when the plane hit there, literally down the hall from their cubicle. They were shaken by the blast but immediately made their way to the lawn outside the burning building and soon were reporting live from the scene. Thankfully, they were not injured.

Although ABC News didn't lose anyone that morning, I learned a few days later that for a time it looked as if we might have. I spent the week of 9/11 in my office, in the control room, and on the floor with Peter. We

ABOVE: *Roone Arledge (left) and I, clowning around for* Fortune Magazine *at the start of my tenure.* (© Fortune Magazine)

BELOW: (Left) *Presenting Barbara Walters with her Lifetime Achievement Emmy in September 2009.* (Right) *Appearing at the semiannual press tour with (from right to left) George Stephanopoulos, Ted Koppel, and Peter Jennings in Pasadena, California, where we announced plans for our coverage of the 2004 presidential race—including the debut of our first-ever 24-hour streaming news channel.*

TOP: *Jackie Judd, reporting here for 20/20, broke the controversial news about Monica Lewinsky's now-infamous blue dress on January 23, 1998. When President Clinton denied having had a sexual relationship with Lewinsky, the public and the media cast a disparaging eye on our reporting; it wasn't until late July that we were vindicated.*

ABOVE: *Election night, 2000: the first of our two mistaken projections of the presidential winner in Florida. Our inaccuracy cast doubt on the Decision Desk's process and on the media's overzealousness in predicting election results.*

ABOVE: (Left) *Ted Koppel in Iraq, where he contributed reporting from the earliest days of the war.* (Right) *The opening title for* Nightline's *"The Fallen" on April 30, 2004. The episode listed the names of the war dead in Iraq; some commentators feared a political motivation. Claiming the episode would be a one-sided, biased attack on the war, the Sinclair Broadcast Group elected not to air our broadcast on its seven ABC stations.*

BELOW: *With Kate O'Brian (left), head of news coverage, and Robin Sproul (far right), Washington bureau chief, at the news desk on the evening of 2008's Super Tuesday primaries.*

*Bob Woodruff in a U.S. Army helicopter over Iraq during one of his several tours there. On January 29, 2006, Woodruff and cameraman Doug Vogt were severely injured by an improvised explosive device in an attack north of Baghdad.*

*On the set of* Good Morning America *with (from right to left) Diane Sawyer, Charlie Gibson, and Elizabeth Vargas the morning after Woodruff and Vogt had been hurt in Iraq.*

*Diane Sawyer and Charlie Gibson covering 9/11 from the set of*
Good Morning America. *Of all the events I faced in my tenure, 9/11 was
undoubtedly the most difficult and catastrophic; it really did change everything.
In the aftermath of the attacks, our coverage ran to 100 uninterrupted hours.*

*Peter Jennings (center, standing) anchoring a special,* Answering Children's Questions, *about the terrorist attacks of 9/11.*

*With Peter Jennings in the newsroom, presenting the staff with the George Foster Peabody Award we'd received for our 9/11 coverage.*

ABOVE: *October 8, 2002: Cuban president Fidel Castro and Barbara Walters walk through the halls of a Havana school; I follow behind them.*

BELOW: *With Senator John Kerry (center) and* Good Morning America *executive producer Shelley Ross (left) at an ABC News editorial meeting that the senator visited during his bid for the presidency in 2004.*

*Answering questions from George Stephanopoulos for one of my closed-circuit appearances from the set of TV 3 in New York.*

*With my wife, Sherrie, celebrating the dawn of the new millennium on the Times Square set.*

had a cameraman named Tony Hirashiki working from a satellite truck downtown near Ground Zero. Tony had been with ABC News since the day in the 1960s when he'd appeared on Ted Koppel's doorstep in Saigon. Ted at the time was our Southeast Asia bureau chief. Tony, a native of Japan, spoke little or no English. But he had a note pinned to his shirt that introduced him, saying that although his English wasn't much, he was a great "shooter." And so he'd proven to be.

The morning of 9/11, Tony had been one of the first on the scene, before the towers collapsed. He'd set out on his own to get video to feed back to the control room uptown. And then, for a time, no one heard from him. The towers crashed to earth, and we were told he'd been seen somewhere near the footbridge before the South Tower came down. Those working on the scene, including our correspondent Bob Jamieson, feared he'd been one of the victims. An hour or two later Tony emerged from the dust and the smoke holding his beta tapes and proclaiming proudly, "I have pictures." Tony's pictures gave us some of the most dramatic video of the story of the death of the World Trade Center.

We didn't lose anyone at ABC News that day, but many of us lost friends. As the days passed, word would come to us about someone or other who'd gone missing and was likely dead. I was in the control room when I heard that Ted Olson's wife, Barbara, had been on the plane that had struck the Pentagon. Ted at the time was the U.S. Solicitor General, working in the Justice Department, and Barbara had been an associate at my law firm years before. I'd worked with her and kept up with her in the years since. I remembered her as the young woman with long blond hair who was so outspoken and energetic, walking through the halls of Wilmer, Cutler & Pickering.

I was also in the control room when I heard that another friend, Neil Levin, head of the Port Authority, had been in the Windows on the World restaurant at the top of one of the towers when the planes came. He was missing. My wife and I had gotten to know Neil through his wife, Christy Ferrer. We'd been to their apartment not long before for dinner. And so it went.

Through it all, the loss and the shock and the flood of news, I had the complete support of the company. I spoke by telephone with Bob Iger and Alex Wallau, the head of the network, often during the week of 9/11, but all they talked about with me was what they could do to help us. The next week, once normal air traffic had resumed, Bob, Alex, and Michael Eisner, the head of the Walt Disney Company, flew in to meet with the news teams at the network and the local station. They had nothing but praise for our efforts. The one thing that never came up, then or later, was any financial consideration. I never knew how much those ninety-one hours and ten minutes of straight coverage without any commercials cost the Walt Disney Company in lost advertising. One press account estimated that all the networks together lost about $100 million a day during those first few days of around-the-clock coverage. But, to the company's credit, it was never an issue. This is one great advantage of being part of a major media company with deep pockets—an advantage that too often is overlooked by those complaining about "media concentration."

Our company may have been supportive, but it didn't take long for some people outside the company to start asking questions about whether we were being patriotic enough in our coverage. We got the first taste of what was to come the day of 9/11 itself. As I've said, President Bush began the day reading to an elementary school class in Florida. By 10:30, we were anxiously watching the empty airspace around Washington to see when Air Force One would return and where it would land. Peter asked Claire Shipman in Washington repeatedly about the president's plans, but there was no guidance from the White House. By noon, we had heard from Mayor Giuliani, Governor Pataki, and Senator Schumer of New York. But we had not seen or heard any more from the president since his brief remarks shortly after the second attack.

Peter discussed this on the air. Saying he didn't want to be "melodramatic," he asked directly, "Where is the president of the United States?" Even as he was asking this, a bulletin came in that the president was about to record a statement at Barksdale Air Force Base in Louisiana.

ABC News got lucky that day in having Ann Compton on the plane with the president. Ann has covered the White House and Washington for many years; no one is more experienced or better. She was one of a handful of reporters sent to cover what everyone had thought would be a routine presidential trip. Ann called in from Barksdale as soon as she could, and we put her on the air live with Peter. In introducing her, Peter noted that "the president and his response to this is part of the psychological package because the country looks to the president on occasions like this to be reassuring to the nation."

Ann reported that the president's plane had flown at well over forty thousand feet from Florida to Louisiana and had been accompanied by fighter planes. She said that he had been in communication with Vice President Cheney, with his cabinet, with world leaders, and with Mrs. Bush. Air Force One had landed at Barksdale at 11:45 a.m. local time, and Ann described the "very emotional" statement he'd made to camera that "freedom has been attacked but freedom will be defended . . . America's military is on its highest state of alert."

And then, when Peter tried to ask some further questions, Ann was cut off as the president's plane prepared for an immediate departure. She explained before ending that she had "no idea" where they were heading or even whether she would be allowed to continue to travel with the president. In an understatement, Ann said, "They are still quite worried about his own security." Even as we all continued to wonder about the whereabouts of the president, Peter repeatedly reassured the audience that "the chain of command in the country is very much in place."

We finally received the recording of the president's remarks from Barksdale about 1:30 that afternoon and broadcast them immediately. The president concluded his remarks by saying that "the resolve of our great nation is being tested, but make no mistake we will show the world that we will pass this test." Peter picked up on this theme, agreeing that "a great nation is being tested and the president reassures the nation and anybody else in the world who will hear this that the nation will pass the test. And there is no doubt about that, I think, in the United States of America. As horrible as this—these incidents are, and as tragic as Oklahoma City was— the great strength of the nation, you know, is always there."

By 3:00 that day, Ann Compton had placed another brief call to us to report that Air Force One had landed at Offutt Air Force Base in Omaha, Nebraska, home of the Strategic Air Command. There, Bush was to have a meeting by secure videoconference in a protected bunker with the National Security Council. Ann was one of only five reporters who had been permitted to travel with the president from Florida to Nebraska, accompanied by a small Secret Service contingent.

Peter recognized that the president's remaining outside Washington strongly "suggest[ed]" that the Secret Service and others at the "highest reaches of government" had concluded that the president should "stay on the move . . . lest there be any security threat to the president." But he also observed that there was "a very delicate line for the president to follow," as we also had reports from Washington that "political operatives in the president's entourage very much want him . . . to get . . . back to Washington to be in control in the place which is familiar to most Americans."

A few minutes before 4:00 p.m., we got the first official confirmation of the president's whereabouts when his close adviser Karen Hughes gave a statement to camera that the president was indeed at Offutt Air Force Base and was "in continuous communication with Vice President Cheney and key members of his cabinet and national security team."

A half hour later, we heard from Ann that Air Force One was about to take off again and that it was likely heading with the president back to Washington. By 5:00 we received word that the president would address the nation that night. It turned out to be 8:30 p.m., and the president spoke from the Oval Office. It was almost twelve hours after the first plane struck the North Tower.

At the time, I thought that Peter had it right in talking about the president's whereabouts. It was understandable that the security team wanted to keep him out of harm's way. But as a citizen, I wanted desperately to hear from the president. I wanted him to tell us as much as he could about what had happened and what we were doing about it. And yes, I wanted him to set the tone for the country. The White House didn't see it that way.

Within twenty-four hours, I began to hear that at least some in the administration were none too pleased with the way we'd covered the president's movements on 9/11. Conservative pundits (especially Rush Limbaugh) claimed that Peter had accused the president of "hiding" on the day of the crisis and had called on him to address the nation about his failure to protect it. The complaining from the White House grew to the point where I decided to call Karl Rove directly and talk to him about what Peter had said. Karl and I spoke on Friday, three days after 9/11, when we were still in sustaining coverage of the crisis. He minced no words in saying that many in the White House were angry that Peter had called the president a "coward." I told Karl that Peter had done no such thing, and I sent him the transcript of what Peter had said. Karl faxed me his response almost immediately; it's fair to say he did not back down.

That I would be talking with the White House about this issue seventy-two hours after the worst attack on U.S. soil since Pearl Harbor shows how emotional a time it was. Those like Karl Rove unquestionably felt a powerful need to circle the wagons and do everything they could to project the image of a strong America and a strong American president. Those of us in the media were extremely sensitive to any claim that our reporting could somehow take away from the effort those in government were making. And let's be frank, all of us had it in the back of our minds that if the audience saw us as unpatriotic, it could damage our long-term reputation with the public.

There's one other point about my exchange with the White House over our reporting: it was all based on a falsehood. After the fact, Rush Limbaugh—to his credit—went back to figure out where he got his information about what Peter had said on the air. It wasn't as if Limbaugh himself had been watching ABC News all day. It turned out that he'd relied on an e-mail from a friend who had claimed that Peter had said President Bush should "quit hiding behind the Secret Service, come out and face the nation and explain the 'President's failure' to protect the country." Limbaugh admitted later that Peter had not said anything close to this.

This was the first glimmer of an issue that would come to loom large. Much of our reporting over the next few years would be viewed through a prism of patriotism. Our nation had been attacked. Was our on-air reporting aiding the enemy? Shouldn't our reporting be shaped at least in some ways by our personal feelings about our country? And if so, how much should it be shaped? This became a heated discussion from time to time, sometimes making it into the press and sometimes fought out behind the scenes with the government.

While we were dealing with criticism of Peter's language, questions came about the patriotism of our coverage from a different direction. I was in the control room in the middle of our nonstop coverage when our communications vice president, Jeffrey Schneider, came to me. Some in the media were noting that Fox News anchors were wearing American flag pins on their lapels. Would we do the same? ABC News had had a long-standing policy that no one could wear pins or buttons of any sort on the air (or, for that matter, in the office). I'd never really thought about this policy much, but the reason seemed obvious. We were there to report the news, not to espouse any particular cause—even when that "cause" was our nation.

This was admittedly an unusual situation. Thousands of innocent civilians had been murdered by terrorists—in New York, in Washington, and aboard a plane that crashed in the Pennsylvania countryside. How could we not "show the flag" on our lapels? How could anyone fail to support the United States in every conceivable way? Given the circumstances, would I change our policy?

I thought about it for a few minutes and then said that we would stick with our rule: No one should wear a lapel pin on the air. Several things went through my mind at the time. It was hard to argue against being for America. But the flag pins could be taken as indicating something more than support of the country. All members of the administration were wearing American flag pins whenever they appeared on television. There would likely come a time when doing our job would mean questioning or even criticizing what the government was doing in response to this crisis. I didn't want ABC News reporters to be wearing what appeared to be part of the administration's uniform while they were questioning whether the administration was doing its job. At this of all times, I didn't want there to be any confusion over our respective jobs.

It also passed through my mind that not everyone we put on the air was an American citizen. Indeed, Peter Jennings himself had yet to become a citizen; he was a loyal citizen of Canada (which he remained to the end of his life, even after he'd added his loyalty to the United States by becoming a U.S. citizen a few years later). If some of our on-air people began wearing American flags on their lapels, would there be pressure on everyone to do so? What if some refused? Would they be singled out as unpatriotic?

In all honesty, this lapel pin issue seemed to me to be first and foremost a distraction. We had an important job to do—to find out what had happened and tell the American people. Worrying about lapel pins (or for that matter American flags incorporated into sets and graphics, which came soon after for some news networks) seemed superficial—or even cynical. We had more important things to worry about. Right or wrong, ABC News would stay true to the standards that had served us well for many years.

My decision was not well received in some quarters—including some quarters of ABC News. I looked up one evening during our nonstop coverage to see our White House correspondent Terry Moran wearing an American flag pin on his lapel on the air, contrary to our policy and contrary to my decision. I called our Washington bureau chief, Robin Sproul, and said she had to instruct Terry to remove the pin. She called back after talking with him to say that this was a real problem and that he was likely both to disregard my order and to call me directly.

Terry and I then had a pointed discussion over the phone. I reminded him of our policy and of my decision. He insisted that this was a special circumstance. I stood firm; he did as well. Toward the end of the conversation, Terry said that as much as he thought of himself as a journalist, he was an American first. I responded that he was both an American and a journalist. As a journalist, the most patriotic thing he could do for his country at that moment was to report the truth—and make sure that his audience *believed* he was telling the truth as an independent reporter, rather than as an adjunct government spokesman. The lapel pin would have to go.

Our lapel-pin policy drew a fair amount of commentary from the outside as well. Some experts supported our position, such as Bob Steele of the Poynter Institute, who said that "journalists should remain independent in both substance and symbolism. That doesn't mean we should throw away our beliefs, but we shouldn't wear them on our lapels." On the other hand, some local station managers took issue with our policy. Roger LaMay of WTXF-TV in Philadelphia said that "newspeople don't have to sacrifice their objectivity to show solidarity with their country." And over on the Fox News Channel, Brit Hume, who had been a longtime White House correspondent for ABC News, thought our policy "an example of a well intentioned idea not being properly thought through . . . Our flag is not the symbol of the Bush administration, and Fox News is not located in Switzerland." Ten years later I was still receiving sporadic e-mails from people who'd apparently just read about it on the Internet and criticized the rule as foolish and unpatriotic.

Although it was a quick decision, looking back on it more than ten years later, I still believe it was the right one. I respected Terry Moran's sincerity. The question that Terry had posed was not an easy one to answer. We are journalists, and we owe a certain allegiance to the meaning of the term. But we also are citizens of a country to which we owe loyalty. Indeed, but for the values upheld by our government—values embodied in the protection of freedom of speech and of the press in the First Amendment—we wouldn't be able to do our jobs as journalists. Which is our higher duty? When is there a true conflict, and when is the conflict only apparent?

The question was posed in stark (if somewhat unrealistic) terms in a hypothetical situation back in 1987 in a Fred Friendly seminar presided over by Charles Ogletree and broadcast on PBS. Two of the panelists were our own Peter Jennings and Mike Wallace, of CBS News. The question posed to the panel was what you would do if you were a journalist covering a war from the enemy's side and were with enemy troops about to ambush U.S. soldiers. Would you stay true to the journalistic principle that this was an undercover operation done with an understanding that you would not blow the enemy's cover? Or would your loyalty to your country override the duty to journalism and allow you to warn the U.S. troops?

Peter and Mike Wallace had different responses. Mike did not hesitate in saying he would cover the story and report it without giving any warning to the Americans. Peter said that he would probably try to warn Americans.

But as provocative and interesting as the discussion was, it didn't have much to do with the issues that came up in the wake of 9/11 and then the wars in Afghanistan and Iraq. As strongly as people feel about the American flag lapel pin, let's face it, whether one wears it on the air is not a matter of life and death.

All of us are proud of the flag. We fly it at home on holidays; I fly it from my 1962 Corvette on Memorial Day every year in the local parade. We don't give up our personal sense of patriotism and loyalty to our country when we decide to become journalists. But even as we retain our personal feelings, we do give up some of our rights to express those feelings as part of our journalism. Citizens can do certain things that journalists can't—or at least shouldn't. Journalists don't make contributions to political campaigns. Journalists don't campaign for candidates—or even support them.

The days following the attacks of 9/11 were special, and many people had special roles to play. First responders rushed in to save people; the military and other security agencies tried to assess the threat and protect us against the next attack; our leaders did their best to rally us together. Those of us covering 9/11 as journalists had our own duty. The country needed us at that moment to do our best to report the truth—and to be seen as telling the truth. As important as independence and objectivity are for journalists every day, they're that much more important in times of war or other serious threats to the country and its citizens. The last thing we needed right then was for the American people to think we might be reporting things not because we'd checked them out and concluded they were true but because the government wanted us to report them.

A few months after 9/11, Bill Kovach, the former *New York Times* Washington bureau chief, put it well in addressing the Organization of News Ombudsmen: "A journalist is never more true to democracy; never more engaged as a citizen; never more patriotic than when aggressively doing the job of independently verifying the news of the day; questioning the actions of those in authority; disclosing information the public needs but others wish secret for self-interested purposes."

I'm pleased to say that in the end, Terry Moran complied with our policy—pleased not so much because I'm sure I was right as that I didn't want to lose a gifted reporter from our air at a critical time.

There were other issues raised about our coverage during the week of 9/11. The same Friday as my exchange with Karl Rove, Ari Fleischer, the White House press secretary, summoned the Washington bureau chiefs for the networks and gave them something between a request and a demand. He prefaced his remarks with the statement that the nation was "at war and there have to be different rules." One of the new rules from the White House was that none of us would report the whereabouts of the president, the vice president, or any member of the cabinet without prior White House approval. And this rule apparently was to continue for the duration of the war. We were told this was for security reasons.

Before responding to the White House, I conferred with my colleagues at the other networks, some of whom were inclined to go along. I had reservations. What would we do, I asked, if we learned that Vice President Cheney had been admitted to the hospital with a heart attack (something sadly all too realistic, given the vice president's history of heart disease)?

In the end, we promised the White House that for the time being only, we would not report the whereabouts of the president or vice president unless we first notified the White House. This would give officials an opportunity to make their case that reporting what we knew could jeopardize national security. But the ultimate decision of whether and what to report would remain with each of us individually. And there would be no restrictions on reporting on members of the cabinet.

During this time, I tried to persuade officials at the White House that this was ultimately in the country's best interest—and even theirs. My reasoning came straight from my thinking about lapel pins. The last thing the American people would want to learn when there was so much anxiety in the air was that the White House was making secret deals with the media to withhold sensitive information from the public. If we had agreed to withhold information about the location of the vice president and all the members of the cabinet, what else were we holding back? No one at the White House seemed to think much of my argument. We had been attacked, and as far as I could tell, they firmly believed that as much secrecy as possible was the best defense of the nation. In the end, we never had to withhold reporting on the location of the president or vice president, and the new restriction went away on its own without further discussion.

About a month later, the White House was back with a new request. It was two days after the war in Afghanistan had begun, and I was driving home with my wife after attending a reception at the residence of the UN secretary-general, Kofi Annan. Earlier that day, we (and the other networks) had broadcast part of a new videotaped statement released by Osama bin Laden. We'd done our best to verify that it was bin Laden, to translate it, and to cut it down to the most interesting and relevant parts. (Frankly, the complete statements were too long and repetitive to hold the interest of most of the audience.)

When my cell phone rang, it was the switchboard at the White House saying that the national security adviser, Condoleezza Rice, wanted to speak with me urgently. Rice said they were concerned that al-Qaeda might be burying secret messages to its cells around the world in these long prerecorded statements. I told her I would certainly want to be responsive to any legitimate national security concerns. But these statements were news and had to be reported in some way. What specifically should we be looking for in the statements that could be a hidden message? She said she didn't know but would check. She asked me to join a conference call the next morning she was arranging with my counterparts at the other networks to discuss the matter with her.

By the time I got home at 11:00 that night, I had messages from Robin Sproul and Jeffrey Schneider telling me that Condoleezza Rice had called and convened a meeting by telephone of the news division presidents for the next morning to talk about the bin Laden statements. I was surprised that word had gotten out so quickly about what I'd thought was a private conversation. I'd learned that as irritating as leaks were, there never was much use in trying to find out where they came from: you couldn't usually tell, and if you guessed, you usually got it wrong. But most often the leak came from someone who would benefit most. On this one, I couldn't figure out whether that might be someone at the White House who thought it would make the administration appear strong or someone at one of the networks who wanted people to understand how patriotic they were being in cooperating with the government.

On the conference call the next morning, Rice formally requested that all of us agree not to air videos coming from Osama bin Laden or other al-Qaeda officials. She repeated that members of the national security team were concerned that these videos might contain hidden messages to al-Qaeda operatives. Although she admitted that she still had no specifics about buried messages, she emphasized the propaganda value of the videos. We agreed to consult among ourselves and get back to her.

After Rice hung up, we had a short but vigorous discussion covering the range from declining her request altogether to acceding to it. In the end, we chose a middle course. We'd hold off on airing any videos until we'd viewed them in their entirety. This would in theory allow us to pick up on any unusual gestures that might be some sort of signal—although we had no specifics from the government about what to look for. And we would limit our airing of video to those segments that we thought were newsworthy, avoiding simply airing them in their entirety (which we hadn't been doing anyway).

We then called Rice back and relayed our decision. Within minutes, we watched the White House spokesman Ari Fleischer spend the greater part of his daily press briefing describing the "cordial" discussions we'd had with Rice and referring to the prerecorded messages as "at best insidious propaganda" and "at worst" some sort of hidden message to bin Laden's followers. Though pressed, Ari declined to characterize what networks had decided to do.

Unfortunately, *The New York Times* was not as restrained. On October 11, 2001, the *Times* reported prominently on its front page that the "five major television news organizations" had agreed to a White House request to "abridge any future videotaped statements from Osama bin

Laden or his followers to remove language the government considers in-flammatory." The *Times* got it wrong—and *The New Yorker* made the problem worse by publishing a Talk of the Town piece based on the erro-neous *Times* report without checking with any of us on the call about what was said or agreed to.

As a group, the news division presidents wrote a letter to the editor of *The New York Times* explaining that we had never agreed to excise language that the administration found "inflammatory," or to excise any particular language at all. The only thing we'd said was that we'd watch the statements in their entirety and put on the air what was newsworthy. The *Times* de-clined to print the letter, saying it had a policy against publishing letters to the editor that pointed out where their factual reporting had been wrong. If they'd gotten something wrong, it should be handled in a correction—not a letter to the editor. It took another two weeks before we could get the *Times* to run a correction of its mistake, which it put among a number of other corrections inside a Saturday edition of the paper.

As wrong as our print critics were on the facts, they were right on a broader, more important point. We had not handled the situation at all well. There were no specific reasons given to curtail our reporting; it was merely the flimsiest of "maybes." By trying to reach an understanding with Rice, we'd opened the door for others to misinterpret what we'd done. In retrospect, we should have done what the then editor of *The New York Times*, Howell Raines, did: thanked the White House for the advice and taken it under advisement.

What I learned from the incident with Rice was that we shouldn't allow ourselves to be summoned together on an editorial matter in the first place. It was up to each of us to exercise our own, independent judg-ment. Getting us all together on the telephone in what was still a time of national emergency had the natural effect (whether intended or not) of starting a competition to see who could show themselves to be the most patriotic. Anything Rice had to say to me, she could have said in the car the night before on the way home.

Don't misunderstand me; I don't blame Condi Rice. She was doing her job in the energetic way she thought best. No, the fault lay with us in how we responded. Even if we agreed to no more than we would have done anyway, the appearance that the media collectively was making arrange-ments with the government not to report things sent an unhealthy message to our audience—the very sort of message I'd been trying to avoid when dealing with the lapel pin policy and the White House request not to report cabinet officers' locations.

What makes these issues more difficult is that sometimes the individual news organizations *should* work with the government to protect national security interests. An example came on another day also in October 2001. We were several days into our coverage of the Afghanistan war. Late in the afternoon we learned that U.S. Special Forces were in the middle of a raid behind enemy lines outside Kabul. This came to us only shortly before our evening newscast, and we wanted to report it on *World News Tonight* that evening. When we sought confirmation from the Pentagon, we were told that, yes, the raid was ongoing but that if we reported it before the troops returned, we could put them in danger.

For me, this was an easy call. The information we had was definitely newsworthy, but we weren't agreeing to suppress it altogether—only delay it for a few hours. The American people deserved to know about the raid, but I couldn't see why they needed to know at that moment. On the other hand, I accepted the Pentagon official's claim that there was some slight chance that the enemy might pick up on our reporting and take action. To be sure, it's a bit far-fetched that a Taliban or al-Qaeda official sitting in a bunker in Afghanistan would be watching *World News Tonight with Peter Jennings*, but in the world of the Internet it was at least possible that a version of the report could be picked up in the war zone.

I learned the hard way, though, that holding a story for national security reasons—no matter how justified—can come with a price. Much later, in October 2004, we obtained a videotape through sources in Pakistan that appeared to be a statement from an American identifying himself as "Azzam the American" and threatening terrorist attacks on the United States. From our other reporting, we believed that this was a young man from the West Coast who had taken the name Adam Gadahn (though he was born Adam Pearlman). The FBI earlier in 2004 had said that they were looking for Gadahn and suspected he was plotting with others from al-Qaeda to commit attacks.

We thought it was Gadahn on the tape, but we weren't sure. So we gave a copy of it to the FBI for them to review and confirm our suspicion. They agreed to check into it and get back to us.

As far as we knew, the FBI was still vetting the video when, two days later, Tony Snow on his Fox News Radio show reported as an exclusive that we had the tape and that it had come from al-Qaeda. As far as we could tell, there was no way that Fox News could have gotten this information unless it had come from the government. We were furious, and the FBI was somewhere between baffled and sheepish. We'll probably never know how Fox News ended up scooping us on our own reporting, but years later we were told that the FBI had provided the information to the Justice Department and the White House and someone (we suspected a political appointee) had given it to our competition. Nonetheless, we got our confirmation that it was Gadahn on the tape, and we aired our somewhat compromised "exclusive" on *World News Tonight* the evening of October 28, 2004.

A little over a year later, we got another tape made by the same American al-Qaeda member, and once again we sought government confirmation. By this time, Michael Chertoff had taken over as the head of Homeland Security. Secretary Chertoff called me at home over the weekend. He'd heard about our last experience with giving the government copies of our videotapes, and he didn't ask for a copy. Instead, he asked whether a senior FBI official could travel to New York and view the videotape in our offices to see whether there was anything in Gadahn's statement that could be a hidden message to terrorist cells (reminiscent of Rice's concerns about the bin Laden tapes three years earlier).

I agreed, and so late on a Saturday the FBI official came to our edit suite in New York to review the tape. This time there was no competitor preempting our reporting, and we aired the second Gadahn statement on *Good Morning America* the next day, a Sunday. By the way, the government found no hidden messages, but it did agree with us that it was Gadahn.

Much has been said and written about risks the press can pose for national security when it is reporting things the government wants kept secret. In my experience, the question never comes up the same way twice. Everyone has his own opinion about where the right balance is between national security and freedom of speech and of the press. Contrary to what some may believe, however, major news organizations like ABC News take these issues extremely seriously and struggle to come up with the right answers.

There is more of a give-and-take between the government and the major news organizations than people may realize. This doesn't happen every day, but it does happen many times during the course of a year. At any time, an organization like ABC News may be working on one or more issues that touch on sensitive matters of national security. Members of the government learn of the possible story, often because the reporters tell them as part of the confirmation process. Then someone from the government calls to register his or her objection. Sometimes this comes in the form of confirming the story but asking that it not be reported—at least not right away or at least not with complete details—because of a concern with national security. Often, if the story is particularly sensitive, the government declines either to confirm or to deny the story but argues that reporting it would be detrimental to the national interest. In my experience, this amounts to a tacit confirmation. The government is never shy about telling reporters when they've got it wrong.

After a few go-arounds of this sort, I developed two policies I followed in all cases. First, if we had a story that we believed would be sensitive for reasons of national security, we had to seek confirmation from the government agency most directly involved. This made sense first and foremost to make sure we got it right. But it also gave the government an opportunity to make its national security case to us. The opportunity to have a substantive discussion with those in government who know so that we can take into account their concerns is valuable—indeed, essential.

Second, I learned from experience that if a governmental agency was raising a red flag, then we needed to hear from someone at the top. If the national security issue was important enough for the government to be asking us to kill, postpone, or modify a report, then it was important enough for the head of the agency to pick up the telephone and call me. That's why Michael Chertoff himself called me at home on a Saturday to ask for the FBI to review the second Gadahn tape.

Beyond making sure we had open discussions with the government on issues of national security, I learned that the factors to be considered are surprisingly similar no matter how unique the particular circumstances. How specific can the government be in describing why our report would harm national security interests? How plausible is the claim? How important is it that the American people hear what we have to report? Do they need to hear it now, or can it wait (if the waiting will address some or all of the concerns about national security)? How much detail needs to be in the report for it to be helpful to our audiences (again, if taking some of the detail out will take care of the national security concerns)?

And finally, the decision whether or not to publish a report over the objections of a government official should always be made by individual news organizations—not collectively. There's no real need for collective action, and it can lead to unintended consequences, including a perception that the press is colluding with the government to control the flow of information.

Keeping our nation secure, its people safe, is about the most important responsibility that any of us can have. The tragedy of 9/11 brought the importance of that responsibility home for us all, including those of us covering the events and their aftermath as journalists. There are times when national security requires secrecy, something that journalists must appreciate and respect. But ultimately our national security does not lie in secrecy alone, not even in times of war. Making sure people know what has happened, how it happened, and what their government is doing about it is also essential to keeping our nation safe.

When the country is under attack, when the facts are far from certain, that's when journalists come under the greatest pressure to defer to our government. The pressure can come from responsible government officials who are pursuing their duties with the dedication we would want and who truly believe that secrecy is the best course. But it also can come from officials simply using any argument available to keep the news media from reporting something against the government's wishes. This is the time when the audience *needs* and deserves a stronger and better news media than it may *want* in the heat of the moment. It's the responsibility of journalists in these times of crisis to resist the pressures and draw for themselves the line between reporting that will cause specific, real damage and reporting that the government just doesn't want the people to see or read. The long-term security of our country requires no less.

# 6 | War and Bias: Portraits of the Fallen

Our goal tonight was to elevate the fallen above the politics and the daily journalism. Some of you doubt that. You are convinced that I am opposed to the war. I am not, but that's beside the point. I am opposed to sustaining the illusion that war can be waged by the sacrifice of the few without burdening the rest of us in any way.

—Ted Koppel, "The Fallen," <u>Nightline</u>, April 30, 2004

In April 2004, the executive producer of *Nightline*, Leroy Sievers, had an idea. He called me and said that he and Ted Koppel wanted to take one entire *Nightline* program and devote it to reading the names and showing the faces of every man and woman in U.S. uniform who had lost his or her life in the Iraq War to that point.

It had been almost a year since ABC and the other networks had shown President Bush landing on the aircraft carrier *Abraham Lincoln* off the California coast as it returned from combat operations in Iraq. Instead of coming in on the helicopter used by other members of the administration that day, the president flew in on a Lockheed S-3 Viking, a navy combat plane used to fly missions over Iraq. He climbed out of the copilot seat dressed in a navy flight suit. It was a dramatic entrance and a powerful image of the commander in chief, who himself had been a pilot in the Air National Guard more than thirty years before.

The president addressed an enthusiastic crowd of sailors that day, standing on the flight deck under a large banner proclaiming "Mission Accomplished." In fairness, the White House said later that the banner was the navy's idea, and the president did not use the words "mission accomplished" in his speech. But he did say that "in the Battle of Iraq, the

United States and our allies have prevailed." Back at the Pentagon, Defense Secretary Donald Rumsfeld declared at about the same time that all major combat operations had ended in Afghanistan as well.

It was easy to get caught up in the euphoria expressed on that aircraft carrier back in May 2003. Whatever reservations anyone had about the invasion of Iraq, things seem to have gone unbelievably well. Sure, there were reports of widespread looting and some remaining pockets of resistance, but it felt, at least for a moment, that we as a country were emerging from the nightmare that had begun on September 11, 2001. I was in the control room watching as the president climbed out of that navy plane, and I thought I could feel the sense of relief and optimism among my colleagues; I couldn't deny that I felt some of it myself.

But by the time Leroy Sievers called me nearly a year later, that optimism was gone. It was apparent to just about everyone that the president and his secretary of defense had spoken too soon. Battles were still being fought, and men and women were still dying. In August 2003 there'd been major attacks on the Jordanian embassy in Iraq and the UN headquarters, killing nearly thirty people, including the UN special representative Sergio Vieira de Mello. Vieira de Mello was a UN veteran of conflicts around the world, including Bangladesh, Cyprus, Mozambique, and Yugoslavia. As the UN high commissioner for human rights, he was thought by some to be a serious candidate to be the next secretary-general of the United Nations. His loss was devastating, not only to the UN, but to diplomats and international aid workers around the world.

There were also repeated attacks on Iraqi civilians, attacks that killed dozens and sometimes more than a hundred people at a time. In March, four private U.S. contractors were dragged from their car in Fallujah, murdered, and their bodies mutilated, burned, and hung from a bridge. Perhaps most striking, when the president proudly told us that "the United States and our allies have prevailed" in Iraq on May 1, 2003, a total of 138 American soldiers, sailors, and marines had died in the war; by the spring of 2004, the number had grown to more than 700. In the month of April 2004 alone, 137 U.S. troops gave their lives—almost as many as had died up to the point when we all saw the "Mission Accomplished" banner on the deck of the USS *Lincoln*. If this was a victory, it sure didn't feel like one.

While things were getting worse in Iraq, we saw the size of our audiencc for thc story dwindling. The American people were growing weary of the war. I had the sense that they embraced the "Mission Accomplished" idea in part because it put a nice, neat end to the story. At ABC News we were committed to continuing our reporting on the war, and we talked often in our editorial meetings about what we could do to make sure someone was paying attention.

One of the things we tried was to put the "kinetics" of the violence into a larger context. The afternoon I watched the horrific story of the explosion that took Vieira de Mello's life, I wondered whether we were really giving a full account of what was going on in Iraq—whether we even knew what was really going on. Was this an isolated, awful event, or did it reflect more broadly on how the war was going? And so I commissioned a series of reports we called "Where Things Stand," in which we reported not only on the violence but also ways of measuring the quality of life—things like the delivery of electricity and local government and education and employment all around the country. We put two of our strongest news executives in charge, Tom Nagorski (the foreign editor for *World News Tonight*) and David Reiter from the news desk, and dispatched three reporting teams to different parts of the country.

The first installment aired in November 2003, three months after Vieira de Mello's death. We did our reporting jointly with *Time* magazine, where my friend Jim Kelly was editor. I'd called Jim early in our preparation, and he'd enthusiastically committed some of *Time*'s reporters to the project. For our part, we aired a series of reports throughout all of our broadcasts over several days to reach as many people as possible. And we repeated the effort every few months over the next eight years, winning a series of Emmy Awards. I'd like to think that we helped our audience gain a better understanding of what was going on, not just on the battlefield but in towns and villages across Iraq. As so often happened, it was difficult to get a real sense of whether our reporting was making a difference, but at least we were trying.

It was against this backdrop that Leroy called me with his idea on an April afternoon in 2004. As president of ABC News, I didn't pretend to approve in advance each and every one of the stories appearing in the thirty-plus hours of original programming we did each week. I'd have a pretty good sense of what was happening from our morning and afternoon editorial calls, at which we'd talk about both the "news of day" and future plans. When it came to special programs, though, we didn't rely on the editorial calls. The executive producers would make sure to bring me into their thinking enough in advance so that I could weigh in and ultimately sign off on their plans. What Leroy and Ted were talking about was clearly a special program. It's not every day that you take a half hour of network TV, break format, and simply read names with photographs attached.

Leroy was the first to admit that the idea, though powerful, wasn't really original. In June 1969, *Life* magazine had run a cover story titled "The Faces of the American Dead in Vietnam: One Week's Toll." Inside, it published photographs of the 242 American soldiers, sailors, and marines who had died in one week on the battlefield. When Leroy first called me about Ted's and his idea, he invoked the *Life* precedent.

It didn't take me long to agree to the *Nightline* they described. There was no more important issue than the war in Iraq, it wasn't going away any time soon, and—as I've said—I was looking at the time for new ways to hold the attention of the audience. At first we thought we'd simply use our regular, half-hour *Nightline* time period including commercials. But as the number of deaths rose and we focused on how long we would need to show each soldier, we quickly figured out that we'd need more time to do it right. At one point we got a call from a grieving father whose son had been decorated for valor in combat and then died on his way back from military action when the truck carrying him crashed. He'd heard we were thinking about doing a program devoted to those who'd died "in combat." Technically, his son was not among that group. He asked us how in good conscience we could exclude his son. The simple truth was that we hadn't thought about those who'd died as the indirect result of combat. The father was, of course, right. So we expanded the list to include non-combat deaths in the theater.

When it became apparent that we'd need more than the thirty minutes, I went to the man who by then had taken my old job as head of the network, Alex Wallau. One of the things network heads do is referee between different network "day parts" (between news and entertainment, for example) about how network time will be divided up. If *Nightline* was to go long, we'd be taking away from *Jimmy Kimmel Live!*, the entertainment show that came after us. The ABC Network had made it a priority to find a successful entertainment show in late night to rival Jay Leno and David Letterman, even going so far as to offer the *Nightline* time slot to Letterman in 2002, two years before. After Letterman declined, the entertainment division developed a late-night show for Kimmel, a comic best known at the time for *The Man Show* on Comedy Central. ABC premiered *Jimmy Kimmel Live!* immediately after *Nightline* in January 2003, and there was no doubt in my mind that growing the show was a priority for the network; moving it back even a few minutes for us to recite names of those lost in Iraq certainly wouldn't help Kimmel. Despite this, Alex agreed—and did so readily. He shared our belief that it was important to cover the story and, like me, he was from a generation that remembered the *Life* story from the Vietnam War.

With Alex's support, we went back to work on the special *Nightline* episode. The next complication came when our sales department checked with advertisers and warned us that none of them would want to keep their advertisements in our special *Nightline*. I couldn't really blame them. Having television commercials show up in the middle of a reading of the war dead would be jarring, to say the least. At first we thought we might persuade one advertiser to be a special sponsor for the program, with some appropriate statement at the beginning and the end. But that didn't work either. We still wanted to proceed, but of course this meant I had to go back to Alex and get his agreement. Now we were not only cutting into *Jimmy Kimmel Live!*; we were proposing that we give up hundreds of thousands of advertising dollars.

There are all sorts of situations where covering the news doesn't maximize corporate profits—at least in the short run. Presidential elections? They cost a lot of money to cover and don't realize much in revenue at all. (People think about all the money candidates spend on TV commercials, but almost all of this goes to local stations—not to the networks.) Covering natural disasters like Katrina or, for that matter, wars like the one in Iraq? Very expensive, with limited commercials and most advertisers not wanting to be associated with them anyway. But doing a program like *Nightline* on those lost in the Iraq War wasn't a presidential election or a national emergency. It was a judgment call, something I needed approval for. Sometimes I got the approval and sometimes not. Sometimes I knew that I would have made a different decision if I'd been back in my job running the network. But the fact that I had had that job made me understand how tough some of these calls were. More important, I knew even when I was overruled that it didn't say anything about the commitment of company management—both Alex and his boss, Bob Iger—to covering the news well. Both Bob and Alex believed in news. But that didn't give them the luxury of handing us a blank check.

I'm proud to say that the *Nightline* special edition was one the company fully supported. We went ahead preparing an extended, commercial-free edition of *Nightline* devoted entirely to showing the faces and reading the names of the Americans who had given their lives in the conflict. We knew that we were getting extra time from Jimmy Kimmel and that we wouldn't be getting any commercial support. What I hadn't known, of course, was how our audience would react.

On the one hand, I'd thought those against the war might see our broadcast as glorifying it or waving a patriotic flag to distract attention from how the war was really going.

On the other hand, I thought some who supported the war might object because we were shining a spotlight on the ultimate price we as a nation were paying. I certainly had some inkling of where the Bush administration would come out. Just before the war began, in March 2003, the Pentagon had issued an edict stating "There will be no arrival ceremonies for, or media coverage of, deceased military personnel returning to or departing from . . . Dover [Delaware] base." For most of the Iraq War, the media couldn't show those iconic images of the flag-draped coffins returning home. But I still thought that at least some of those who supported the war would see the program as a fitting tribute to those lost in a valiant and worthwhile cause.

Ted put it best at the time:

> I truly believe that people will take away from this program the reflection of what they bring to it. I think it is just as possible for a staunch supporter of the war to come away from this program very moved and content that it was done as it is for someone who is an opponent of the war to come [away] with exactly the same feeling. I also have no illusions. I think it's entirely possible that people who hold those differing points of view will watch the same program and come away wishing it had not been done.

After working on the program for two weeks or so, we announced on April 27, 2004, that we would air a special edition of *Nightline* titled simply "The Fallen." Initially, we had thought that the right time would be on Memorial Day. But then we thought better of it, concluding that the holiday should be for honoring those who served in *all* wars, not just those who died in the most recent war. So the special *Nightline* was set to air the following Friday, April 30.

With our announcement, we started a firestorm.

Talk radio and the blogosphere exploded with criticism of ABC News, decrying what we planned as a politically motivated antiwar campaign. William Kristol, the conservative commentator, said that "this was a statement with a capital S, and it's a stupid statement." Neal Boortz, speaking on CNBC, said, "It is not news. It is grandstanding. They are trying to make a political statement . . . I think the intent is quite obvious here." Brent Bozell, president of the right-of-center media watchdog group Media Research Center, criticized the program's "partisan nature" and said its true goal was "to turn public opinion against the war." Bill O'Reilly of Fox News was more measured, worrying that the program might undermine morale if it tried to "exploit casualties in a time of war."

Most dramatically, the Sinclair Broadcast Group decided it would not air our broadcast on its seven ABC stations, claiming it would be a one-sided, biased attack on the war. As David Smith, the president of Sinclair, wrote in a letter, the planned program "appears to be motivated by a political agenda designed to undermine the efforts of the United States in Iraq." Unless we found alternative ways of distributing the program, this would mean that our audiences in cities such as St. Louis, Mobile, and Columbus would never see what we were doing.

Sinclair's decision itself triggered its own controversy. Senator John McCain wrote to the head of Sinclair, decrying his decision. In McCain's words: "Your decision to deny your viewers an opportunity to be reminded of war's terrible costs, in all their heartbreaking detail, is a gross disservice to the public, and to the men and women of the United States Armed Forces. It is, in short, sir, unpatriotic."

One of the more bizarre criticisms of our plans came from a media critic at *The Washington Post*, Lisa de Moraes. In a column the week of the broadcast, she noted that we were "telecasting this thing on the second night of the May sweeps," which made it "appear like an unseemly sweeps ratings grab." (The May sweeps are an annual ritual in which all television broadcasters try to get the best ratings that they can in hopes that they can sell their advertising through the summer based on these high numbers.) As Ted pointed out in a letter to the editor of the *Post*, if the goal had been to boost *Nightline*'s ratings, there were surer ways to do it than to spend forty minutes reading out the names of those who've died in war: "There are ways to artificially boost *Nightline*'s ratings and they could involve a list of names. Kobe Bryant, for one; Scott and Laci Peterson [the convicted wife killer and his victim] seem to attract a lot of viewer attention, as, of course, does Michael Jackson."

Ted was right that there were much surer ways of getting high ratings than what we were planning. It was also true that we were trying to reach and hold an audience to focus on the Iraq War. But this was an unusual case where the size of that audience had absolutely nothing to do with the money we would be taking in, much less with the May sweeps period. As I've said, we'd already decided not to include any commercials, so we wouldn't be making any money at all—not even the amount we would have made with an ordinary program. What's more, the only sweeps ratings advertisers look at are the ones for programs with commercials in them. Programs without commercials are called "sustaining" and don't count in the sweeps rating "book." Because we weren't airing any commercials in our program, it would be excluded from the official results—no matter how well or how badly it did. Of course, the critic could have called us and asked us about what we were planning, but she didn't. Often, those most vocal in criticizing what we were doing (or what they thought we were doing) had taken the least time to get the facts right.

On the eve of our Friday broadcast (and just after our announcement and Sinclair's much-publicized letter), we had the annual White House Correspondents' Dinner. This evening is a close cousin of the Radio and Television Correspondents' Dinner—like the one where I'd been the subject of President Clinton's roast. Once again, we were in the ballroom of the Washington Hilton with over a thousand journalists and Washington leaders dressed in black tie. This time, President Bush was the keynote speaker, and I'm happy to say that neither ABC News nor I was the center of the president's humorous remarks. We did, however, have some Bush administration luminaries sitting with us as our guests, including Secretary of Defense Donald Rumsfeld and Karl Rove, President Bush's senior political adviser. I was seated between the two.

I didn't know Rove well. I'd met him when we'd gone down to visit then–presidential candidate George W. Bush in Austin five years before, and I'd seen him a few times since. The only real business I'd had with him was our testy exchange about Peter Jennings's talking about the president's whereabouts on 9/11. Karl Rove was not, in my experience, a shy man. He was on a mission, and the mission was doing his best to persuade all around him that his view of the world was not only right, but the only view worthy of serious consideration. Rove was smart and tough and very effective.

Rove didn't waste much time wading into the brewing controversy over our plans for *Nightline*. Nor did he hesitate to register his extreme displeasure. For Rove, this was just one more powerful piece of evidence for how the "left of center" major media outlets were pursuing their political agenda even though, according to him, the country was "right of center"—like the president and like Fox News. We just didn't really know our audience.

I tried my best to persuade him of the merits of what we were about to do—merits that in my mind didn't lie to the left or the right. But I soon realized that we weren't going to agree on this. So instead, I shifted the discussion to the fact that it was Ted Koppel and ABC News who were doing it. Was it possible that the perception of bias came not from the substance of the broadcast but from the source? Could it be that he was objecting not to *what* we were doing but to the fact that *we* were the ones doing it? I asked, "What if Fox News put on the exact same program with the exact same content? Would your reaction be different? Would they be showing an antiwar bias?"

"No" was the simple answer. To his credit, Rove didn't hesitate. In his mind, such a program aired by Fox News would be entirely different. It would not be "antiwar." Bias for him (and, I believe, for others) doesn't lie in the eye of the beholder. It doesn't even lie in the substance of what's being said. Bias is for some a question of who's saying it. People were reacting the way they were because they "knew" (in his words) that both Peter Jennings and Ted Koppel were "left of center" and against the war. Anything we did had to be seen through that prism.

Despite the controversy, on Friday, April 30, we aired "The Fallen." It was forty minutes long and included no commercials. Over the course of the program, we showed photographs of 721 American men and women, all of whom had given their lives in the Iraq War. As Ted read the name of the person on the right of the screen, we slid their photograph to the left, so that two images would be on the screen at any given time. We did this so that the image of each would be on for longer than it took simply to read his or her name.

At the end of the broadcast, Ted Koppel addressed the controversy directly. He did his best to make it clear that it wasn't the war he was against; he was against our ignoring the price being paid in the lives of young men and women.

As is so often the case, the reaction to the broadcast after the fact was much more subdued than the debate leading up to it. Those who believed we were acting out of bias beforehand likely didn't change their view, if they watched the program at all. And what of those seven Sinclair stations that refused to air "The Fallen"? In the end, we found other ways to broadcast the program in six of the seven markets. And even though we didn't get "credit" for the ratings in the May sweeps book, that special edition of *Nightline* attracted 20 percent more audience than the program was usually drawing at that time. It may not have had the draw of Scott Peterson or Michael Jackson, but someone out there certainly was interested.

At the time, I found the furor baffling. Some programs we knew from the beginning would get us into hot water with someone or other. Certainly we'd hoped this program would get attention and perhaps trigger discussion. But this one wasn't something I thought would be nearly as inflammatory as it turned out to be. Our nation singles out its war dead in all sorts of ways without anyone taking it to be a campaign against armed conflict. Has anyone ever suggested that Arlington National Cemetery across the Potomac from the White House is a pacifist shrine? What about all the memorials across the country honoring those who fell in World War I or World War II or the Korean conflict? What about the Vietnam Veterans Memorial in Washington? For that matter, what about all the statues erected to Confederate soldiers who died in the Civil War that can be found throughout the South? How could anyone object to what we were doing? Could it have been a reflection of a growing anxiety within the country about the Iraq War itself?

It didn't help my understanding that the accusations of bias didn't line up with anything I'd heard or seen behind the scenes. I was there, and I can tell you that Ted, Leroy, and I never conceived of what we were doing as an indictment of the war. Both Leroy and Ted had told me that they were troubled by the disconnect between more and more Americans being asked to give their lives in Iraq and fewer and fewer Americans at home paying attention. They thought we owed it to the brave people who had given their lives to spend at least a moment looking into their faces and hearing their names.

Leroy and Ted felt a particular responsibility to those serving: they'd been embedded for almost two months with the Third Infantry Division of the U.S. Army in March and April 2003 as it came across the border from Kuwait, through southern Iraq, and into Baghdad. The Third Division was the "tip of the spear," as they said, an armored division whose mission was to thrust quickly across Iraq and take Baghdad. They'd spent days and nights in all their gear, sometimes including hazmat suits for protection against the chemical weapons we all thought Saddam had deployed throughout the country. They'd traveled hundreds of miles in ninety-degree heat in vehicles with windows closed to keep out the sand kicked up by the armored vehicles in their column. They'd slept in their vehicle in the cold desert nights. And they'd suffered the loss of their colleague and friend Michael Kelly from *The Atlantic* magazine when Kelly's Humvee had come under fire and, in seeking cover, had flipped into a ditch. Like Ted and Leroy, Michael had been embedded with the Third Infantry on the drive to Baghdad.

I didn't have the experience that Ted and Leroy had, but I agreed completely with their stated reasons for doing the special. The story of the Iraq War wasn't just about battles or territory or politics. It was also the individual stories of the men and women who were giving their lives. I felt an obligation to those risking and giving their lives—and to their families. An obligation that had little to do with ratings and nothing to do with whether one agreed or disagreed with the decision to go to war in the first place (or with how the war was being conducted).

I also felt an obligation to the country overall. It was wrong for us to be paying the price we were in young lives without talking about what that price was. Looking back on it now, I'm struck by how prescient Leroy and Ted were. Whatever estimates the government made about the ultimate price of the Iraq War in blood and treasure turned out to be wildly off the mark. Whether the Iraq War was justified or not, it is dangerous for the American people to think that war, any war, is too cheap or easy. Deciding what we should do as a country isn't the job of any news organization. But journalists cannot and should not let the nation go ahead without careful consideration of what it is sacrificing.

The problem, of course, was that our critics weren't particularly concerned with either the substance of our program or our real motivation for putting it on the air. Karl Rove got it right. It wasn't *what* we were doing; it wasn't really *why* we were doing it. It was simply that *we* were the ones doing it. Our critics came to the program believing we were biased against the war because of what they believed about our politics. There was nothing we could do to persuade the Karl Roves or the Sinclairs or the talk radio hosts that our motives were pure. They knew better, not because they knew us or had talked to us about our thinking, but because they knew us to be "biased." And that very bias made anything we had to say on the subject untrustworthy. So it shouldn't have come as a surprise that these critics would have strong objections about what in another context, done by someone else, they would likely have applauded.

Throughout my time at ABC News, somebody somewhere was accusing us of bias every single day—and usually many times in a day. Entire websites are given over to pointing out perceived bias in major news organizations. The charge of bias came up all the time, and I always found it the most difficult criticism to answer.

Not all the criticism came from outside the company. For a time, one of the directors of the Walt Disney Company was certain that ABC News in general, and Peter Jennings in particular, were deeply biased against Israel in our coverage of the Middle East. I would hear from him from time to time. At one point, he confronted me with the charge at a dinner Bob Iger was hosting for the Disney board and senior management. And that's just the part of it I heard. I have no doubt that Bob was shielding me from a good deal more of the same. Even as I tried my best to answer the charge, I could sense that the more I tried to argue that we weren't biased, the more someone could take my defense itself as proof of just how biased we were. We had such a set view of the world that we couldn't even see that we were biased.

I never found a clear, simple way of responding to charges of bias in our reporting, but I took it to be just about the most serious criticism any-one could make of what we were doing. We went to elaborate lengths to try to get the story right, whatever the subject. We trained young journal-ists how to gather facts and check sources. We had checks and balances within the chain of command for a given reporter. We had a staff of sev-eral people outside the chain of command to vet reporting in advance if we thought there was any danger we might have it wrong. And on top of all that, we had several in-house lawyers from the general counsel's staff to check what we were reporting. It's no exaggeration to say that I spent some of my time just about every day I was at ABC News trying to make sure we were right about one story or another. All of this was because we wanted to be telling the audience as much of the truth as we could find about everything we covered. To say that all of this was simply a charade, that even after all we went through we were really telling people only what we wanted to be true, was pretty devastating. In my mind, it turned us from truth-tellers (however imperfect) into mere advocates marketing a particular point of view just the way our advertisers were marketing their products during the commercial breaks.

What made it even more difficult to answer the charge of bias was that, in one sense, it always carried a germ of truth. No matter how hard you try, you just can't deny that all of us—journalists and non-journalists alike—are biased one way or another. We wouldn't be human if the sum total of all we are and what we've experienced didn't lead us to prefer some outcomes over others. As humans, we are imperfect.

What's more, during my time at ABC News, I thought I sometimes saw real bias in the way other journalists sometimes covered us. I once was on a panel with Bill Keller, the *New York Times* editor, who said, "The best experience for any journalist is to be covered by other journalists." Boy, was he right. I came away from ABC News convinced that some of the major print news organizations have a clear editorial point of view (I would say a bias) that television news is an oxymoron. You can have tele-vision, and you can have true news reporting. But you can't, according to this point of view, have both. I'm aware that my defensiveness probably leads me to overstate the bias. That's probably my own bias. And I'm sure that some print reporters would say that their point of view is justi-fied, that they've had experiences with TV news that they've found much less than satisfying. It also occurs to me that some of this may come from jealousy, particularly over what has historically been a very different pay scale for TV journalists compared with their peers in print. But whatever its origins, I believe there is a general bias in much of print coverage of TV news.

So, even for those in the media, the question is not whether there is bias that makes its way into some reporting. The question is, what can be done about it? From my platform, I saw news organizations take one of two approaches: either they admitted the bias and embraced it, claiming justification in the bias of others; or they fought against the bias in the hope of doing better, knowing they could never completely eliminate all bias from even the best reporter's work.

Newspapers in England are an example of the former. For many years, some of the most prominent English papers have associated themselves with one political side or the other—"The Torygraph" (as *The Telegraph* is sometimes referred to) leaning to the right and *The Guardian* tradition- ally leaning left. During the time I lived in London in the early 1980s, it didn't take a careful student of British politics to detect the preference of either paper in the race between Margaret Thatcher and Michael Foot for prime minister. And I'm not talking about just the editorials and col- umns. You could tell from the front page just about every day.

Whatever they may sometimes claim, this is pretty much the approach of both Fox News and MSNBC today in the United States. Both have de- cided that on average and over time, they will present the news from a particular political point of view. It doesn't mean that all of their reports are skewed; they're not. But they have a specific audience with a specific point of view that they're targeting. And addressing that audience is more important to them than worrying too much about whether some biased reporting shows up on air.

This is one approach. But it's not the only approach. Instead, you can admit the bias and use it not to justify biased reporting but as a starting point for reducing bias where you can. This was why we had all the checks and balances on our reporting at ABC News. It's the approach I em- braced—embraced more closely the more I was exposed to the fairly constant charges of bias from all directions.

I found that the only way to seriously address bias was to try to under- stand all we could about our own biases wherever we could find them. The analogy I used time and again at ABC News (my colleagues might say "overused") to illustrate the point is the annual ritual that is the Michigan versus Ohio State football game. I attended the University of Michigan for seven years—four as an undergraduate and three in the law school. What's more, the seven years I was there (1970–77) were the heyday of the intense rivalry between Bo Schembechler and Woody Hayes. For those of us sitting in the student section down in the end zone of the Big House, this was far more than just a sports contest. This was personal. I was there to witness the moment when the Ohio State Buckeyes came out of the tunnel and, instead of running to their benches right by the tunnel, ran out onto the field and ripped down the banner held up at every home game for the Michigan Wolverines to jump up and touch for good luck. Fortunately, I've never seen murder and mayhem on a college football field. But if the thousands of Michigan students had acted on what was in their hearts that day, the Buckeyes would have paid a heavy price—helmets and pads or no.

If I were covering a Michigan–Ohio State football game, I'd have a hard time separating my feelings from my reporting—and I'd know it. Knowing that I had my bias wouldn't excuse me from the responsibility of at least trying my best to cover the game as if I didn't have the loyalties I had. If I were doing my job as a journalist, I'd admit my bias and try to overcome it. But I'm not sure I'd succeed.

Recognizing how hard it would be for me to put aside my "Go Blue" mentality, I think it would be better if my bosses either put someone else on the assignment or, failing that, made sure someone joined me for the coverage, someone who didn't share my bias, could recognize it, and would keep me honest. Maybe even someone who loved the Buckeyes just as much as I loved the Wolverines.

Over and above all that, I really should make a point of explaining to the audience my ties to the University of Michigan. That way, the audience could judge for itself whether my reporting was impartial, even if deep inside what I felt was completely partial.

That's a metaphor for what we tried to do at ABC News. We were constantly on the lookout for circumstances that might make it too difficult for particular reporters or producers to work on a particular story. Even if their work was straight down the middle, it might be perceived otherwise. And if our reporting was challenged, it might make us all more vulnerable. When Chris Cuomo's brother ran for governor of New York, we all agreed that Chris shouldn't be assigned any stories related to New York State government. When Bianna Golodryga became engaged to Peter Orszag, President Obama's director of the Office of Management and Budget, we made sure that her reporting didn't go near the administration's plans for the economy. And so it went with any financial or personal or other ties we could identify throughout the entire organization (an approach I believe we shared with most other major news providers).

We also put the responsibility on staffers to be thinking about bias, to avoid allegiances and connections that might compromise their reporting whenever possible. We had policies that served as reminders of this responsibility, such as the ban on contributing to political candidates or on displaying partisan political badges or signs—either inside or outside the office—or on even attending political rallies. The ban on wearing lapel pins that my White House correspondent disagreed with me over right after 9/11 was ultimately based on the need to avoid even the appearance of bias—and to remind everyone how important that was every day.

In cases where we simply couldn't avoid reporting on something where we had a stake that could make us biased, we did our best to make the stake apparent to the audience. This came up most often when we were reporting on things having to do with our parent company. The company itself was sometimes in the news, and we did our best to report the story—good or bad—straightforwardly. But we also did reviews on *Good Morning America* of Disney films, and we reported on things ESPN was doing. Whatever the story, whether straight news or a movie review, we had a standing policy of always saying on the air that Disney was the parent company of ABC News. Sometimes my friends at corporate would ask why this was necessary. My reply was always the same: We need to make sure that the audience can judge for itself whether what we're saying is being influenced in any way by our corporate ties.

But just as my trying not to be biased or my telling the audience of my Michigan loyalty probably wouldn't be enough, so I found it to be in the newsroom at ABC. The critics have a point when they say that one of the most pernicious things about bias is that sometimes you may not even recognize you have a particular slant on how you see the world. I may have been a bit more sensitive to this when I came to ABC News, not only because I was from outside journalism, but also because I wasn't from the

East Coast. I was from Flint, Michigan. My father and grandfather had worked in auto plants. My background was very different from that of many of those in the leadership of ABC News. Sometimes things were said in the newsroom that I thought showed a lack of understanding of some of the things I'd grown up with—some of the hopes and fears of the industrial manufacturing communities in the middle of the country, how they sometimes regarded Washington and New York, their ties to faith and to church. Because I was there, I did my best to get people at least to consider this point of view, which can be different from what is often found on the Upper West Side of Manhattan. You could say that people were biased, or you could say that they just weren't aware of other points of view. But it really came down to the same thing in the end.

It was largely because of concerns with alleged media bias that I came to believe so strongly in diversity in the newsroom. No matter how hard you try, you really can't address the dangers of editorial bias if you aren't exposed regularly to a wide range of viewpoints. This certainly includes racial and ethnic diversity. We spent a fair amount of time, for example, talking about the disproportionate effects Hurricane Katrina had on African Americans and what we should do about the issue in our reporting. It helped enormously that we had African Americans in editorial positions who could relay some of what they were hearing of the criticism— the charge that both the media coverage and the aid were less than they would have been if the racial makeup of the victims had been different. People can come to their own conclusions about whether the charge was fair. But I saw how important it was that we hear it, hear it loud and clear, and carefully consider its merits.

As I came to appreciate the importance of newsroom diversity, I saw that true editorial diversity only began with race and ethnicity. The different viewpoints that can come into play in covering the news include politics (yes, that's right—liberals *and* conservatives); religion; socioeconomic backgrounds; geographic origins; and on and on. For example, in the wake of 9/11, it became very important that we had some way to hear the viewpoints of people who'd grown up in the Islamic faith. Most of us didn't really know all that much about Islam and how it worked (a notable exception being Peter Jennings, who'd spent so much time in the Middle East and had studied Islam closely for years). It helped enormously, for example, when Diane Sawyer did a documentary on Islam that we could include our reporter Lama Hasan, who was born in Qatar and raised in London and whose parents are Palestinian.

All of the things we did—the vetting, the reassignments, the policies, the disclosure, and the pursuit of greater newsroom diversity—were done to identify and reduce bias wherever possible. And by this, I mean the sort of bias that comes from the reporter having a predetermined point of view based on their experience, allegiances, or interests. But there's also another kind of "bias" that I saw in some journalism. This bias comes not from the reporter approaching the story with a predetermined outcome in mind but from the reporter deciding too early in the reporting process what the "right answer" is and then gathering evidence for the conclusion reached prematurely. From what I saw, this problem wasn't talked about much, but it was surprisingly common.

I first saw this sort of bias before I even went to ABC News—when I was the source a reporter was hoping would confirm the story he'd already decided to tell. I was running the ABC Network when the Telecommunications Act of 1996 came into force. One of the act's provisions required television set producers to include a new technology called a V-chip in all sets over a certain size. The networks were called upon to adopt a ratings system along the lines of that used for many years by the motion picture industry. Each TV program was given a rating that specified what age children should be watching it based on the language, violence, and sexual content. The theory was that parents could use the V-chip to police their children's viewing even when the parents weren't in the room. I'd publicly expressed skepticism about the V-chip because I didn't believe that many parents would take the time and trouble to use it (which has largely turned out to be the case, according to a 2007 Federal Communications Commission report).

When the act came into force, *World News Tonight* did a piece on it. I was visiting our ABC offices in Los Angeles, and an ABC News reporter called asking that I appear in the piece. I declined, mainly because I was busy and I didn't think I had much to add to the discussion. The reporter was very insistent, however, saying my contribution would be critical, and I reluctantly agreed. I went to a conference room in our L.A. offices where they'd set up a camera and microphone manned by two people. It turned out that I wasn't going to be interviewed by the reporter. Instead, the producer asked all the questions, and even he wasn't present. They had him on a speakerphone from New York. It was clear right from the start that they didn't really want to hear what I thought about the V-chip. What they wanted was a good sound bite to support their thesis that the V-chip would actually *increase* sex, violence, and bad language on TV because it would allow the networks to do whatever they wanted and hide behind the new V-chip to protect the kids.

I thought this was ridiculous. There were all sorts of reasons to use—or not to use—racy content in TV shows that had nothing to do with the V-chip. I'd never even considered that we'd change our programming because of the new technology, and I'd never heard anyone else suggest it. But the producer essentially asked various forms of the same question, trying to get me to say what he had already concluded would be the unintended effect of the new act. After about a half hour of this, he gave up and ended the interview. By the way, nothing I said ended up in the piece that aired—none of the interview that it had been so crucial for them to get. I always suspected it was because it didn't fit the reporter's thesis.

I don't know where the reporter and the producer got their idea about what the true effect of the V-chip would be. There's no reason to think they had any particular stake in the issue one way or the other. I wouldn't be surprised if they talked to someone in the industry at an early stage of their reporting who suggested the thesis, it sounded interesting and plausible to them, and they never went back to consider that it might be wrong. Psychologists have identified an innate bias humans have in favor of whatever information is gathered first. If the first part of a reporter's gathering of information tends to point in one direction, it may color how he or she views all the information gathered after that.

You can't ask reporters not to make judgments about what's true and what's not; you can't ask them to leave behind all their relevant experience every time they begin work on a story. More than that, you wouldn't want them to. Part of the reason you turn to a reporter to tell you the story is because you want her to do her best at coming to some conclusions about what's really happening based on her judgment and experience.

It's hard to draw the line between jumping to conclusions and using your experience as a precedent. I saw the interplay of experience and jumping to conclusions firsthand in the coverage of the Monica Lewinsky scandal. By the time the attorney general gave Ken Starr authority to investigate the circumstances surrounding President Clinton's relationship with Lewinsky, many in the press—and especially in the Washington press corps—had tired of what they saw as cynical attempts by the White House to spin stories ranging from the circumstances surrounding the Clintons' investment in Whitewater to the president's dealings with campaign donors. Later, senior White House officials would write about their efforts to leak negative stories in ways that would be least damaging to the administration and to outright lie to reporters. These experiences may have predisposed some reporters to believe the worst about Clinton. The question is whether their experiences made them better prepared to cover the story or gave them a bias—not because of a view about the merits of the administration's policies, but a bias based on jumping to conclusions.

As I watched all of us struggle to find the right balance between drawing from experience and prejudging, I realized that I'd seen something like this before. When I worked for Justice Powell, I'd seen the way judging was done on the Supreme Court, which came to influence my views about good reporting. One of the things I admired was Powell's ability to bring all of his rich life experience to bear and yet keep an open mind long into the judging process. He always wanted to hear and consider all of the arguments on all sides of an issue. I remember one case in which another justice circulated a draft opinion for the majority. When we received the draft, I took one copy, and Justice Powell took the other. In reading over it, I was troubled by something in the opinion and quickly wrote five or six pages setting out my concerns. I walked into the justice's chambers to give him my memo only to learn that he had already sent a note to the author saying he would join in the opinion. When Powell told me that, I said he wouldn't need to read what I had written. Quite the contrary, he said, he wanted to consider arguments against his position even after he'd gone this far along in the process. There was still time to change his vote, as the opinion wouldn't be delivered by the Court for several days.

But Justice Powell never let his openness keep him from making up his mind once the time came. In fact, I suspect it was easier for him to finalize his views because he was satisfied that there weren't issues out there that he hadn't considered. By the way, after reading my memorandum, the justice stuck to his position and to his vote.

Keeping an open mind as long as possible is hard when you're operating in an atmosphere as politically charged as the period beginning with

9/11 and continuing through the war in Iraq. This was a time filled with raw emotions and strong talk, particularly when it came to matters of national pride, national security, and what some people saw as tests of patriotism. When you're in the pressure chamber, the natural tendency is to become defensive, rejecting out of hand charges of bias, knowing that some of those making the accusations have their own agendas—agendas that may have little to do with the truth. And yet, in my experience, taking everyone's criticism seriously is the first and best line of defense against making mistakes.

Karl Rove and the Sinclair Broadcast Group had strong points of view about "The Fallen." And it was important that we consider what they had to say. After all, they might have been right. Behind the scenes we asked ourselves some tough questions about why we wanted to have a special edition of *Nightline* to read the names and show the faces of the war dead. I concluded that the motives Ted, Leroy, and I could recognize in ourselves were pure. Could there have been some deep, unconscious desires that we didn't recognize? Everything is possible, especially when it comes to the human mind playing tricks on itself. But to this day I believe "The Fallen" was just what it purported to be: a respectful reflection on the awful price paid in war that everyone should consider. I don't believe that that message was biased. And if it's the messenger we need to consider as well as the message, bias is often a two-way street. All too often those making the harshest and loudest complaints about media bias are themselves the most biased.

None of us is immune from bias; there is the frailty of humans inside all of us. But that doesn't mean we can't learn. Or that we can't try to overcome the biases we bring from our various pasts; or that we can't surround ourselves with people who both have a different point of view and are not afraid to express it; or that we can't try to put ourselves in the shoes of the person or people we're covering. And if we do all of this, we have a hope, at least a hope, not of eliminating all biased reporting but of reducing it by a good margin. I believe we tried to do just this at ABC News. We tried because we believed that even in making the effort, consistently over time, we would accomplish something worthwhile. It was always for the audience to judge how close we came to our goal.

# 7 | The Swift Boat Saga: Is Balance Overrated?

One of our producers this morning raised a question that I suspect a number of you may have on your minds. Why, just when the presidential candidates are starting to focus on real substantive issues, devote yet another program to what John Kerry did or didn't do in Vietnam?

Here's why: Questions have been raised about John Kerry's character and honesty. We were offered the chance to set the record straight on one discrete chapter in Mr. Kerry's war record. We didn't know what we were going to find when our crew went into Vietnam. You have the right to expect that we would have reported it either way. And we would . . .

Our interviews don't prove that John Kerry deserved his Silver Star, but they are consistent with the after-action report and his citation for bravery.

—Ted Koppel, "What They Saw," Nightline, October 14, 2004

In July 2003, Senator John Kerry came to the ABC News offices in New York for an editorial meeting. We were a year away from another presidential election, and it was the senator's turn to come and let us get to know him a bit, as we would do with his rivals for the Democratic nomination.

The country had known John Kerry as the junior senator from Massachusetts for almost twenty years. He'd figured prominently in national discussions on issues ranging from the Iran-Contra affair to relations with Vietnam because of his service on the Foreign Affairs Committee and the Senate Select Committee on POW/MIA Affairs. We knew he was intelligent and experienced, even if he was somewhat awkward at times as a politician. We got to see both sides of him when he came into town to meet with us. Whenever we met with a presidential candidate, we had a big turnout. Well over fifty people from ABC came to talk with Senator Kerry, ranging from anchors such as Peter Jennings, Diane Sawyer, and Barbara Walters to our most senior producers to junior off-air political reporters and assistants on the news desk. All were eager to hear what he had to say.

He started out by surprising us. Every other candidate or newsmaker we had in for a meeting came early, mingled with the crowd beforehand, and sat down with ease to make a few remarks and then take questions. But Kerry showed up twenty minutes late and then insisted on going into an office to take a phone call. By the time he emerged, we had a restless crowd of ABC News people. But instead of jumping right into the planned meeting, he decided to go around the entire room, stopping in front of each anchor, correspondent, producer, and desk assistant to introduce himself and have a short, awkward exchange while the rest of us listened and waited for him to get to us. And then, after this oddly stilted beginning, he proceeded to answer a wide range of questions clearly, cogently, and with a real command of the material. We got to see both sides of John Kerry that day: the accomplished, thoughtful statesman and the ill-at-ease, studied candidate who seemed to be learning politics as a second language. We had plenty of questions for the senator—some of which we asked directly and some of which we tried to get a sense of in watching his interaction with us. His track record of actually getting legislation through Congress was surprisingly thin, given his long tenure. He'd tended to do more presiding over high-profile hearings than he had legislating. His position on the Iraq War was convoluted at best. There were stories that he was not always beloved by those who worked most closely with him. And so on.

But whatever questions we may have had, the one thing we thought we knew best about John Kerry was that he was a genuine war hero. This part of Senator Kerry's biography loomed particularly large, given that the country was at war in Iraq and Afghanistan and was actively combating terrorism around the globe. President George W. Bush, on the other hand, had avoided combat by serving in the Air National Guard, and questions had been raised during his first presidential campaign about whether he'd even shown up for all that service. (At that point, we were still more than a year away from Dan Rather's controversial *60 Minutes II* report challenging what Bush did during the war.)

Senator Kerry's reputation as a war hero was based in large part on the five medals he'd been awarded for his service in Vietnam. The most prestigious of these was the Silver Star, which he'd received as the result of a firefight in the hamlet of Nha Vi on February 28, 1969. At the time, Kerry was a navy lieutenant (junior grade) who had graduated from Yale less than three years before. He was in command of a group of three swift boats patrolling the Mekong River delta on the Bay Hap River in western South Vietnam.

What were commonly called swift boats were actually Patrol Craft, Fast (or PCF) boats designed to transport men and ammunition quickly along the rivers and streams that penetrated the Mekong Delta all the way to Cambodia. They were fifty feet long, had a shallow draft, could move as fast as twenty-four miles an hour, and were armed with .50-caliber machine guns mounted on top of a cabin at the forward part of the boat. The usual crew was one officer and six enlisted men. Kerry later said that when he volunteered for the swift boats, "they had little to do with the war. They were engaged in coastal patrolling and that's what I thought I was going to be doing." But shortly after he went to the swift boats, the U.S. military launched a new offensive called Operation Sealords that depended in part on using the swift boats to patrol the delta, draw enemy fire, and destroy enemy positions. Kerry's mission became one of the most dangerous at that point in the Vietnam War.

The official citation awarding Lieutenant Kerry the Silver Star recounted that he was in command of three swift boats on February 28, 1969, as part of an operation to insert thirty South Vietnamese troops into the Mekong Delta. Going up the Bay Hap River, they "came under heavy enemy small arms fire from the river banks." Kerry ordered "his units to turn to the beach and charge the Viet Cong positions" and then "expertly directed the fire of his craft at the fleeing enemy while simultaneously coordinating the insertion of the [South Vietnamese] troops."

But his day wasn't over yet. Kerry's swift boat and one of the other two went farther up the river to investigate a location where there were reports of enemy fire. Someone from the riverbank fired a handheld rocket at Kerry's swift boat. In response Kerry "ordered his units to charge the enemy positions." He beached his own boat "in the center of the enemy positions," and when an enemy soldier "sprang up from his position not ten feet from [Kerry's boat] . . . and fled," Kerry "without hesitation . . .

leaped ashore, pursued the man . . . and killed him, capturing a [rocket launcher] . . . with a round in its chamber." Before the day was done, Kerry and his units would come under fire twice more, both times returning and suppressing the enemy fire.

Beyond receiving the Silver Star, Lieutenant Kerry was also awarded a Bronze Star and three Purple Hearts for other action he saw during his tour of duty. It's hardly any wonder that all of us who knew anything about Senator Kerry considered him a war hero. If the issue of combat service came up at all in the presidential race, it just made sense that it would be to Kerry's benefit.

Most of us also remembered what the young John Kerry had to say about the Vietnam War after he came home. Kerry returned from Vietnam to a military posting outside New York City in 1969. Two years later, after completing his service, he became the center of national attention when, on April 22, 1971, he testified against the Vietnam War before the Committee on Foreign Relations. He spoke about what he described as "war crimes" committed "on a day-to-day basis" by U.S. soldiers in Southeast Asia with "the full awareness of officers at all levels of command." He spoke of the guilt that American soldiers carried after their service was ended. He spoke of the shabby treatment given returning veterans of the Vietnam War. And he famously asked, "How do you ask a man to be the last man to die for a mistake?"

As if this weren't enough, he participated in a demonstration outside the gates of the White House. On national television, John Kerry took his medals and threw them over the fence in a symbolic rejection of the war.

So, in addition to Kerry's distinguished service in combat, there was certainly the possibility that some would object to his anti–Vietnam War stance, taken in so public a way. But even this was something most of us took to be a possible counterpoint, rather than a contradiction, to the heroism he'd shown under fire.

Then, on May 4, 2004, only sixty days after the "Super Tuesday" primaries, when Kerry effectively clinched the nomination, an unusual press conference was held in Washington, D.C. A group of Vietnam veterans, calling themselves the Swift Boat Veterans for Truth, came forward to claim that at least some of what we thought we knew about Senator Kerry's war record was a lie. The group's leader was John O'Neill, a Houston lawyer and former U.S. Navy officer who had taken over command of

Kerry's swift boat when he returned to the United States in 1969. O'Neill had been asked by the Nixon administration back in 1971 to debate Kerry publicly on his condemnation of the Vietnam War.

Over thirty years later, when Kerry decided to run for president, O'Neill gathered two hundred other swift boat veterans to challenge Kerry's claims about his war service. At the press conference, O'Neill was joined by some of his supporters, including one who had served on a boat Kerry commanded, several who had not, and some who had commanded Kerry during his service. Most of their complaints were about what Kerry did on returning home—the claims he'd made of war crimes and his testifying against the war. But they also questioned whether all of the wounds Kerry had suffered were serious enough to merit the Purple Hearts he received. They did not, at that initial press conference, question whether Kerry had earned the Silver Star and Bronze Stars.

The May press conference got some coverage in the print media, including an article in *The New York Times* titled "Veterans Group Criticizes Kerry on His Record in Vietnam." The conservative media criticized those of us who didn't immediately give the story national attention, and the Swift Boat Veterans decided they would get the word out on their own by raising money and producing a series of campaign spots criticizing Kerry for his war service.

In the meantime, O'Neill had been working on a book, *Unfit for Command*, which came out in mid-August, two weeks after John Kerry's official nomination at the Democratic convention in Boston. In his book, O'Neill drew together a comprehensive indictment of Kerry's war service and of his conduct after Vietnam. For the first time, O'Neill directly challenged whether Kerry deserved the Silver Star, claiming that his act of beaching his swift boat to race ashore, far from being heroic, "display[ed] stupidity." His encounter with the Vietcong soldier was really only the "dispatching of a fleeing, wounded, armed, or unarmed teenage enemy" dressed "in a loincloth."

The first of the Swift Boat Veterans for Truth spots aired in August, a week after O'Neill's book was published. In the commercial, several of the veterans appeared on camera, saying things like "John Kerry has not been honest about what happened in Vietnam" and "He is lying about his record." Once again, there was no direct challenge to the account of the events that had led to Kerry's Silver Star. Instead, the spots included an allegation that "John Kerry lied to get his Bronze Star" and stated flatly that "John Kerry is no war hero."

On August 9, right after the ads began to run, *Nightline* devoted a program called "Trial by Fire" to the Swift Boat Veterans' accusations. In the program, *Nightline* presented the sharply conflicting points of view of the various veterans weighing in on Kerry's service record, talked about where the financing for the ads was coming from, and discussed the possible political effects on the campaign.

For the rest of August, questions raised about Senator Kerry's record pretty much dominated coverage of the presidential race. According to one critic (who later argued that the story had been given far too much play), *The Washington Post* ran twelve front-page stories on the Swift Boat Veterans attacks in the second half of August 2004. During the same period, each of the broadcast news networks aired somewhere between seven and nine pieces on the same story. One indication of how seriously some were taking the story came when Republican Senator John McCain on August 19 weighed in on the subject, saying of the first Swift Boat ad, "I think the ad is both dishonorable and dishonest and I condemn it. I hope that the President will also condemn it."

Try as he might, Senator Kerry never really put the Swift Boat Veterans attacks behind him for the rest of his campaign. To those of us covering him, it didn't appear that Kerry or his campaign really had a command of the facts from the outset, which kept them from immediately putting out the truth and taking the steam out of the story. The media focused like a laser (or perhaps more like a fire hose) on the claims and counterclaims. We soon learned (and reported) that the Swift Boat Veterans were being funded by, among others, Bob J. Perry, a well-known backer of Republican and conservative causes. When protesters showed up at his house to object, he increased his contribution from $250,000 to $7 million. Eventually, 140,000 people contributed to the Swift Boat Veterans for Truth, and they raised $27 million. Members of the group appeared on cable television. Then other veterans came forward to support Senator Kerry's version of the events. There were counterattacks questioning the bona fides of at least some of those participating in the Swift Boat Veterans effort.

There's little doubt that the Swift Boat Veterans had a real effect on the 2004 campaign. According to a postmortem in the *National Review*, "One post-election survey of actual voters found that 75 percent of them were familiar with the Swifties and their allegations about Kerry's qualifications for the presidency."

What was the media's role in all of this? Were we covering a legitimate news story and presenting both sides in a "fair and balanced" way? Or were we pawns being manipulated by partisan politics? One thing is certain. The media did what it does best: it covered the controversy. It covered it as a political story about liberals and conservatives, Democrats and Republicans, and how modern campaigns for president are conducted. If we had any concerns at the time about our coverage, it was about whether we were being "fair" to both sides. Were we giving both sides a full airing? Were we being "balanced"?

The problem was that this approach missed the most important point. This was not the usual political fight over who would take the country in a better direction or whose qualifications better prepared him for the Oval Office. This was a dispute about historical fact. Whether John Kerry on that February afternoon did or did not turn his boat into oncoming fire, whether he went ashore to engage a serious and dangerous enemy in the face of real danger, was not a matter of opinion. There were two sides to the argument, but one of those sides was just plain wrong. If we had been there on the shore of the Bay Hap River in 1969, the answer would be plain to us. Either John Kerry did what he said he did (and what the military report at the time said), or he didn't. He was either a hero or a liar. And it mattered which he was. We were, after all, deciding whether we would elect him to be our next president.

Considering how important the factual question was, shockingly little media coverage of the story was devoted to trying to determine how much of what the Swift Boat Veterans were saying was true. How many members of the group were actually there at the time? How many of them were in a position to see what happened? Who else was there? What could they tell us about the events of that day?

*Nightline* undertook just such an effort. An independent producer, Jed Duvall, approached us in the early fall of 2004. Duvall was married to a Vietnamese woman and spoke Vietnamese. He proposed that we send him and an ABC News staff producer to Vietnam to see what they could learn about what had happened thirty-five years earlier. At first, the Vietnamese government was reluctant to give us permission, saying it didn't want to get involved in the U.S. presidential election. But eventually we got the okay, and Duvall, joined by our own Andrew Morse, set out for Vietnam, where they were joined by a government driver.

They drove for nine hours and then took a two-hour boat trip up the river, following a detailed Vietnamese map and checking it against a map showing the coordinates of the 1969 firefight. When they got to the village that had been at the center of the battle, the first person they interviewed was Vo Van Tam, a fifty-four-year-old man who said he'd been a Vietcong commander during the war. With his wife, who was there in 1969 and said she'd witnessed the events, he told a very different story from what John O'Neill had written in his book. Instead of a solitary "fleeing, wounded, armed, or unarmed teenage enemy" dressed "in a loincloth," the former Vietcong described the fighting as "very fierce." According to the *Nightline* report, "The area was a hotbed of guerrilla activity. They had recently been reinforced by a twelve-man unit, supplied with small arms and one B-40 rocket launcher. [Vo Van Tam] said the reinforcements had been dispatched from provincial headquarters specifically to target the swift boats."

Our team talked with several villagers who said that they'd been innocent bystanders to the firefight. Like Vo Van Tam, they contradicted the story being told by the Swift Boat Veterans. Where O'Neill had said that there had been "little or no fire," those who had been there described fire from several directions at once. In the citation for Lieutenant Kerry's Silver Star, he is credited with chasing after an enemy soldier with a rocket launcher and killing him. This is the person John O'Neill describes as a "lone" young person in a loincloth. Although the Vietnamese could not say for certain how this man died, they did identify him as Ba Thanh, a "26- or 27"-year-old Vietcong dressed in black (not a "loincloth") who had been sent as part of the reinforcements from provincial headquarters. As one villager in his eighties remembered it:

> I didn't see anything because I was hiding from the bullets and the bombs . . . It was very fierce and there was shooting everywhere and the leaves were being shredded to pieces. I was afraid to stay up there. I had to hide. And then, when it was over, I saw Ba Thanh was dead. He may have been shot in the chest when he stood up.

Intriguingly, it turned out that we were not the first to go to Tran Thoi and try to re-piece the history of the swift boat firefight. One of the villagers told us that another American had appeared about six months before, bringing with him a cameraman. He told the villagers that one of the swift boat veterans was running for U.S. president. He also said that "he didn't do anything to deserve the medal." We never found out who this other American was.

The *Nightline* visit to Vietnam didn't resolve all the questions that were raised about Kerry's service. It didn't pretend to. Thirty-five years had passed. Memories could be flawed. Those with whom we talked could have had reason to change their stories. But the more important point was how quickly the media jumped over the question of what actually happened—how reluctant most were even to ask the question—in the rush to present the controversy. The bulk of the coverage (and there was a lot of coverage) consisted of the Swift Boat Veterans' version of the truth "balanced" against Kerry's account and the accounts of those awarding the medals. Then the media quickly moved on to the horse race of what it meant in the polls, mingled with a great deal of unsubstantiated opinion.

"Fair and balanced" is a phrase that Fox News has co-opted to great effect in its marketing. And balance is certainly important in some of journalism. There are questions—important questions—on which reasonable minds can differ. Should a woman have the right to terminate her pregnancy, and if so, at what point in her term? What are the limits that the state can or should place on our constitutional right to bear arms? Should the government provide us with universal health care? How far should we go in using the tax code to bring greater equality of wealth among our citizens? What's the best energy policy for the country? Should the United States become involved in foreign conflicts on humanitarian grounds? Should we engage in preemptive warfare when we believe our security is threatened? The list goes on and on.

When it comes to questions such as these, journalists can't come up with "the answer" no matter how much reporting we do. It doesn't matter how many reporters we assign or how hard they dig, we still will be left with a basic judgment call that is for each individual citizen—not for those in the media—to make. In reporting on these kinds of questions, journalists have no right to impose their own views on the audience. Our job instead is to make sure that people have heard all relevant sides of the story so that they can make up their own minds. This is when "balance" is essential.

But there are plenty of news stories that aren't just about different people's opinions or values. Sometimes there is a single right answer, even if it's hard to find. Every day medical studies and polls and other issues arise in the news that are susceptible to scientific validation. Not all medical studies are created equal. They can involve too few people in the research to be reliable or might be sponsored by companies with a stake in the outcome. Those in a position to know can often tell us which are reliable and which are not. Similarly, statisticians tell us that some "polls" are not worth the paper they're written on (or the Internet digits they're based on). Where there is a scientific or other expert consensus—and particularly where that consensus is overwhelming—journalists have an obligation to tell their audiences the truth, not just give them two sides to the story.

Sometimes the most important stories hold out at least the promise of having an answer. I put the Swift Boat Veterans for Truth story in this group. Another is the question of whether Saddam Hussein did or did not have weapons of mass destruction (WMD) before the United States and its allies invaded Iraq in March 2003.

During late 2002 and the beginning of 2003, Peter Jennings and I had more than one discussion about the war, which at that point seemed increasingly inevitable. We talked about whether war was justified, whether the United States would prevail, how long it would take, and what would likely come after the war was over. Every time we talked about it, whatever the answers were to questions such as these, I thought one thing was certain: if the U.S. armed forces went in, they would find weapons of mass destruction. And every time, Peter would say, "Don't be so sure."

I had plenty of evidence on my side. We knew that Saddam Hussein had used WMD on his own population back in 1988, when he'd gassed his own Kurdish citizens in the "Halabja genocide." Our reporting from confidential sources was that all the intelligence showed that he still had WMD. And that reporting was right as far as it went. The overwhelming weight of the intelligence did give every indication that Saddam had WMD.

After the fact, Ken Pollack, one of the principal government experts on Iraq and WMD from the Clinton administration, went back over the intelligence that led up to the war. He quoted from a classified U.S. National Intelligence Estimate from 2002 that concluded that Iraq

> has continued its weapons of mass destruction (WMD) programs in defiance of UN resolutions and restrictions. Baghdad has chemical and biological weapons as well as missiles with ranges in excess of UN restrictions; if left unchecked, it probably will have a nuclear weapon during this decade.

Pollack went on to recount a 2002 meeting he attended with twenty UN weapons inspectors, none of whom doubted that Iraq had WMD. And he said that Israel, Russia, Britain, China, France, and Germany all had concluded the same based on their intelligence.

On top of all that, Saddam himself had seemed to confirm that he had something to hide by manipulating and avoiding the UN process for WMD inspection until the very end, when it seemed to dawn on him too late that he might well be provoking a war.

Those of us in the media may have had plenty of reasons for accepting the government's assertion that Saddam had WMD. The problem is that we were wrong. The question wasn't about what governments thought was there; it was whether Saddam actually had WMD. This question was a matter of fact, not opinion, just like the question of what happened to John Kerry in Vietnam. No, we couldn't send undercover reporters into Iraq to search for the weapons (at least not without exposing them to ridiculous danger). But if we could have, then we would have known the truth.

Almost all of us in the news media let our audiences down at a time when they really needed us. It was our job to do all we could to examine the evidence, find new evidence, and come to our own informed view that we could share with our audiences. And that job was critically important, given that this factual question was to determine whether or not the United States would go to war.

This is what Peter was saying when he questioned the government's assertion of fact. It wasn't that he had access to special information that none of the rest of us had. He didn't. Instead, he had the experience of covering that part of the world for many years. He knew how some governments and leaders used posturing and false impressions to keep themselves in power—particularly when faced with near adversaries (Iran) and countries farther off (the United States and much of western Europe). He'd watched the United States and other Western countries make mistakes before in the Middle East. That experience had taught him to be skeptical. Peter was saying that we—all of us in the media—had a duty to dig deeper to see what facts we could uncover about the WMD claim.

What made our failure even more glaring was that a handful of journalists did press hard for the truth—harder than the rest of us did. Most notable was a series of reports by two Knight Ridder reporters. In report after report in the fall of 2002, Warren Strobel and Jonathan Landay wrote that some within the U.S. government were questioning the strength of the intelligence, and they described open disagreement about whether various activities were truly part of a WMD program.

Our failure to pursue the WMD story more aggressively is a powerful reminder of how important it is to do all we can as journalists to find the truth whenever there is a single truth to be uncovered. Let's face it, no single member of the public was going to go all the way to Vietnam to find out whether John Kerry did or did not distinguish himself in a skirmish in the Mekong Delta some thirty-five years earlier. No private citizen was going to develop the relationships with government officials and members of the intelligence community to double-check what we were being told about how strong the evidence was of Iraqi WMD. That's why we invest in journalists: to stand in our stead to ask the difficult questions that we can't.

I don't pretend that sorting out the answerable from the unanswerable is always easy. It isn't. We see this right now, for example, in the debate over global warming. Despite a great deal of time, effort, and money expended trying to learn whether the globe is truly warming—and if so, by how much and how much of it comes from human behavior—a debate continues to rage in some circles over these very important questions. More disturbing, there's even a debate about whether there is a debate. One side claims that there is an overwhelming consensus on the most important points of global warming among scientists qualified to know.

For them, there is no "other hand" for reporters to worry about. The other side argues that there is dangerous groupthink going on among many of the scientists, who have persuaded the media to disregard a legitimate "other hand" to the argument.

After watching George Will express his strong views on *This Week* that the science just wasn't there to support the claim that humans contribute to global warming, I decided I should do my best to figure out for myself whether or not there was a true scientific consensus. We brought in several scientists for off-the-record editorial meetings at ABC News to address just this question. I read as much as I could understand of the literature. I thought it was important that we know whether climate change fell into the category of opinion, requiring balance on the air, or fact.

I took two clear truths away from all this. First, climatology (at least for those of us who are not experts) has to be one of the most complicated and inexact of sciences. Second, you don't want to get into the middle of a fight among scientists. They can be ruthless in their criticism of one another.

That said, the fairest conclusion I could draw based on what the scientists told us and the reports I read is that there is nothing close to an even "balance" in the weight of scientific opinion on the subject of global warming. The overwhelming majority of qualified scientists have concluded that the earth is warming, that the degree of that warming raises at least the specter of substantial changes in the ways we live our lives, and that human behavior is a big part of the cause. This is the view supported by all the scientific papers addressing these questions in peer-reviewed journals.

Does this make it all certain? Certainly not. As I've suggested, climatology is too inexact a science. Even the scientists who have reached consensus on the basics can disagree over degree and timing and what could be done. There is always the possibility, as my former colleague George Will has argued, that the reason for the scientific consensus is that scientists know that research funds will go only to those who believe in global warming, introducing a skew to the results. And of course none of this tells us what we should do or whether the costs of taking dramatic steps to change our carbon footprint are justified by the benefits we would gain.

I ultimately concluded that there are answers to the most basic climate change questions. If I am right, if there is a yes or no answer, presenting both sides of the argument is no virtue. It can, in fact, be a vice.

On all of these issues—everything from John Kerry's war record to climate change—it's the journalist's job not only to look at serious questions as they are raised, but also to answer as many of these questions as we can. In reporting that we put a man on the moon, journalists surely aren't required to "balance" their saying so with the conspiracy theory that it was all done on a soundstage in Hollywood. In reporting that nineteen hijackers from the Middle East flew planes into the World Trade Center, the Pentagon, and a field in Pennsylvania, journalists shouldn't be required to "balance" what they say with a countervailing view that it was all a government conspiracy. It would be wrong if they did.

Why is it that we sometimes rush to report the "balance" instead of striving to find the truth? From my vantage point, I saw two reasons.

First, it's easier and cheaper to present two sides to an argument than it is to figure out the answer. When you can enlist colorful personalities to turn a phrase (or at least fashion a catchy slogan) and do your arguing for you, airing various opinions about a subject can be entertaining—often more entertaining than a carefully prepared report getting at the truth.

We've seen how effective it can be to air competing opinions, rather than reporting the truth, on cable news and talk radio and the Internet. Everywhere we look, we see an array of people expressing their forceful opinions. Often this is done in a cross-fire type of format, where someone representing one side of an issue is pitted against someone representing the other. Many of the same people move from one channel to another throughout the day and night, repeating the opinions they've expressed elsewhere. We certainly saw this sort of news coverage done on stories like the Swift Boat Veterans' attacks on John Kerry; we see it today in much of the climate change coverage.

There's nothing wrong with the expression of opinion in the news media—but only if it's addressed to questions for which there is no real answer and only when it's clearly labeled as opinion. As I've said, a wide array of important questions are covered in the news for which there is no single "right" answer. There is a long tradition of opinion in journalism—much of it noble—for dealing with such issues. Just consider the editorial and op-ed pages of our major newspapers.

But I never took the low cost and high octane of opinion as an excuse to avoid digging for the truth. Even when we were dealing with subjects that were legitimately matters of personal opinion, we tried to do as much factual reporting around the controversy as we could. It's all well and good to have people (at least people who know what they're talking about) give their views about whether we should have universal health care in the United States. But before we get to that discussion, shouldn't we spend some time and effort getting our facts straight on who doesn't have health coverage now and what the real consequences are? It's fine to have a roaring debate about the size and scope of government entitlement programs, but don't we need to know the facts and figures about Medicare and Social Security and the projections going into the future before we try to decide what to do about it? And on and on.

Opinion is interesting—and valuable—only if it is based on facts. George Will estimates that 90 percent of any good opinion piece consists of facts—not opinion. And he has a fair amount of experience writing some pretty effective opinion pieces.

Even the most informed opinion can never be a substitute for reporting. The problem is that the sort of reporting that seeks the truth is hard work. It takes time. And it costs money. It requires developing or hiring reporters who truly know what they're reporting about. It requires following leads that may lead nowhere. At a time when most news organizations are beset with financial difficulties, it's awfully tempting to cut back on the reporting and seek an audience through the expression of opinion. Often vivid opinion. Extreme opinion. And let's face it, these days you can find an "expert" or a pundit on just about any side of any issue. They show us every day how eager they are to get some more airtime.

During my time at ABC News, I watched opinion come to dominate more and more of what we call news. For the most part, opinion on ABC was confined to the interviews and roundtable on *This Week* every Sunday morning and interviews done with one side or another in a controversy covered on *Good Morning America*. When we had people on to express their opinions, whether on these programs or others, we did our best to make sure that it was clear to the audience we were now going into matters of opinion, not reporting the facts.

But not everyone does as good a job of distinguishing between opinion and fact. As a result, audiences can see people who look like one another on sets that look alike with similar graphics either expressing strong opinions or reporting the facts. Is it any wonder that audiences start to believe that it's all the same—that pretty much everything they're hearing is some form of opinion? Over time I became increasingly concerned that the audience was learning to regard everything it saw on the news as an expression of someone's opinion.

It wasn't just the audience I was concerned about—it was the journalists. Given the limited resources for covering the news and the need to attract and hold an audience, we might come to value truth less and value opinion more. It's too easy in this new environment to lose sight of truth as the ultimate goal. Journalists can think that they've fully reported a story if they've just gotten competing viewpoints included in a piece. If we're not careful, we could end up in a world where, implicitly, none of us—not the audience and not the reporters—even believes any longer in the pursuit of the truth.

This may seem a radical—even a ridiculous—suggestion. How could it be that we would give up our belief in the truth? But consider the reporting of most media outlets on the Swift Boat Veterans for Truth allegations. Or, more recently, consider an example coming not from journalism but from the U.S. Senate. In the middle of a debate about the funding of Planned Parenthood in April 2011, the Senate minority whip, Jon Kyl of Arizona, took to the floor to say, "If you want an abortion, you go to Planned Parenthood, and that's well over 90 percent of what Planned Parenthood does." When confronted with the facts—that less than 3 percent of Planned Parenthood's activities is related to abortions—Senator Kyl's office issued a statement saying that "his remark was not intended to be a factual statement, but rather to illustrate that Planned Parenthood, an organization that receives millions of dollars of taxpayer funding, does subsidize abortions."

Either Lieutenant Kerry charged ashore in the face of a Vietcong ambush in 1969 or he didn't. Either 90 percent of Planned Parenthood's activities are related to abortions or they're not. We can have strong opinions about whether Kerry should have been president or whether the government should be supporting Planned Parenthood, but facts are facts. Too much of what passes for reporting on television today skips over the distinction. Increasingly, we don't even ask whether something is true or false. We jump over this basic question and go straight to an analysis of who's doing the talking and why. What is their background? What is their affiliation? What hidden motive may they have for saying what they're saying? What are the likely consequences for those directly involved? We don't bother to go back to Vietnam and ask what happened of the ones who were there. Or check the public records on what Planned Parenthood does.

Journalists have a hard job. They can get it wrong either way. They do a disservice to the audience by reporting something as fact when it's very much in legitimate dispute. This is the criticism most often leveled at reporters: that they dress up their opinions as facts. But journalists do every bit as much of a disservice to the public if they present their audiences with discredited viewpoints and leave it to them to sort them out, implying that one view is as good as the other. My experience taught me that sorting out the positive from the normative is an important part of the responsibility of a journalist—made more important by the rapid growth of so many outlets for every conceivable point of view.

I've said that turning news into opinion is cheap and effective, but there's a second reason it's so seductive. It can deflect criticism—particularly partisan criticism. Partisan groups of all colors and stripes have used the "unfair" and "unbalanced" charge to ridicule us—on the Internet, on talk radio, in print, and on cable news shows—and some in the media have become understandably a bit gun-shy.

To this day I wonder whether unconsciously some of us held back on challenging the claims of WMD in Iraq because we knew we would come in for tremendous criticism if we challenged the Bush administration on the facts. I know this was not in my conscious thinking at the time. But there's no question that all of us knew what would come our way if we seriously challenged the claims of Western intelligence on this crucial fact. After 9/11, the country was caught up in a wave of patriotism. These attitudes formed a backdrop for the discussions and debates that led to the United States and a coalition of forces invading Iraq in March 2003. Those of us in the news media were not immune. And our critics were quick to charge us with being less than patriotic whenever they got the chance.

We at ABC News got a taste of this when we were criticized for being insufficiently patriotic in our coverage of the buildup to the war. We thought we were devoting our reporting, including a three-hour special in prime time on the eve of the war, to telling the public about the circumstances leading up to the war, the military buildup, and how the war was expected to proceed.

Our conservative critics didn't see it that way. They singled out instances where they felt we had given too much time to opponents of the war—things such as asking Iraqi children how they felt about the impending war, covering antiwar protests in Washington and Europe without noting that one of the organizers had expressed support for China and Cuba, and reporting a drop in support for the war without noting that the numbers were coming back down after a spike. They also took issue with Peter Jennings's interview with the commanding general, Tommy Franks, on the eve of the war when Peter asked the general whether he had enough troops. Whatever one thinks of the merits of these particular criticisms, they show the extent to which some partisan groups were flyspecking everything the news media reported at the time. One can only imagine the reaction if we had taken on the task of disproving what intelligence agencies from so many countries had found about Saddam's WMD.

I don't necessarily blame those with an agenda for using the tool of criticism to try to influence our reporting (although some of it can get pretty extreme and personal). It's like a basketball player or coach yelling at a referee on the sidelines about his call, not so much because it was wrong or because he thinks the ref will change his mind, but more in the hope that he just might take the criticism into account on the next call and lean a bit in the other direction. It's human nature.

I was concerned throughout my time at ABC News that if we weren't careful, this sort of criticism could influence our editorial judgments. It's entirely understandable that people in news organizations may react to some of the relentless and often vitriolic charges of the left or of the right that we are "unbalanced" or "unfair." It's understandable, but it's certainly no excuse. And it can have severe ramifications.

I've said already that journalists need to be open to criticism—to consider whether we may have made a factual mistake—just as I've said journalists should always be open to considering whether they may be biased. But if the question is a matter of fact, and if they believe that

they've got their facts right, then they really have little choice but to report what they believe to be the truth no matter what the consequences.
Not every coin has two sides, and when there's only a single side that is
true, reporters owe it to the people to tell them that—even when some
may not want to hear it.

Presidential campaigns bring some of the highest partisan pressures
to bear on the journalists covering them. Maybe that's part of the reason
more news organizations didn't pursue the facts surrounding Senator
Kerry's war service the way that they might have. Or it may have been just
too hard to try to go back thirty-five years and come to a firm conclusion
about what a handful of people had witnessed halfway around the world.
But whatever the reasons or excuses, we journalists owed it to the people
to do what *Nightline* tried to do: find out the truth. And those in the audience should expect and demand no less. They should always be asking
themselves whether the questions raised in a news story can be answered.
And if the questions can, why the news organization isn't giving them the
answers.

Another presidential campaign taught me a different valuable lesson
about the uneasy relationship between the facts and the truth: sometimes
the "truth" is misrepresented by the facts. With some stories you can report the facts accurately but nevertheless lead the audience to a conclusion that is the opposite of true.

One afternoon in the middle of the presidential primaries, I received
a surprise telephone call from a candidate who was clearly upset. He told
me our reporters were working on a story for our newscast that evening
that would allege he had twice been to a private club that excluded blacks.
He admitted to me that this was so. His parents had belonged to this
club, and he had on two occasions (one Thanksgiving and the other
Christmas, as I recall) dined with them, not knowing about the club's policy. Since then, both of his parents had passed away. At the end of our
conversation, he asked me simply, "David, do you honestly believe that I'm
a racist?"

I had no good answer for him. I didn't know the candidate well, but I'd
long followed his career, and I knew his outstanding record. I didn't believe that whatever his other strengths or weaknesses, this man was prej-
udiced against people of any race or ethnicity. I went to *World News
Tonight* and asked about the story. They confirmed that they were work-

ing on it, but they had not yet made a decision whether to go with it. I asked them the same question the candidate had asked me. Do we really believe he's a racist? And if not, why are we going with the story? We never aired the report.

Going the other way would have been completely defensible. We knew the facts to be true. The club at the time did have a policy of excluding blacks; the candidate himself had confirmed to me that he had been there with his elderly parents. But this was a case where, in my judgment, the literal facts led away from the truth, not toward it.

# 8 | Is Any News Report Worth Dying For? The Bob Woodruff Story

We have some breaking news to report, disturbing news for us here at ABC News. We need to report that our co-anchor of <u>World News Tonight</u>, Bob Woodruff, and his cameraman, Doug Vogt, were injured in an attack this morning in Baghdad, near Baghdad, in Taji, a city in Iraq. Injured in an improvised explosive device attack.

          —Kate Snow, anchor of <u>Good Morning America Weekend</u>, January 29, 2006

The telephone woke me from a sound sleep just before 5:00 a.m. on a Sunday in the middle of the winter. The call came in on the office line, which meant it wasn't good news. On the other end was Paul Slavin, our executive overseeing news coverage. You couldn't normally detect emotion in Paul's voice, but I could tell he was upset from the moment he began speaking. There'd been an attack on an ABC News team north of Baghdad in a place called Taji. Bob Woodruff and his cameraman, Doug Vogt, had been injured. We didn't know much about the injuries, but Bob's arm was hurt; Doug may have had a head injury. Days later, I would learn that the attack had happened at 12:10 local Iraqi time—less than an hour before Paul's call to me.

My immediate reaction was to call Bob's wife, Lee. My wife and I had gotten to know the Woodruffs well. Like me, Bob had come from Michigan and graduated from the University of Michigan Law School (although he came a decade after me). They had children close to the same ages as our own, and our families had spent time together. Paul told me, however, that Bob asked us not to talk to Lee because he wanted to be the one to call and reassure her. I took this as a promising sign, so I didn't call

Lee right away. Doug and his wife, Vivianne, lived in the south of France, and our London bureau would be calling her.

My wife, Sherrie, had heard my half of the conversation, and when I got off, I told her what I knew. Like me, she was shocked and horrified. She'd developed a close personal relationship with Lee, and I think she couldn't help but identify with her, both as a friend and as a mother.

I got dressed and waited for updates in my study at home. I called Anne Sweeney, who oversaw the ABC Television Network, and Bob Iger at home in Los Angeles, even though it was the middle of their night on the West Coast. Over the next couple of hours we began to learn more. Bob and Doug had been with two other ABC News colleagues, Vinnie Malhotra, Bob's producer, and Magnus Macedo, who was handling Bob's audio. The team had been in an armored vehicle on a road near Taji when an improvised explosive device (IED) went off. Vinnie and Magnus were not injured. But each report about Bob brought worse news.

By 7:00, it was clear that Bob was not going to be able to call Lee any time soon. It wasn't just an injury to his arm he'd suffered. He was unconscious. Like Doug, he'd suffered some sort of head injury, and now we heard that Bob's was even worse than Doug's. First I was told that the two men were being taken by helicopter for treatment in Baghdad. Then I learned that they'd be moved again, this time to a major medical trauma center for the U.S. forces in Balad, north of Baghdad. Their condition was unknown.

I knew I needed to get in touch with Lee whether Bob wanted me to or not. Of all people, she and Vivianne deserved to know what was going on. And they needed to hear it from us. I was concerned that the story might soon be picked up by the media. Throughout the wars in Iraq and Afghanistan, we'd had an unwritten understanding with other news organizations that when one of our colleagues was kidnapped, injured, or worse, we could call one another and ask that the story not be reported until we'd had the opportunity to sort things out. This had happened several times when we'd learned of a print or TV journalist from another company who'd run into trouble. Think of it as our version of the military's policy of not releasing names of casualties until next of kin can be notified. Some people might criticize this unwritten understanding as suppressing the news, but it wasn't meant to keep the public from knowing altogether, typically applying only for a few hours. And let's be frank, right or wrong, when it comes to one of your own who's a casualty, your priorities change—something that it doesn't hurt for journalists to remember when they're covering others suffering loss.

One of the first things I'd done when I got Paul's call that morning was to make sure we'd alerted other news organizations and asked them to hold the story. But a serious injury to Bob Woodruff was a particularly big story. Only one month earlier, I'd announced that Bob and Elizabeth Vargas would be co-anchors of *World News Tonight*. It had been only three weeks since Bob and Elizabeth had stepped into the role that had been empty since Peter Jennings had died in August.

Whenever there was a change in the evening news anchor at one of the three broadcast networks, it was big news. Peter, after all, had anchored the program for over twenty years. The media covered his illness and passing extensively—and then speculated endlessly about who would replace him. After Peter's death, I waited four months to fill the job. This was first and foremost out of respect for Peter. But it was also because I wanted to take the program in a different direction.

All three evening newscasts had been in steady decline for years, not because they were any less strong, but because there were many more ways for people to get their news. The format for these programs had not really changed since the days of Walter Cronkite. They were essentially studio programs done with a dominant anchor in New York introducing live and taped reports from correspondents in the field. There was nothing wrong with this format. It provided a concise, well-written, and well-edited synopsis of the day's most important and interesting news. But I thought it was time for a change.

With Bob and Elizabeth, we'd have two anchors. This in itself was not new. Chet Huntley and David Brinkley had done it successfully on NBC when I was a boy. When Roone Arledge took over ABC News in 1977, Harry Reasoner and Barbara Walters were co-anchoring the evening news (an experiment that, according to everyone involved—including Barbara—did not work). Roone replaced the two of them with not two but three anchors, Frank Reynolds in Washington, Max Robinson in Chicago, and Peter Jennings in London. And more recently, Dan Rather and Connie Chung had a dual-anchor format for a time.

But my idea for Bob and Elizabeth was different. We weren't going to have our two anchors in the studio together most nights. Instead, the goal was to have at least one of them in the field, reporting from the scene of a major story. They'd also do much more than appear during a half hour of television. For the first time, we would produce an entirely new program for the West Coast every night, which typically gets only a version of the East Coast program broadcast three hours later. And they'd be expected to provide reports through the afternoon and evening that would appear on the Internet and on mobile devices. We would have two anchors not only to change the look of the telecast but also because we'd need two people to do all the work for all the various platforms that we planned to program for.

Because we were trying something different, there had been more press attention than normally came with anchor changes. In the first three weeks of their joint program, Bob or Elizabeth had broadcast from New York, Washington, West Virginia (the scene of a mine disaster), San Francisco (where Bob anchored from Google headquarters), Los Angeles, and Israel (twice). Sandwiched in between was a quick trip to Los Angeles, where they joined me for an appearance before the semiannual gathering of television critics to lay out what we were doing and why.

That Bob was in Iraq was itself part of the new model. As we approached the end of the first month with Bob and Elizabeth in the anchor chairs, the big story we were covering was the president's State of the Union address. All of us knew that most of the speech that year was going to focus on the war, which was not going well. Traditionally, the evening news anchor goes to Washington to cover the State of the Union, for which the networks preempt their prime-time programming. But we had an opportunity to demonstrate the strength of our new approach. Elizabeth would go to Washington, and Bob would go to Iraq to share the anchoring from there.

Bob knew the Iraq story well. He'd been embedded with the U.S. Marines for the march to Baghdad in March 2003. Since then, he'd been back to report from there several times. He knew the leadership of the U.S. military. On this trip, Bob had first gone to Israel and then the Palestinian territories to report on the elections in Gaza. From there he had moved on to Iraq. On Friday, he had reported for *World News Tonight* from the streets of Baghdad, where he visited an ice cream store that was open for business, showing that some normalcy was returning to the lives of ordinary people. This was Bob Woodruff at his very best, reporting with care and intelligence from the field. And it showed the strength and range of ABC News. All in all, it was a good plan—until it turned into a disaster.

Given the attention to the war and to our new approach, I had plenty of reason to be concerned that word of Woodruff's injuries would spread quickly. So, shortly before 7:00 a.m., I decided to go ahead and call Lee despite what I'd been told about Bob's request. It turned out she was visiting Disney World in Orlando with her children. The desk was trying to get the number for the Beach Club, where they were staying. I asked the desk to make arrangements for a charter plane to be ready to carry Lee and the children back to New York, anticipating that she'd want to get home as quickly as possible.

I called Orlando information to get the resort's number myself. Before placing the call, I carefully went over in my mind what I needed to communicate and in what order. Before the Iraq War, we'd brought in a grief counselor to teach us what to say to the families of those injured or killed covering the war and how to say it. I tried my best to follow those guidelines as I remembered them. I'd calmly tell Lee that Bob had been wounded, that he was being treated by the military, that there appeared to be some injury to his head, that we didn't have complete information, but that I'd tell her as soon as I learned anything more.

After going over this in my mind, I placed the call. I got a groggy Lee on the line, clearly waking up from a sound sleep. As soon as I'd identified myself, she came fully awake and knew something was wrong with Bob. I got only about halfway through the points I'd gone over in my head before she interrupted me. "David, is my husband alive?" This should have been where I'd started the conversation. I quickly assured her that Bob was indeed alive. But we'd been told that he'd been hit in the head by shrapnel.

Lee's next question was even more pointed: Why on earth was he with the military convoy to begin with? I told her I wasn't sure, but I'd been told the original plan was for him and his crew to have a down day on Sunday in Baghdad before reporting on Monday for the upcoming State of the Union address. Apparently, a one-day embed with the Fourth Infantry Division had come up at the last minute, and Bob and his team had decided to go. The Fourth ID was operating in and around Taji, north of

Baghdad, and was having success with mixed units of U.S. and Iraqi soldiers patrolling together. They were eager for Bob to report on that success, and Bob was eager to see it firsthand. So Bob had gone with his crew to tell this story.

Lee said she had to collect her thoughts and call Bob's parents in Michigan and her own parents in New York. She'd call me back as soon as she could. While I waited to hear from her, I called the Beach Club a second time, explained the situation to the manager on duty, and asked for whatever help the resort could give Lee and the children to get packed and in a car we were arranging to be waiting for them to take them to the airport.

A short time later, Lee called back, speaking from her cell phone in the hallway so as not to wake her children. We went over arrangements. I gently explained that we were doing our best to keep a lid on news of the attack, but it was getting increasingly difficult. I thought it was time to report the news ourselves to make sure the story was factual, rather than based on rumor. Lee agreed.

Lee needed an hour and a half to get the kids up, explain to them what was happening, get everyone packed, and head out the door. But she wasn't sure how to tell her children. They ranged from fourteen down to five. It would be difficult to tell any child that his or her father was seriously injured half a world away; the age range just made it harder. Lee asked to speak with Sherrie. Besides their being friends, Lee knew about Sherrie's work as a senior executive at Sesame Workshop overseeing a fair amount of research about children and how they process information. Lee wanted to walk through with her how best to talk to her kids.

I called the newsroom again, telling my colleagues it was okay for us to report the attack and to release other news organizations from the embargo. I went over the rapidly growing list of logistics we were working on, including getting Lee and the kids home. And then I sat at my computer to write an e-mail to all ABC News personnel. They needed to hear what was going on, and they needed to hear it from me. This would be a traumatic event in the life of any news organization. But it had been only ten months since I'd had to write everyone about Peter Jennings's diagnosis of lung cancer, only five months since I'd had to tell them that he had passed away. How much the organization had been through—how much shock and how much sadness—weighed heavily on me as I wrote. But I always thought that more information, promptly given, was better in a crisis. And so I sent a short e-mail out to the entire ABC News Division just after 8:00 a.m.:

> Bob Woodruff and his cameraman, Doug Vogt, were injured in an IED attack near Taji, Iraq today. They were embedded with the 4th Infantry Division, traveling with an Iraqi Army unit in an Iraqi mechanized vehicle. Bob and Doug are both in serious condition and are being treated at a U.S. military hospital in Iraq. At this point, we don't know much more than this. We'll keep you posted as we learn more. I know that all of us will keep Bob, Doug, and their families in our thoughts and prayers.

This would be the first of six e-mails I'd send that day, followed in the coming days by many more, letting people know how Bob and Doug were doing.

Then I headed into the newsroom. As I left, Sherrie gently asked about a trip I had scheduled for Iraq less than two weeks later. George Stephanopoulos and I were to go over together; George would anchor *This Week* from there and I would meet with our team on the ground, as well as with U.S. officials. Ironically, part of our itinerary involved a trip to Taji to see the success the U.S. military was having integrating with the Iraqi armed forces—the very trip Bob and Doug had gone on. Didn't this mean the trip was off? Sherrie wanted to know. Or at least couldn't I postpone it? I told her we'd need to wait to see how things sorted themselves out, but we'd certainly take a new look at whether I should go. Later, I learned that George's wife, Ali Wentworth, had been a bit more forceful with George—when she heard what had happened to Woodruff's team, she simply told George he wasn't going.

By the time I reached West 66th Street, a group had gathered around our foreign desk, including foreign editor Chuck Lustig; Mimi Gurbst, our head of news gathering; Paul Slavin; and a few others. We were soon joined by Diane Sawyer and Phyllis McGrady, who came in unasked to give their moral support.

Over the next several hours, bits and pieces of information trickled in—from our Baghdad bureau, from our London bureau, and from the U.S. military. Our national security correspondent Martha Raddatz was in direct contact with General George W. Casey (the top commander for all forces in Iraq and Afghanistan) and with Lieutenant General Peter Chiarelli (in direct command of U.S. forces in Iraq). Some of the best, most reliable information we received about Bob and Doug during these difficult hours came from General Casey and General Chiarelli, with Martha as the conduit. General Jack Keane, retired army vice chief of staff and a consultant to ABC News, called in to tell me I should reassure Lee that Bob was in the best hospital in the world for dealing with head trauma. The unfortunate truth was that Balad had more such experience than any other medical facility on earth, given all the injuries from IEDs in Iraq.

Throughout the morning, the news continued to get worse, at least as far as Bob was concerned. At the Balad hospital, Bob and Doug had been taken straight into surgery. The plan was to fly them to the U.S. military hospital in Landstuhl, Germany, once they had come out of surgery and had stabilized. But for now they were in surgery, and there was precious little news coming out of the operating room. The desk had established telephone communications directly with the hospital in Balad so we could learn as soon as the surgeries were over. It was left to us to wait. I asked someone to start making arrangements for Lee and whatever group she chose to fly to Germany that night after she'd gotten back from Florida.

After an hour or so, we learned that Doug had come out of surgery well and that he was expected to survive. I called Vivianne in France to check on her and assure her we would do anything we could to help her and her family. Robin Wiener, our deputy bureau chief in London, had taken over communicating with Vivianne. London was making arrangements for Vivianne and Robin to meet the next morning in Frankfurt and then travel to Landstuhl together.

But Bob was still in surgery. For those of us waiting for word in New York, it seemed a very long time. I fought against the thought that came repeatedly to my mind: Brain surgery that took this long could not be a good thing. At one point we got a call from Balad. The surgeons were asking for a number to contact Bob's next of kin. Lee was in the air on her way home to New York and unreachable. Our contact in Balad insisted that the doctors had to have a number in case they concluded it was hopeless and wanted approval to stop their efforts to save Bob. They weren't saying that they'd reached that conclusion yet, but that it might come to that. With a gulp, I told them they should call me. Fortunately, that call never came.

After five long hours we received word that Bob was out of surgery and was stable. A sigh of relief, mingled with more than a few tears, ran through the newsroom. Just after 1:00 that afternoon, I was able to write to the ABC News staff that both Bob and Doug were out of surgery and in "stable condition." Saying that the next few days would be "critical," I explained that they would be evacuated to Landstuhl, probably overnight.

At last I was able to talk with Vinnie, Bob's producer, who had made it to Balad on his own while the helicopters whisked Bob and Doug away, first to Baghdad and then to the trauma hospital. From Vinnie I learned that the ABC News team had originally been in a U.S. Army armored personnel carrier. At one point during the morning, the convoy had stopped at a checkpoint along the road. Bob had pressed the U.S. Army officer in charge, a major, to let the ABC team switch to an Iraqi armored personnel carrier for the next leg of the journey. The major was reluctant, I think simply because he felt that he would have more control over the team's safety in one of his vehicles. But Bob pressed, arguing that if the point of the story was to show how the Iraqi military was working more closely and successfully with the U.S. military, it only made sense that they get the opportunity to report some of the story from the Iraqi perspective.

So it was agreed that Bob, Doug, Vinnie, Magnus, and their Iraqi translator, Omar, would switch to the Iraqi vehicle. They set out, and Bob's armored vehicle took the lead position—something I'm not sure anyone expected—as the convoy moved farther down the road. When the attack came, Bob and Doug were standing up in hatches in the back of the tank to film a "stand-up," the bit of a news piece where the reporter talks to camera about what he is seeing and reporting. This was to be a moving stand-up, done while the tank was proceeding down the highway to give the audience a sense of what it was really like. They'd been having trouble getting the stand-up right because the roar of the tank's motor made it difficult to hear Bob. Magnus, Vinnie, and Omar were down in the vehicle directly below Bob and Doug, working on the audio.

It was as they tried the stand-up again that the bomb went off. Both Bob and Doug had their protective body armor and helmets on. But they were otherwise exposed from the waist up. Immediately after the blast, Bob fell down into the tank, bleeding and badly injured. Vinnie did his best to catch Bob. The team was in shock, but Omar was a veteran of twenty-seven IED attacks, and he recovered the fastest. He yelled at Vinnie to stop Bob's bleeding, and Vinnie used his bare hands to apply pressure to Bob's neck and head. The convoy stopped. A U.S. medic ran to the back of the Iraqi vehicle. Even as all this was going on, they started taking small-arms fire from the surrounding trees. Despite the ongoing attack, the U.S. soldiers got Bob and Doug out of the tank and onto a helicopter for evacuation. Bob was conscious at first and had yelled at Vinnie. But whatever he yelled, it wasn't the request not to call Lee that got relayed to me. We never did figure out where this had come from in the confusion of getting word back to me in New York about what had happened.

Vinnie confirmed what our military sources had been predicting: Bob and Doug would be transported as soon as possible to Landstuhl. From there, they would ultimately be coming back to the U.S. naval hospital in Bethesda. Doug had a serious injury to the brain, but the doctors did not seem to be as concerned about him at that point. Bob was alive, but his prognosis was far less certain. The left side of his skull had been removed to relieve pressure from his swelling brain. The piece of the skull that they'd removed was so "compromised" that they'd had to throw it away. They had taken what pieces of shrapnel, skull, pebbles, and other debris that they could out of the brain itself, but couldn't get it all. In addition to all that, Bob had some pretty serious injuries to his left shoulder. We couldn't be sure whether he would live. If he did, we had no idea what shape he would be in. We didn't know what effects the brain injury might have on his speech, mobility, or cognitive functions. Simply put, we didn't know whether we'd get Bob back.

I asked Mimi Gurbst, who knew Bob and Lee well, to go and meet Lee at the airport and take her home to pack. That Sunday night, Lee, traveling with Bob's brother Dave, her sister's husband, Sean McLoughlin, and her good friend Melanie Bloom (widow of David Bloom, the NBC News correspondent who had died covering the initial invasion of Iraq), took an overnight flight to Frankfurt, where a waiting van took them on to Landstuhl. My colleague Bob Murphy flew with them to make sure they had whatever they needed. Robin Wiener flew to Frankfurt from London, where she met Doug's wife, Vivianne, and they took a separate van to Landstuhl. In the meantime, Bob and Doug had been placed on the medevac plane bound for Landstuhl about 7:30 that evening.

Just before I left for home late that Sunday night, someone from the *Good Morning America* staff came and asked me to be on the program the following morning to talk about Bob, Doug, and the attack. I was initially reluctant. Dozens of Americans were being injured or killed each month in Iraq in early 2006. Should we be giving any more coverage to our friends and colleagues than we typically gave to others in similar situations? I didn't want this story to be about us. But as I talked it through with my staff, I began to realize just how big this story really was. Everyone else would be covering it extensively, and it would be odd if we were the only ones who didn't. So in the end I agreed to go on *GMA*.

Shortly after 3:00 a.m., the desk called me at home to let me know that Bob and Doug had arrived safely in Germany. They had been admitted to the intensive care unit and remained in stable condition. Overnight, Lee and her group and Vivianne and Robin made their way to Germany.

I got up early for my *GMA* appearance, checked in with the desk for an update, and headed for the Times Square Studio. I appeared on the set that morning with Diane Sawyer, Charlie Gibson, and Bob's co-anchor, Elizabeth Vargas. Before we went on, Jim Sciutto, our correspondent in Landstuhl, laid out the basic facts for the audience. I frankly don't remember much of what Jim reported that morning; my mind was elsewhere. I do remember seeing Bob's brother Dave live from Germany as part of our piece and marveling at both how good he was and how much he reminded me of Bob.

When it came time for Elizabeth and me, Diane turned to me and asked what had gone into the decision to send Bob. Did he ask to go? Charlie followed up, asking how we made the calculation about what risk was acceptable and how involved we were back in New York. I talked a bit about Bob, about his experience, and about how badly he wanted to be over there covering this story. And I said that we were constantly reviewing with our people in the field what an acceptable level of risk was. But I also noted that "the irony in part from my point of view is we spend literally millions of dollars every year for the security of our people in Iraq. Particularly in our compound and going off our compound [unilaterally]. We have perhaps a false sense that when we're embedded with the U.S. military, there's a particular sense of safety. And in fact, there's nowhere in Iraq that's safe."

Diane and Charlie then went on to talk with Elizabeth about her recent experience in Iraq. She had herself just returned from being embedded with U.S. forces, and her cameraman had been Doug Vogt. So she could speak from firsthand experience about both Doug and the situation in which he and Bob had been injured.

Toward the end of the segment, Charlie asked me whether what had just happened to our team would change our approach to covering Iraq. I hadn't yet given a thought to that question. I'd been too consumed with worrying about Bob and Doug and their families. I admitted this on the air. And then I spoke about all the things that had been going through my mind since I'd received that first call just over twenty-four hours earlier. That the assignments I'd been authorizing were so very dangerous. That we tried our best to take precautions, but even with all the precautions in the world someone was going to get hurt. That sending someone on these assignments was really assigning the entire family. And then, after running through all these contradictory thoughts, I came to the only conclusion I really could reach, a conclusion that I hadn't consciously thought of until that moment. I asked: "What choice do we have? As long as the United States is over there and our men and women are over there and they're in harm's way, this is a story that we have to . . . cover."

The segment ended just before 7:20, and as I walked off the set, the *GMA* production staff came up to me to ask why I hadn't gone into more detail about Bob's condition. They'd been monitoring the competition, who'd gone into graphic detail, including that part of Bob's skull had been removed to relieve the pressure on his brain. I'd known all of this and more since my first talk with Vinnie from Balad the afternoon before, but I'd consciously not discussed any of it out of respect for the privacy of Bob, Lee, and their family. At that point, we didn't know whether Bob would come back to us. Assuming he did, I wanted him to decide what he told the world about what he'd been through.

From an office just off the *GMA* studio floor, I called Lee in Germany to see how she was doing—but also to make sure that I wasn't being too circumspect. As I called, I thought to myself that this was probably the last thing she wanted to be thinking about, but she expressed surprise that anyone would be reporting details about Bob's medical condition. I'd been right in my understanding, and so I sent the word not only to *GMA* but to our other outlets that no matter what the competition was doing, we would respect Lee's wishes.

After that, Monday was largely a day of waiting. I monitored the situation as best I could, talking frequently with Bob Murphy in Germany (and doing my best not to bother Lee again), Martha Raddatz, who was our pipeline into the military, and our own medical editor, Dr. Tim Johnson, to learn all I could about traumatic brain injury, or TBI (an affliction I'd never heard of before). As important, I was doing my best to deal with a badly shaken staff.

In the middle of all this came a minor contretemps with our friends at *The New York Times*. At midday, I got a call from Bill Keller, the *Times*'s executive editor. I knew Bill from having been in some meetings with him a few years before when he was the deputy to Joe Lelyveld and we'd talked briefly about some form of cooperation between our websites. After expressing his sympathy over Bob and Doug, Bill got to the reason for his call. He'd heard from some *Times* reporters on the ground in Landstuhl that they might not be given the same access as other reporters because ABC News was upset over the way the *Times* had covered the story that morning on its front page. He apologized for raising it with me, as I probably wasn't even aware that some people in my shop were upset.

Had I heard about it? I'd heard about it since the moment I got to *GMA* that morning. People were furious that after a headline saying that this was the "latest blow to [the] network" (referring to our losing Peter Jennings months before), the *Times* had said in its subheading: "Field Reports Were a Ratings Strategy." The idea that we were sending men and women into harm's way to cover the war in Iraq simply to get ratings was as insulting as it was absurd. People at ABC News interpreted it as *The New York Times* taking yet another shot at television news at a time when we were most shaken and most vulnerable.

I told Bill I was very much aware of it. As I put it to him, he had managed in one morning to do something I'd been working on for years: bringing all fourteen hundred people of ABC News together to think as one. Everyone was deeply offended and angry. Bill and I then had a full and frank exchange about the merits of what *The New York Times* had written. I pointed out to him that if ratings had been our goal, the last place we would go would be Iraq. Viewers were tired of the story, and every time we put it on, our ratings went down. Bob Woodruff went to Iraq to report because we thought it the best way to cover an important story it was our duty to cover. He was no more there to get ratings than John Burns (the outstanding *New York Times* reporter in Baghdad at the time) was there to increase the newspaper's circulation.

In the end, we agreed to disagree. But I assured Bill that we wouldn't let it affect how we dealt with them—at Landstuhl or otherwise. And I sent word to Germany to make sure that we didn't. I did write a letter to the editor that the *Times* published early the next week. In it, I made the points that I'd made to Keller, saying that what the *Times* had written "demeans what two brave men did for the right reasons." I explained that Bob and Doug "sought nothing more than to inform our audiences" and that as such they were like "the many other ABC News personnel—and personnel from so many other news organizations, The Times included—who have put their very lives on the line to report things that are important for the American people to know."

Remarkably, by 7:00 that evening, Bob and Doug were back in the air on the way to the Bethesda Naval Hospital, once again on a military transport along with other injured soldiers and marines. Doug was alert and talking with the doctors and nurses; Bob remained in a coma. The next morning, I flew to Washington to join Bob's and Doug's families, including Lee and those who had gone with her to Germany, Vivianne Vogt, and Bob's parents and brothers. On the way down to Washington, I read several articles (some too technical for me to understand fully) that Tim Johnson had sent to me. They set out some of the unique problems presented by the war in Iraq—a war in which medical advances meant that soldiers who would have died on the battlefield in Vietnam were now surviving, but were having to deal with issues the nation had not seen before and was not prepared to handle. Many of these soldiers' wounds came not from gunshots but from IEDs like the one used against Bob and Doug. It was clear that we were in the very early stages of understanding TBI and its treatment. We as a country would need to come to terms with the debt we owed these wounded warriors for many years to come. What quality of life could they expect to enjoy? And what about their families?

I learned of these issues because of Bob Woodruff and Doug Vogt. With time, millions of other Americans would be introduced to TBI, its consequences for so many of our veterans, and what we need to do for them because of the valiant efforts of Bob, Lee, Doug, and Vivianne. But that Tuesday, as we waited to visit the naval hospital in Bethesda where Bob had just arrived, all of this was well in the future. For the moment, our concern was that Bob remain alive.

I met Lee and her family at the Bethesda Marriott. We'd booked a group of rooms, as well as a suite where people could gather or hold meetings as needed. I saw Lee for the first time since Bob's injury in the lobby of the hotel and met her brother-in-law Dave (whom I'd watched on camera from Landstuhl the morning before), Vivianne, and Melanie. Up in the hospitality suite, I met Bob's parents, who'd flown in from Michigan, as had Bob's brother Mike; his third brother, Jimmy, had come from California. After talking for a bit, we got into a van for the short ride to the hospital. As we went in, we drove past a congregation of satellite trucks, lights, reporters, and cameras near the gate, just inside the grounds. They were eagerly awaiting any news they could get about Bob and Doug.

A naval officer greeted us at the door and took us upstairs to a conference room for a detailed briefing by the team of physicians who had taken over caring for Bob on his admittance to the naval hospital. The leader of the team, Lieutenant Colonel Rocco Armonda, was a neurosurgeon. He explained that his co-leader, Commander James Dunn, a trauma surgeon, couldn't join us. He was up at the Capitol as part of the medical team assigned to the president in case of any incident during the State of the Union address. It struck me as I sat there that this speech was the reason we'd sent Bob to Iraq; now the lead doctor on his team was at the Capitol, and we were sitting in a conference room in Bethesda desperate to learn whether Bob would be coming back to all of us—and, first and foremost, to Lee and their children.

Dr. Armonda led the briefing, with contributions from various specialists in turn. At the outset, he made it clear that these doctors had treated these types of injuries hundreds of times both at Bethesda and over in Iraq. They were the most experienced in the world at treating injuries like these. Together, the doctors went over Bob's condition in detail. It was horrific. The damage to his skull and to his brain was extensive. That he had survived at all was both miraculous and a testament to the extraordinary skill of the military medical personnel, from the medic who first ran to his aid in the Iraqi tank to the surgical team in Balad to the doctors and nurses at Landstuhl and now to this trauma team at Bethesda. We were seeing firsthand what medical science made possible.

But despite all the medical skill and resources being brought to bear, the range of possibilities remained stark and wide—from full recovery to death. Bob had only just begun his journey back. And it wasn't only the trauma he had to survive. We learned, for example, about a particular virus unique to Iraq, a virus the medical team was concerned might lead to an infection that could kill him.

Throughout the hour or so briefing, Lee kept careful notes and asked focused, direct questions. Later, she'd write that she was dazed and that her notepad was left largely blank, but that's not the way I remember it. She was truly remarkable. After the briefing was over, Lee and Dave were invited to go in to see Bob. Lee asked me whether I'd like to join them, but I declined. I felt this was a private moment for the family. It also occurred to me that an awful lot of people would want to see Bob in the coming days and weeks. I wanted Lee to be able to tell everyone else at ABC News that I hadn't been to his room, so the fact that they were kept away wasn't meant as disrespect.

After the family visit, we agreed that Dave and I would go speak to the reporters waiting by the gate, both to give them an update and to distract them as the van took Lee and the rest of the group back to the hotel. After making a brief appearance, we returned to join everyone in the hospitality suite. Together, we watched the State of the Union address on a television in the hotel suite. Elizabeth Vargas anchored from Washington as originally planned. But instead of Bob Woodruff co-anchoring from Baghdad, Charlie Gibson was with Elizabeth in Washington.

Most people know the story from that point on. Doug was released to an outpatient facility at Bethesda a week later; two weeks after that, he and Vivianne were on their way home to France. Doug still had lasting effects from his serious injury to the brain, but he was on his way back.

Bob remained in a coma for weeks. Lee stayed at his side, sleeping in that hotel room in Bethesda when she wasn't with Bob. I'd talk to her on the telephone regularly, and I went back down to visit her in Washington from time to time, just to make sure she had everything she needed and to give her what moral support I could. After various procedures and a fair amount of healing, the doctors slowly started to reduce Bob's medication, bringing him out of the coma. There were various glimmers of hope, but still not enough to have any sense of how this would all end.

And then, on March 6, after thirty-six days, Bob miraculously awoke to talk with Lee—not all that coherently, but talk nonetheless. We still didn't know the long-term prognosis, but from that point on Bob pretty much performed as well as even the most optimistic experts said was possible—and quite frequently even better. Within ten days he was on his way back to New York—not quite yet to home, but to work on his recuperation at New York-Presbyterian Hospital. Three weeks later, on April 6, Bob finally returned to his home in Westchester. Given how much play the story had gotten, we were concerned that paparazzi would stake him out at home to try to get a photograph at an unguarded moment. So we arranged for our own photo of Bob to be taken as he arrived home, which we distributed to the press.

While Bob was still in the hospital in the early stages of recovery, I turned my attention to something I'd put off: screening the videotape that had been taken from Doug's blood-smeared camera. Vinnie Malhotra had taken the camera with him to Balad and never let it out of his possession until he turned it over to Bob Murphy in Landstuhl. Bob took custody of the camera and kept it secure until he could turn it over to me. We believed Doug had been taping at the moment of the explosion, and we didn't want to let anyone see it for fear that it might contain grisly video of the attack and its aftermath. It was brought to New York, and I set up a monitor with a beta machine in my office. Until that point no one—not Vinnie, not Bob, no one—had seen what was on the tape. By myself, with the doors closed, I put the tape in and watched several minutes of Bob in the armored vehicle and the Iraqi countryside passing by. I saw the failed attempts to get Bob's stand-up right and heard the loud noise of the APC's engine interfering with the audio. And then the camera simply tilted sharply to one side and the tape went to black. Our fears were unfounded. The video really showed nothing at all. It turned out that the explosion had sent a burst of air that hit the camera even before the shrapnel and the rocks flew up from the road. The explosion of air simply stopped the camera from recording anything more.

In June 2006, less than five months after that blast on the road, I got a call that Bob was coming up in the elevator to pay a visit to the newsroom. I ran down the stairs to join a large group quickly gathering to greet him as he walked in. There was a lot of hugging and tears and jubilation. By the fall, he was back to work, both at ABC News and writing a book with Lee about their life together and the ordeal they'd gone through. *In an Instant* became a bestseller.

Bob's first major television project was an hour-long prime-time documentary, "To Iraq and Back," which told the dramatic story of Bob Woodruff and Doug Vogt. For someone else that would have been enough, but Bob used these stories as the jumping-off point for turning a bright spotlight on the plight of so many men returning from Iraq and Afghanistan with TBI. It was the beginning of an effort that continues to urge that we as a nation do more for these valiant warriors. The anchor of the documentary? Bob Woodruff himself.

Bob has been a full-time anchor and reporter for ABC News since the fall of 2006. Any doubts I had about whether he'd come back were erased the first time Sherrie and I went to visit him after he'd come home in April. That day, there was a story about Iraq on the front page of *The New York Times*, and Bob—still wearing a helmet to protect his head because his skull had yet to be restored—asked about going back to Iraq to cover the story. Nothing he'd been through had taken anything away from his determination. I told him no that day in his kitchen—and more than once in the months that followed even as he continued to heal. We'd almost lost him once. And no doctor could predict what effects a concussion would have on a brain that had been through so much.

But Bob wouldn't give up. After asking my permission for over two years, he went over my head to Admiral Mike Mullen, the chairman of the Joint Chiefs of Staff, to persuade me it would be safe for him to travel with Mullen back to Iraq. The admiral assured me that they wouldn't let anything happen to Bob. Nonetheless, I resisted. As they continued to press, I asked what Lee thought, and Bob assured me she would be okay with it. Not that I don't trust Bob, but I called Lee directly just to make sure. In the end, I concluded that about the safest way to go to a war zone is with the senior-most officer in the U.S. military, so I reluctantly went along. And privately, I had a sense that Bob needed to do this for himself. He needed to go back to bring an end to an important chapter in his life.

In 2009, Bob returned to the region with Admiral Mullen. Their first stop was Iraq, where Bob hoped to visit the hospital facility in Balad where they'd saved his life. But when the military aircraft landed in Mosul in northern Iraq for refueling, a sandstorm made it impossible for them to go on to Baghdad. After spending the night in Mosul, Mullen decided they would skip Baghdad altogether for fear that they might get tied down there by the storms. So they flew on to Kabul. Bob was disappointed that he wouldn't make it to Balad after all, but in an ironic twist he unexpectedly met in a hospital in Kandahar two of the people who had cared for him when he was first injured—one a doctor who'd helped stabilize him on his arrival at Landstuhl, the other a nurse who cared for him while he was in a coma in Bethesda.

Bob distinguishes himself every day in his anchoring and his reporting on a wide range of subjects, covering everything from the tsunami and nuclear crisis in Japan, to North Korea, to Prince Harry's trip to the Arctic (which, of course, Bob tagged along on part of). It was no coincidence that Prince Harry's trip was with British veterans who had suffered serious injuries in Iraq or Afghanistan. Bob makes a unique contribution in his coverage of the issues surrounding our soldiers, sailors, and marines returning home wounded from Iraq and Afghanistan. No one—and I least of all—would ever have wished to put him and his family through the hell they experienced. Yet, but for the horrific events, he never could have made some of the important contributions—to our audience and to the nation—that he has made since the attack. He and Lee contribute even more directly through the charity they created, the Bob Woodruff Foundation, co-chaired by Bob's brother Dave and supported by his brothers Mike and Jimmy. Even now, years after his injuries, Bob continues to improve, defying what used to be the conventional wisdom that whatever recovery there may be from TBI would happen within the first two years.

Questions of life and death don't come up every day in covering the news, but they arise more than you might think. Often—too often—some of the most important stories involve danger, whether it's an armed conflict or a natural disaster.

The first time I had to approve someone from ABC News going into a dangerous situation, I said almost reflexively that "no story is worth dying for." And I repeated the phrase often, privately and in large meetings. It was a convenient way of reminding myself and others that we should always err on the side of personal safety. I was always concerned that people might take chances for the sake of reporting the story (or even for the sake of their own career) that weren't warranted. Journalists are not, after all, soldiers or police or fire department first responders. It's not part of journalists' creed that they put their lives at risk to save others.

But when Bob and Doug came so close to death on that January Sunday in Iraq, I had to admit to myself that I had never really come to terms with the issue. Did I really mean that no story—no matter how important—was worth a reporter's dying for? If so, then why did I ever allow colleagues to put themselves in situations where, let's face it, death was a possible consequence? If I really meant that no story was worth dying for, shouldn't we just keep everyone at our headquarters on West 66th Street in New York and report the news from there? Surely the chances of dying were greater on the streets of Baghdad or Kabul than they were on the Upper West Side of Manhattan.

My first thought when I heard that Bob's life hung in the balance was to ask myself what I had done—not what Bob had done; or his crew had done; not even what the insurgents had done; but what I had done. Had I deprived four young children of their father? Had I deprived Lee of her husband? I knew it was the insurgents in Iraq who were truly responsible. I knew Bob had wanted to be there. But I was the one who had made it possible for Bob to be in the place where this could happen to him. If I hadn't agreed to the assignment, he would have been safe at home with his family on that Sunday morning. And I'd done it for the sake of the story, ultimately for the sake of ABC News. It wasn't for "ratings," as *The New York Times* had suggested. But it was for the sake of getting the story.

So, after what happened to Bob and Doug, what was left of my maxim that no story is worth dying for? With time, I came to understand that the question was much too hard for a simple categorical statement like "no story is worth dying for." I had to break it down into several parts.

First, any assignment involving real danger has to be strictly voluntary. Not just voluntary in the sense that people have to step forward, but voluntary in the sense that whether someone does step up or not should have no effect on his or her career. That said, how can you ever eliminate from young correspondents' minds the possibility that they may be the ones to be in the critical place at the critical time that will put them on the map in television journalism and move their careers along? You can't, but you can do everything in your power to make sure there are no ramifications for those who do not step forward.

Second, making dangerous assignments voluntary doesn't relieve management of the responsibility of deciding what reporters can volunteer for. The people in the field are in the best position to judge the danger involved. But it's unwise and unfair to place the burden on their shoulders entirely. That's the job of news management, to make the decision and take the heat in deciding when enough is enough. In the lead-up to the Iraq War in early 2003, for example, we had our correspondent Dan Harris and his producer, Nick Watt, in Baghdad. I would speak to them several times a day with our foreign editor Chuck Lustig to assess the danger of remaining in the city. Officials at the Pentagon at the time were giving us regular warnings that the war could start any day, and they could not ensure the safety of any reporters in Baghdad when the bombing began. Every time we talked, I made it clear both that I wanted their best assessment of the danger and that the decisions whether and when to pull back would be mine alone. Three days before the bombing began, I ordered Dan and Nick to evacuate. They were not happy. Indeed, Dan was quoted in the press as disagreeing with my decision. But I was fine with that. The decision was mine to make based on all the information I had and my judgment of the risks.

After the attack on Bob and Doug, I implemented a new policy requiring my personal approval of all embeds. That isn't to say I would have made a better decision than Bob and Doug did that day. General Chiarelli went out of his way to tell us that having reviewed the incident carefully, he could not fault one bit of the judgment they'd shown. I doubt I would have prevented their going to Taji even if I had known in advance. As I've said, my own plans for going to Iraq a short time after Bob and Doug had me traveling along the same road where they were attacked. But requiring my personal approval of all embeds was a way of making sure that all of us, up and down the line, were thinking carefully about the risks involved— not just the possible rewards. And given what we'd gone through with Bob and Doug, we were awfully strict on approvals from that point on.

Third, assuming that someone truly does want to volunteer for a dangerous assignment and that news management has determined that it's right to go ahead, you then have to do everything in your power to minimize the danger. This begins with training. ABC News didn't send anyone into a dangerous situation without training—typically from outside professionals (former military and often former Special Forces) about what to prepare for and where the greatest danger may lie. We hired professionals in Iraq and Afghanistan both to advise us on situations as they arose and to provide personal security for our people in country. Our ongoing security costs regularly ran at least as high as our other costs associated with covering the wars in those countries. At the peak, our security costs for our Baghdad operation alone ran several million dollars a year. If our outside security team told us that we shouldn't go somewhere or do something, then we didn't, even when it sometimes angered our reporters on the ground. Make no mistake: we missed stories as a result.

Preparing your people and making sure that they have access to experienced hands who know what they are doing in a war zone may seem obvious, but it's not. Too often, I saw news organizations send their people into danger without the necessary preparation or supervision. I've seen good reporters who, frankly, didn't know what they were doing and took chances that they shouldn't have been taking.

No matter how voluntary the assignment and no matter what training and protection you provide, you need to make sure that you send the right reporters into danger zones. This is most often a matter of experience, but it can be temperament as well. At ABC News we were fortunate to have some very experienced field producers and assignment editors and war correspondents who had handled some of the most horrific situations and knew their own limitations—and those of the people around them. I think, for example, of Clark Bentson, an outstanding producer who has covered it all, from Iraq to the tsunami.

In March 1999, Clark was heading a large ABC News team in Belgrade covering the conflict between the Serbs and the Kosovars. The first night of the NATO bombing, Clark was in his hotel room at 2:00 in the morning when three men—one from the hotel, one from the local television station, and a thug—beat on his door and demanded that he come with them. They put him on the back floor of a car and drove him to the bank of a river (Clark never knew whether it was the Danube or the Sava), where they pulled him from the car. The thug pulled a pistol, waved it around, and held it to Clark's head, all the time shouting in Serbian. The only things that Clark could understand were words like "democracy" and "Clinton." Clark believed they were going to shoot him. For some reason, they piled him back in the car, drove him a long distance, held him in a cell until the following night, and ultimately dropped him along with two other captive journalists near the Croatian border.

As with Bob Woodruff, none of us would have wished for Clark to have gone through any of this. But there's no substitute for the types of experiences—in Belgrade, in Moscow, in Haiti, and in so many other difficult and dangerous places—that Clark had been through. One of the things that news organizations have to do is make sure they have some Clark Bentsons in a position to advise and to make decisions, even in this time of cutting back. Clark is soft-spoken and reserved. But there is no one better at knowing what to do—and what not to do—in getting the story in the face of danger.

And yet, after you've taken all the precautions you can—you've limited yourselves to true volunteers and you've picked the right people and you've trained those people and directed them as well as you can—you're still left with the basic question: Is any story worth risking someone's life to cover? Doug Vogt had been a cameraman in war zones and other dangerous places for fifteen years. All of our colleagues who had covered wars during that time had been with Doug in difficult situations; they trusted him completely and knew him to be the very best. As I've said, Bob had extensive experience in covering the wars in both Afghanistan and Iraq, including training with the U.S. military in preparing for his embed with the marines in 2003.

Bob Woodruff and Doug Vogt were among our most experienced war reporters. They wanted to be there. They had all the training and all the gear. They were embedded in a U.S. military convoy. The U.S. military thought it was basically safe (or as safe as any operation can be in a war), or they wouldn't have agreed to let them come along. But despite all of this, none of us was under any illusion that the assignment was free from risk. It wasn't the same as sending them on assignment to New York or Chicago or Los Angeles. Nor, for that matter, the same as having Bob co-anchor the State of the Union address from a studio in New York or from the Capitol or from our bureau in Washington.

Ultimately, the decision to send people into danger to cover stories means that whether we like to talk about it or not, we do believe, deep down, that some stories are so important for the world to know that good men and women—men and women with bright futures and wives and husbands and children—should go report and risk their lives. Never risk them foolishly or unnecessarily, but risk them nonetheless. That basic judgment makes it our responsibility when something goes wrong—not so much that it is our "fault" as that it is what we have done; it involves decisions we have made and consequences with which we must live. This means recognizing the import of what we are doing in advance, thinking about it, and coming to terms with it as best we can. This is the only way we can hope to make the right decisions about what stories do merit taking risks with peoples' lives.

# 9 | Can We Afford the News? Why ABC News Lost a Quarter of Itself

I know how committed you are; I know how searching you are; I know how passionate you are. Passionate in the pursuit of truth—as much truth as you can find, recognizing that there will always be some truth left to discover . . . So, even as you have all these changes, there will be some things that remain the same . . . In three weeks it will be time for me to get off the playing field. I've been here long enough. But I'm going to be up in the stands. I'm going to continue to be your biggest fan.

—My remarks to ABC News on the naming of Ben Sherwood
as my successor, December 10, 2010

February 24, 2010, was the day I decided it was time to leave ABC News. It was just before our daily editorial meeting in the conference room off the newsroom floor. I'd been attending these meetings virtually every weekday I was in the office for almost fourteen years. They'd changed in some ways since that first editorial meeting I'd attended back in March 1997, but the basic format was the same. We'd convene a group of people responsible for news gathering, for our TV programs and our other outlets, such as ABC News Radio and ABCNews.com. We'd be joined by hundreds of others from around the country and around the world. Most of the people participated by telephone, but a few years before I'd added video, with links to various locations, including Washington and Los Angeles and London. Most days I would limit my contribution on these calls to weighing in on particular stories that I wanted us to pursue (or pursue more aggressively or in a different way), asking questions, and making sure we were coordinated across all of our operations. I'd also use the calls to draw everyone's attention to something I thought we'd done particularly well—or could do better. But on some days something special had happened—either in the news or in the life of ABC News itself. Then I'd break format and take over the meeting, explaining to everyone what I knew about what was going on, telling the group what we needed to do about it, and inviting questions.

The morning of February 23 was one of those special days. Just before the call, I turned to my computer and pushed "send" on an e-mail to all of ABC News that I had been working on for several months. In my e-mail I reviewed the things that we'd already done to adapt to changing circumstances, and I said how proud I was of how strong we still were despite all of it. But I also said something everyone already knew: we found ourselves in the middle of what I called a "revolution—a revolution in the ways that people get their news and information." I told my colleagues that it was time for us to anticipate change, rather than respond to it, and that we needed "to ensure that ABC News has a sound journalistic and financial footing for many years to come, and to serve our audiences even better." I announced a "fundamental transformation that will ultimately affect every corner of the enterprise." I listed several specific areas subject to this transformation, and I admitted that these changes would inevitably mean we'd be reducing our workforce substantially.

After sending my e-mail, I walked down the two flights of stairs to the "Crazy Eddie" conference room (named long ago after the old New York electronics store commercials with all the television sets on the wall). I'd taken this same route down these same stairs hundreds of times, but I knew that this particular day would be different. It would begin not with the big stories we were covering but with my talking about the e-mail I had just sent. As I walked the last few steps to the third floor of 47 West 66th Street, I thought back on the other times I'd walked down to talk with my colleagues and friends about some difficult thing we needed to face together. The morning when employees in our New York bureau feared for their health after we'd discovered anthrax in the work space of *World News Tonight* and our executive offices were taken over by FBI agents and officials from the Centers for Disease Control and the New York Police Department. The day after Peter and I had announced that he'd been diagnosed with lung cancer. The Monday after Peter had died, when Tim Johnson and I had walked down these stairs to talk with the entire division, linked together by satellite, about Peter's death the night before.

The Monday morning only a few months later when I'd addressed the staff about the grievous injuries that Bob Woodruff and Doug Vogt had suffered the day before in Iraq.

And as I thought back over all of these moments and more, I wondered to myself whether this wasn't enough. Whether it wasn't time for someone else to handle the next one. Maybe it was time for me to move on to other challenges. I've always admired those who left before it was over.

A host of factors brought us to the place we found ourselves in broadcast news at the beginning of 2010. Most immediately, there was the overall state of the economy. As a country, we were facing the worst economic downturn since the Great Depression. For those of us at ABC News, this was a big story to cover, but it was also something that affected us directly. As one of my colleagues put it, we had to cover a major flood while water was pouring into our own basement.

In late 2008, I began to focus our editorial meetings specifically on the economy. Over the years, we'd invited a wide range of newsmakers and experts to come in for off-the-record question-and-answer sessions. These sessions were one of the perquisites of working at ABC News, but they also were an effective way to improve our coverage by making sure people throughout the organization were exposed to issues and to those who knew the most about them. Certainly we needed the help in trying to sort through the huge story of the economic crisis. From academia, we talked with Kenneth Rogoff, Martin Feldstein, Elizabeth Warren, and Jeffrey Miron, all from Harvard, and Joseph Stiglitz and Jeffrey Sachs from Columbia. From government, we talked with Federal Reserve Chair Ben Bernanke and Larry Summers at the White House, Peter Orszag from the Office of Management and Budget, and Sheila Bair from the FDIC. From the private sector, our guests included Jamie Dimon from JPMorgan Chase, Lloyd Blankfein from Goldman Sachs, Vikram Pandit from Citigroup, Mohamed El-Erian from PIMCO, Roger Altman from the private equity firm Evercore, Bob Lutz from General Motors, Howard Schultz from Starbucks, and Steve Forbes.

These meetings shaped our reporting on the financial mess we were in, but they also helped me think seriously about what it all meant for the business of ABC News. The people we talked to had a range of views on any number of issues, but the one thing they all seemed to agree on was that things were unlikely to get much better any time soon. Housing prices might or might not have bottomed out (it turns out they hadn't), but it would be years—several years—before they returned to anything close to what we'd seen in 2006. Consumer spending was not there to take up the slack because of unemployment, the fear of unemployment, and the loss of real or apparent wealth by most households, whether from the nominal value of houses against which consumers had been borrowing or from the damage done to people's 401(k)s. Everyone agreed we were in for a long, hard slog economically.

But it wasn't just the overall state of the economy that had challenged the health of broadcast news by 2009. The truth was that things were going on within the news industry itself that meant we had to change what we were doing. We weren't the only ones trying to deal with it. NBC News had just consolidated its operations with MSNBC, and CBS News seemed to announce round after round of cuts. If anything, the robust economy up to 2008 had masked some of the most fundamental problems all of us in television news faced.

Start with the costs. I'd inherited a news division built in times of plenty, when audiences grew and grew and revenues more than kept pace. It's not surprising that in such an environment the costs skyrocketed as well. Television news professionals have long been paid substantially more than their print counterparts, and the disparity tends to grow as you go up the list to the top. Partly this is because for many years television was more profitable.

But there's another explanation for the great disparity between what the best and most well-known print reporters are paid and what the top TV anchors receive. Unlike in print, in television a single anchor can step up and turn around a struggling program, or even an entire news organization. An anchor's talent and hard work can bring in the revenue that pays dozens, or even hundreds, of other people's salaries.

We witnessed just how much of a difference anchors could make at the very beginning of my tenure, soon after Roone had stepped down. By the fall of 1998, our morning program, *Good Morning America*, was in real trouble. Recent anchor changes Roone and I had made were not working. We were losing audience; our revenues were falling fast; and hardly a day went by when there wasn't some scathing piece in the press about the chaos behind the scenes. There was open speculation that the network might take the time period from news and either give it back to the stations or give it to the entertainment division. This could have affected the entire future of ABC News, given how important *GMA* was to supporting our overall effort. There was no question that we had to make a change—fast.

I put together a small team with Phyllis McGrady, our creative muse; Amy Entelis, in charge of talent; and an outside consultant, Stuart Sucherman, to make sure we were thinking broadly. We spent much of that fall considering all our options. The entire program seemed to be broken. The anchors were new and relatively inexperienced; the production team even more so. After talking it through, I realized that we had the best possible on-air team right within ABC News: Charlie Gibson and Diane Sawyer.

Charlie had been the very successful co-anchor of the program during its heyday. No one could quite remember why we'd taken him off to begin with. He knew the program and, more important, the audience knew him well. Putting Charlie in just made sense.

Pairing him with Diane Sawyer wasn't quite as obvious. Diane was about the best-known anchor we had at ABC News. She was intelligent and elegant and innovative and fearless. No one worked as hard as she did. More than that, she was extremely versatile. She could do it all: live and tape, interviews and feature pieces, talking with heads of state and with people on the street. And she had a wide-ranging set of interests, matched with an insatiable curiosity.

Diane had done morning television long before, at CBS, but in the years since she had become known principally for her work in prime time—first at *60 Minutes* and then in creating *Primetime Live* with Sam Donaldson. By the late 1990s, few thought of her as the sort of anchor who would do the softer material typical of the second hour of the morning programs—things like cooking and having animals on the set. It didn't help that Roone thought it was a terrible idea. When I first raised the possibility, he went so far as to say it could jeopardize my career. Roone's thinking was that Diane's natural habitat was the prime-time newsmagazine and that putting her on morning television could damage her prime-time work without saving *GMA*.

By this time, Roone had formally stepped down, and so, despite his warnings, I took the idea to Charlie and Diane. I knew that Charlie cared deeply for the program he'd already given so many years to—and, equally important, he cared for the people behind the scenes who were suffering. Diane didn't have the same investment at that point in *GMA*, and we both knew that failure could leave a mark on her extraordinary career. But she did care deeply about ABC News and she knew how important this was to us all. Diane's and Charlie's ultimate decision to go and save *GMA* was one of the most generous things anyone did for ABC News or for me during my time there.

After some intense discussions in December, we all agreed that we would go ahead, and in January made the announcement to the surprise of just about everyone. *The New York Times* even wrote an editorial about how remarkable it was that Diane would move to the mornings at that stage in her career. The morning of the announcement, we gathered in my office to review last-minute details. While we were talking, Diane's agent called her, and she took the call at my assistant's desk just outside my office, within earshot. From her side of the conversation, I could tell that until that call, the agent had no idea she was going to *GMA*. At a time when Diane could have asked for just about anything in a new contract, she didn't. Instead, she looked at the situation, knew how badly we needed her, and concluded that she could help. The same went for Charlie.

Anyone who follows the morning programs knows how big a success Diane and Charlie proved to be. Diane initially committed to do no more than three months and asked only that I figure out a way to get her off the program if it started to hurt her. The first day they appeared, the *GMA* audience increased double digits, and it just went up from there. Diane and Charlie gave us the time and the stability we needed to rebuild the team around them. Diane stayed on the program for more than ten years; Charlie stayed for just over seven. This sort of generosity and loyalty is a side of some of the big television news anchors that the public doesn't always get to see.

As much talk as there is about how much TV newspeople get paid, there isn't as much focus put on the size of the staffs behind the scenes. These staffs increased substantially through the 1970s and '80s, creating redundancies and layers that weren't really necessary. By the time I got to ABC News in 1997, we had executive producers with no program to produce and anchors with no program to anchor, all of whom were making huge salaries left over from the "good old days."

There wasn't a year during my time at ABC News that we weren't cutting costs somewhere or other. Quietly, without much attention in the media, we cut salaries (and, yes, even of the well-known people), and we cut positions. We shaved tens of millions of dollars from the basic cost structure and made sure that we remained in the black every year I was there, despite declines in the size of the audiences for most of our programs and despite ever-increasing costs. It wasn't fun. I would have loved to have been at ABC News when everything was on the upswing, when they were adding programs left and right and the audiences were only getting bigger. When ABC couldn't get out of the way of the money.

But I wasn't. I was there when the years turned lean and we had to adapt—adapt in ways that made sure we continued to serve the audience with high-quality news programs. Despite the adversity, I took real pride in the work we were doing, as reflected in all the prestigious journalism awards that came our way every year. Throughout my tenure we continued the tradition of great news documentaries; we created and built special units to report in important areas, such as law and justice, medicine, investigations, and business.

In the face of all the cost reductions, we also built an entire new team of outstanding journalists. With Amy Entelis's leadership, we brought in exceptional on-air reporters like John Berman, Lama Hasan, Jon Karl, David Muir, Steve Osunsami, Martha Raddatz, Jim Sciutto, Claire Shipman, Kate Snow, Jake Tapper, Pierre Thomas, Nick Watt, Bill Weir, and David Wright. And while we had to say goodbye to the likes of Peter Jennings, Ted Koppel, Hugh Downs, and David Brinkley, we moved new anchors into position for the future—not just Diane Sawyer and Charlie Gibson, but also Robin Roberts, George Stephanopoulos, Christiane Amanpour, Cynthia McFadden, Terry Moran, Bill Weir, Bob Woodruff, Chris Cuomo, Elizabeth Vargas, Bianna Golodryga, and Dan Harris. Behind the scenes we put together an equally talented group of producers, including Jon Banner, James Goldston, Jim Murphy, and David Sloan. (And that isn't all. Every time I tried to compliment my ABC News colleagues at the morning editorial meeting, I left someone out. Sometimes the most important someone. I know I've done it again. But you know who you are, and I'm sorry.)

Costs were one important part of the challenges we faced as we approached 2010. What had happened to our audience was another. The audiences for just about all broadcast news programs had been declining for years (with the important exception of *GMA* when Diane and Charlie took it over). That would have been bad enough, but while we were shrinking, our competitors over at the cable news channels were growing—dramatically. They started from a much smaller base, which meant that even the most popular cable news program still reached only a fraction of what we did with any of our news programs. But the size of their audience didn't keep the cable news channels from making money. And by 2009, boy, were they making money. This was one of the biggest changes I witnessed during my time in news.

When I came to ABC News, CNN had made its mark during the Gulf War only six years before. It was largely built around live coverage of breaking news—not around controversy or opinion. The most controversial program it had was *Crossfire* with Pat Buchanan and Michael Kinsley. The most popular CNN program? *Larry King Live*, which was often given over to celebrity interviews and wasn't particularly provocative (at least by the standards of today).

Back in 1997, MSNBC and Fox News were just getting started, and at the time we wondered whether the world really needed two more twenty-four-hour channels devoted to breaking news. We didn't see the twenty-four-hour cable channels as much of a direct threat. We thought their main effect would be on CNN, and if anything, we thought that MSNBC would be the bigger issue, given the strength of NBC News. Roone and I met with CNN executives during the summer of 1997 to talk about a possible strategic relationship between CNN and ABC News. I remember sitting in a New York hotel room on the Upper West Side with our CNN counterparts as Roone laid out why CNN should make an alliance with us because of the threat of MSNBC. We didn't even talk about Fox News. Over the next few years, I renewed our talks with CNN several times, once coming so close to a deal that we had the structure for ownership and governance agreed on by the two sides, only to have the AOL–Time Warner board pull back. And all the time we were talking, Fox News was gaining strength.

At the beginning, none of us appreciated what Roger Ailes was planning for Fox News. He wasn't thinking about another breaking news channel along the lines of CNN. He was thinking about something truly different. He was about to mix twenty-four-hour news with polemics. It would prove to be a powerful alliance—both in its effect on the audience and in its financial success. Although all the cable news channels saw audiences grow through the late 1990s and into the new century, none grew like Fox News. From 1998 to 2008, Fox's audience in prime time tripled, while CNN's remained more or less the same and MSNBC's increased slightly. By the time I left ABC News, Fox News regularly had as many people watching it in prime time as CNN and MSNBC had put together. After a few years of trying to develop its own strategy and brand to compete with Fox and CNN, MSNBC decided to take a page out of Fox's successful playbook and embrace opinion—but from the left, rather than the right. And it caught up with CNN in its prime-time audience.

Fox's rise in popularity translated into huge financial success. The Pew Center estimates that Fox first earned a small profit in about 2001, when CNN was making about $300 million. Since then, Fox has grown its profits steadily to the point where by 2009 it was thought to make about $800 million—at least 40 percent more than CNN. MSNBC's profits reportedly were also rising, although they still lagged far behind those of Fox News.

The success of Fox News was big, but how it achieved that success was even more important. Fox went in exactly the opposite direction from the networks and CNN. While the networks sought to appeal to the broadest audience possible by avoiding controversial opinion, Fox embraced controversy. The more partisan, the better. And this approach was every bit as much a matter of shrewd business as it was a matter of ideology.

Unlike the broadcast networks, the cable networks get just as much revenue from subscription dollars as they do from advertising. Every time you pay your cable bill, a portion of your money is going straight to CNN and Fox News and MSNBC—whether you watch those channels or not. The way you maximize subscription revenue is very different from the way you maximize advertising revenue, which is why the most successful cable news channels have come to care more about a zealous audience than about a big one.

Why has passion become so important to news? It's simple. If you're a news cable channel that can get even 10 percent of the audience strongly committed to watching you, then you can get a lot of subscription money from the cable operator. No cable company can afford to lose 10 percent of its subscribers by dropping any individual channel from its system. And that doesn't even mean that 10 percent of the people are actually watching the cable channel—only that they feel strongly enough about the channel that they'll cancel their cable if it's taken away.

In the broadcast world, the opposite is true: no network can afford to lose 10 percent of its audience because of what it will mean for advertising—the only source of revenue it has. As a result, the broadcast networks, and particularly the broadcast news divisions, have historically avoided the sort of partisan opinion that Fox News and MSNBC have come to embrace. Because broadcast networks have depended so much on getting every single advertising dollar they can, there has always been an incentive not to offend, not to take too extreme a view on any subject. Take a controversial position on something and you are sure to alienate at least part of your audience and lose revenue as a result. The way to maximize revenue in the broadcast world has been to keep it down the middle, avoid the extremes, and get the biggest audience that you could.

And so Fox News became very profitable with a small fraction of the audience that the broadcast networks get for their news programs. Even more remarkable, Fox makes far more than CNN, even when CNN reaches more people than Fox. You may think that I'm contradicting myself. I've already said that Fox's ratings were much higher than CNN's. If they have higher ratings, doesn't that mean they reach more people?

No. Ratings tell us how many people are watching at any given time. They don't tell us how many people watch a given channel over time. The truth is that even when Fox gets much higher ratings than CNN, CNN can still reach more people—because the people watching Fox stay for longer and come more often. By late 2009, Fox News was reaching about fifty million people a month, while CNN was reaching over fifty-five million. And neither was in the same ballpark as the broadcast news operations. For example, even though ABC News broadcasts on average just over 30 hours each week (compared with 168 hours a week for the cable channels), when I left ABC, it still reached over a hundred million people each month on television alone—and another forty million or so by radio and over twenty million over the Internet and mobile. Which meant that it was still true that "more Americans get their news from ABC News than from any other source."

So it wasn't just ideology but business as well that led cable news away from the middle of the road and toward partisanship. As I've said, this move toward extreme opinion mixed with the news has some very important implications for how we talk about important issues in this country. Some pretty extreme things can be said—on both the left and the right—without any incentive to rein in the people saying them. All of this is, of course, made even worse by the robust blogosphere of the Internet, which often doesn't have a business model to begin with and so has no constraints whatever on seeking to appeal to even the tiniest sliver of people who are passionate—even rabid—about a particular subject.

As we moved into the fall of 2009, all of these factors were very much on my mind: the overall economic downturn that didn't look as if it would turn around any time soon, the very large cost structure we still had despite years of trimming, the long-term stagnation of broadcast news audiences, and the extraordinary success of cable news channels driven by an approach that we could not mimic—and that I didn't want to copy even if I could. From late 2008 through much of 2009, we'd seen our advertising revenue drop by double digits. It wasn't as big a drop as some others experienced, but it's not just how much money you're taking in that counts; it's how any reduction in revenue compares with the profits you were expecting to make. Traditionally, broadcast television news operations—like the rest of the networks—had operated on pretty narrow margins, rarely exceeding 10 percent and in some years well below that. When we saw our revenues drop by more than 10 percent in 2009, we had to scramble to make sure we remained in the black that year.

I wasn't the only one watching the trends and growing increasingly concerned about where we were headed. The people at the network understandably asked some pretty tough questions—questions that I would have been asking if I'd been back in my old job of running the network. Sure we'd done a good—no, better than good—job at controlling costs and improving quality over the years. But with the revenue situation so uncertain, simply staying one step ahead of the sheriff didn't seem like much of a long-term strategy.

All of this led me to conclude that ABC News needed to be restructured from top to bottom—and restructured in a way that reduced costs substantially and made us viable as a business even as we continued to do great news reporting and moved into the digital age. But recognizing that the restructuring had to happen wasn't the same as saying that I should be the one to do it.

I'd already spent years going through ABC News operations and looking for ways we could be more efficient. There was undeniably excess and waste in what I'd inherited. But there was also excellence. There's a fine line between cutting out the wasteful and compromising your ability to carry out your mission—the important mission of covering the news the way the audience needs it covered. I was always aware of this line, but if I hadn't been, there were those who reminded me of it time and again. One of the most outspoken and perceptive was Ted Koppel. Throughout my time working with him, from March 1997 until he left in November 2005, Ted was never shy about warning me of the dangers in my willingly listening to the "bean counters" (as he would call them) at the network and the parent company. Ted thought I was being used, and he urged me to take a more confrontational stand with the company. He believed strongly that the company should be investing in ABC News in the public interest, even if we lost money.

Was there a chance that Ted was right, that I was simply being used as the tool to do violence to a great news organization? Of course. But two things made me think otherwise. First, I knew the people running the company, and I saw no reason why they would want to damage ABC News if they could avoid it. Starting with Bob Iger, who by that time was running the entire Walt Disney Company, they genuinely believed in our work and took pride in it.

Second, and more important, I could see for myself the powerful forces we were up against. These weren't manufactured—the declining audiences, the flat revenues, and the rise of alternatives on cable and the Internet. I never doubted that if I and all the rest of senior management in the company went away, whoever replaced us would face the same set of challenges. This wasn't a matter of choice; it was a matter of fact. The question was not whether something substantial had to be done. The question was how it would be best to do it—and who should do it. In the end, I concluded that I would be the best one to do the difficult deed of restructuring ABC News. I knew the organization inside out; I knew the outside challenges it was facing and how hostile the environment could be. And, yes, I'd come to love it. I didn't really trust anyone else to do what had to be done. Frankly, I believed I'd do a better job than anyone else even though it would be one of the most difficult and painful things I'd ever done.

So, in the fall of 2009, I began work behind closed doors with a small task force drawn from ABC News and from the network to go over the organization from top to bottom and develop a new way of doing business. We worked through the holidays, starting with a frank assessment of where we were and what was on the horizon. We took what we thought was the worst-case scenario for ABC News over the next five years— projecting continued ratings decline, no increase in advertising rates, and no growth in digital revenues and income. We then asked ourselves what we would need to do to make sure we'd be in the black at the end of five years even if all of these bleak assumptions proved true. From there, we set out to reengineer ABC News from top to bottom to make sure it could weather the storm.

After the fact, I was asked whether all this was imposed on me by the company. My truthful response was that the forces I've described bearing down on ABC News were stronger even than the Walt Disney Company. Make no mistake that the company was holding me to account. That is the job of everyone responsible to the company's shareholders: to make sure they're spending the shareholders' money wisely. And I have little doubt that if I'd buried my head in the sand and refused to deal with reality, someone else would have come along with his or her own approach to fashioning our future. But in the end, there was nothing we did that wasn't my decision. And there was no decision I made that I didn't truly believe was in the best interests of ABC News in the long run—as well as the best interests of the company overall.

Throughout our work in reengineering ABC News, I was committed to four things.

First, I refused to simply pick a percentage by which all costs would be reduced and apply it across the board. I'd seen other large companies take this approach all too often. It's easier, because it doesn't require much study or the choosing of some parts of the organization over others. It's also, in my experience, almost always wrong. The problem is that in any organization at any point there's too much being spent in some places and too little in others. This means that if you cut everything across the board, you're cutting some areas too much and some too little. When it came to ABC News, not to recognize this, not to make the effort to figure out which was which, would be simply lazy and would hurt the organization.

Second, for areas where we thought we could save money, we committed ourselves to doing things differently, rather than asking people to do the same things the same way with fewer resources. We'd already spent years trimming back the more obvious inefficiencies built up through the 1980s and early '90s. I didn't believe that there was still this sort of "low-hanging fruit" to be picked. If we were going to make substantial savings, we'd have to be more radical in our approach.

Third, we tried our best not to impose our business problems on the audience. We might be facing a tough economic and competitive climate, but that was our problem—not the problem of the people who relied on us for their news. What's more, if people saw us sacrificing the quality of our reporting, we could send ourselves into a death spiral of audiences fleeing us ever more rapidly for the growing number of alternatives out there, which in turn would require more cost cuts that reduced quality even further.

And finally, whatever we decided to do, I wanted to do it in the most humane way possible. Because two-thirds of the costs of ABC News were for salaries and benefits, I knew that any real restructuring would mean we'd have to let a good number of people go. These were good people who had given their all, typically over decades of their lives. Many of them had been with ABC News long before I had come on the scene more than twelve years before.

We didn't have a choice about what we had to do, but we did have a choice about how we did it. People deserved to be treated with respect. At the very least, this meant we would be entirely open and honest with everyone about what we were doing and why. And we needed to do whatever we were going to do as quickly as possible. It would be cruel to ask people to give their all in gathering and reporting the news while not knowing whether they'd have a job in six or nine months. People needed and deserved to know as quickly as possible whether they would be staying or going.

The plan we arrived at had many parts, most of which were too detailed to interest anyone who wasn't there at the time. We did things like combine the weekday and weekend staffs of our evening and morning broadcasts, fold our unit doing special events into our programs through the day and night, and rely on more freelance staff for some of our long-form programs in prime time.

The biggest change we made involved how we gathered and produced the news for all of our programs and platforms. For nearly a decade we'd been pushing to use technology in new ways that let producers shoot and edit their own material. This started back in the fall of 2000 with *Hopkins 24/7*, a seven-hour prime-time series that was the brainchild of Phyllis McGrady. Phyllis had always wanted to do a documentary series following what went on in a major teaching hospital over an extended period of time. She and her team persuaded the powerful Johns Hopkins Hospital to let us come in with cameras to shoot behind the scenes for months.

But we couldn't expect to bring the traditional two- or three-person crews with large video cameras, microphones on booms, and arrays of lights into the operating rooms, private rooms, and corridors of a major hospital. Our colleague Rudy Bednar came forward with the solution: we would use some of the new, small, but high-quality video cameras that a single producer could operate by himself. These would be relatively unobtrusive. Indeed, as it turned out, they were so unobtrusive that over time, the subjects we were filming tended to forget we were even there. (We went back after the fact and carefully went over with the subjects what we were planning to air and got their permission.) This approach also made it economical to take a relatively small group of dedicated men and women, move them to Baltimore, and have them spend day after day, week after week, collecting the most intimate details of what went on at Johns Hopkins.

*Hopkins 24/7* was a success in every respect when it aired in September 2000: the critics by and large loved it, we received various journalism awards, and we attracted a healthy audience. One of the producers who'd worked with Rudy on *Hopkins 24/7*, Terry Wrong, went on to use and improve the same techniques in exploring what went on behind the scenes in the City of Boston (*Boston 24/7* in 2002), the New York City Police Department (*NYPD 24/7* in 2004), Johns Hopkins again (*Hopkins* in 2008), and three Boston hospitals (*Boston Med* in 2010). With each project, we learned more about what the digital technology made possible in reporting, shooting, and editing; we also learned about some of the distinctive forms of storytelling that this new approach made both possible and necessary.

In 2005, we took what we'd learned from producing documentaries and applied it to a daily program. Ted Koppel decided in March of that year that he would leave ABC News after forty-two years, which meant we had to make major changes in his signature *Nightline* program. The year before, Ted and I had begun intense discussions about his future. I had wanted him to remain as anchor of *Nightline*, but I thought we needed him on more often than his contract provided for, and I believed the program needed to be done live in the late-night period more often. Ted understandably concluded that at that point in his career, he wasn't in a position to increase his workload. We then discussed other roles he could play at ABC News, including possibly as anchor of *This Week* on Sunday mornings, as I was eager to keep him as a part of the institution that he had had such an important role in helping to build. Ted considered it all carefully over a period of weeks but ultimately concluded that it was best to leave altogether and try some other things.

In an ironic coincidence, Ted called to tell me of his decision to leave ABC News during a short period when I knew, but Ted did not, that Peter Jennings likely had lung cancer, which ended up taking Peter's life in August 2005. Ted's eventual departure came in late November 2005—less than four months after Peter passed away.

Continuing the tradition of *Nightline* without Ted Koppel was a tall order. At the time, many critics and commentators said it just couldn't be done. The entertainment team at ABC on the West Coast had long coveted the late-night slot. They wanted to try their hand at getting the sort of success they had watched with envy on NBC (with *The Tonight Show*) and at CBS (with David Letterman). Ted and I had dodged a bullet only three years earlier when ABC Entertainment almost wooed David Letterman away from CBS—which would have meant the end of *Nightline*.

We spent the summer and fall of 2005 coming up with a plan. I asked my colleague Bob Murphy to oversee the project and turned to Phyllis McGrady once again for creative guidance. We chose James Goldston as the best executive producer for the revamped *Nightline*. James had come to us with Martin Bashir from England, where the two of them had done strong work on projects such as the Princess Diana interview in 1995. They were probably best known for their 2003 documentary on Michael

Jackson that gave rise to a criminal investigation and prosecution. Since James had joined us a few years before, we'd gained a greater appreciation for how strong and creative a producer he could be.

Once James joined the group, we decided to move away from having each half hour cover only a single topic and toward a program covering two or three stories each night. We didn't even try to replace Ted Koppel with a single anchor; it would have been unfair to put someone in who would compare unfavorably with Ted. Instead, we moved to three anchors: Terry Moran, Cynthia McFadden, and Martin Bashir. And we relocated some of the *Nightline* staff to New York, where two of the anchors were based and much of the production was done.

On November 28, 2005, we premiered the new *Nightline*. I'd like to say that we saw an immediate improvement in the ratings. We didn't. For the first few months, the program searched for its new identity. Ratings trailed off, but only modestly. And with time, the program figured out what it wanted to be: a late-night newsmagazine coming after the local stations' late news. Typically covering three stories each night, some on the news and some features. Often unpredictable; always timely and interesting. And the audience began to respond. Gradually, building over the months, *Nightline* went from an also-ran in the late-night space to a serious contender that was consistently at least second and frequently won the time period—competing with the traditional powerhouses of late-night entertainment programs with big names attached like Leno and Letterman. My last full season at ABC News, the 2009–10 season, *Nightline*, anchored by Cynthia McFadden, Terry Moran, and Bill Weir, attracted more viewers than either Leno or Letterman—for the first time in history.

This was a true success, made even sweeter because our doubters and critics said we couldn't do it. But as important was what was going on behind the scenes. In building the new program, we'd substantially reduced our salary costs, but what we'd saved in salary we quickly started spending in production costs. The "classic" *Nightline* of Ted Koppel consisted of a prerecorded setup piece on the subject of the night, followed by a live or taped interview with one or more people to comment on the subject. This was a relatively inexpensive format to produce. But James Goldston was taking the program in the direction of three produced, prerecorded pieces each and every night. Whatever money we thought we might save in salaries was consumed by the costs of shooting and editing all the taped pieces.

I talked with James more than once about the problem. I told him that in order to make the program work financially—and resist the network's temptation to take the time period away from us—we needed to reduce our production costs. The answer to me was plain. We needed to do more live and less tape. James was adamant that if we went to more live, in-studio interviews, we would damage the franchise. And so we were at an impasse.

That's when James showed us all that he was every bit as creative as he was determined. He and his team found a third way. If we needed to do most or all of the program on tape and we couldn't afford tape, then he would need to find a way to make tape affordable. Following the path that Rudy Bednar had blazed with *Hopkins*, *Nightline* began to experiment with having its producers and correspondents shoot and edit their own video. This novel approach wouldn't work for all reports. We weren't about to send an anchor to interview the president holding her own video camera. But there were enough pieces that could be done that way to re-duce our costs substantially. And what's more, as with *Hopkins*, we dis-covered that some stories—not all, but many—we could actually tell more easily and better with this new approach. By the time we were having our secret meetings in the fall of 2009 on how we could fundamentally trans-form all of ABC News, *Nightline* was producing almost half of its pieces in this new way.

There was one more way we'd pioneered use of digital technology that helped us reengineer ABC News. Two years before, we'd begun a new program to use what we called digital reporters to rebuild some of our worldwide news-gathering operations. We recruited seven enterprising, relatively junior journalists, trained them in the use of the digital technol-ogy, and in October 2007 sent them to seven cities around the world—New Delhi, Mumbai, Seoul, Jakarta, Rio de Janeiro, Dubai, and Nairobi. There, they worked out of bureaus of ABC News partners (such as the BBC) or out of their own apartments. They shot their own material, edited it, and sent it back to New York. Originally, we thought the reporters could provide a steady stream of video for our website. If a major news story came up suddenly in their part of the world, they might go on the air for us as a stopgap until we could get more seasoned correspondents into place. They did all that, but what we hadn't anticipated was the number of stories they came up with on their own, stories that made their way onto our programs entirely apart from any localized breaking news.

So, when we met over the holidays in 2009 to figure out how to rebuild ABC News, we had proven results in three different areas—long-form news documentaries, a daily program, and news gathering—each showing ways we could use digital technology to help us save money and either maintain or improve the quality of what we provided our audience. We would move toward a world in which more producers and reporters shot and edited their own material throughout all of ABC News.

Once we'd settled on the changes we would make, we needed to figure out how we would make them. We went through each operation of ABC News and calculated how many people we would need to get the job done in the new ways we were undertaking. This resulted in a reduction of a large part of the staff—approaching 25 percent. Losing a quarter of the men and women who worked at ABC News was going to be painful no matter what. But we sought to ease that pain by giving every single employee—up to and including me—the option to leave voluntarily by a given date in exchange for a settlement over and above what he or she would otherwise be entitled to as severance. The company agreed to our voluntary approach, even though it cost more money. This could not have been done but for the support I received from the head of the network, Anne Sweeney.

And so, on that morning of February 23, 2010, I sent out my e-mail about the profound changes that were coming, and I walked down the stairs to do my best to explain them to the staff on our morning conference call. From that point on, I made myself available to any and all who had questions or comments. I spoke to any member of the press who wanted to report on what we were doing—not because I thought it was all that important that the public follow our internal actions, but because I'd learned that sometimes the most effective way to communicate with people inside your organization is to have them hear it from the outside. You can say and write something internally over and over again, but if people read the same thing in the press (including the trade press) even once, it can get them starting to believe what you've been trying to tell them. I also held several all-staff meetings in New York and Washington inviting any ABC News employee to come and ask questions, make comments, or just complain.

All of this was my attempt to make a very difficult situation a little bit less so. But there's no diminishing the shock and the pain that preparing to say goodbye to as much as a quarter of a workforce causes. This is particularly true in news. Unlike some other businesses, most major news organizations base their success on relationships built among employees over many years. We had people who had been with ABC News for twenty, thirty, even forty years. In this time, they'd worked with their colleagues in very difficult, very stressful, and sometimes very dangerous situations. They'd experienced wonderful accomplishments together; they'd suffered setbacks together.

It wasn't just the staff that was feeling the emotional consequences. From the moment I resolved to undertake a major restructuring more than three months before, I'd known where this was leading. There wasn't a day that it didn't affect me: Was I sure I was doing the right thing? What would happen to all these good people I was sending out into a terrible job market? What would it mean for their families? Could I be putting in jeopardy the future of the great news organization I'd inherited? It took a toll—as it should have.

Despite the ties that were about to be broken (or maybe because of them), people throughout the organization—those staying and those leaving—conducted themselves with extraordinary professionalism through the difficult ninety days between the time of my e-mail and the time when most of the changes were put in effect. No one reduced their effort to gather and report the news. No one allowed the quality of their work to suffer. For the most part, I believe people did the high quality of work that they had always done because of their commitment to their colleagues with whom they worked closely every day—and because they believed in the work they were doing. It was what had brought them to ABC News in the first place and why they'd remained through the years.

By the end of June, we were largely through the worst of the changes. When completed, this plan achieved our goal of ensuring we could remain in the black even under the worst of circumstances. It would give the future leadership a solid financial base from which to build a new ABC News—one positioned to move aggressively into the new, digital world.

And then it was time for me to go. I met with Bob Iger in May to talk with him about my thinking. His first reaction was that he didn't agree—that he thought I should stay. There was more work for me to do. But I thought about it some more and talked with others in the company, and especially with Diane Sawyer, with whom I'd been through so much and whom I respected so greatly. I became convinced that my first instinct was the right one. At the end of July that year, I called Bob and said I'd definitely decided to go. He said he had mixed feelings but wouldn't try to talk me out of it. He undertook personally to make sure that my departure was as smooth as possible. The only thing Bob asked was that I put off the announcement until after Labor Day and that I stay on the job until the end of the year. This was a much longer transition than I would have liked, reminiscent of the long overlap I'd had with Roone at the beginning of my tenure. But I owed it to Bob and to the organization to handle it his way. In December, Bob paid me the highest compliment possible. At a Disney board dinner, he gave a toast in which he said that no one could have done a better job in more difficult circumstances upholding the great tradition of ABC News.

Anne Sweeney conducted a search for my replacement, and by early December they were ready to make the announcement. She chose Ben Sherwood, someone I both liked and respected. Ben had had two different stints at ABC News (the second when I had hired him as my executive producer for *Good Morning America*), as well as at NBC News. Anne Sweeney called me at home late in the evening of December 9, when I happened to be recovering from surgery for a detached and torn retina. She said Ben and she would make the announcement to the news division the next morning and that she was sorry if I couldn't be there because of my eye. I told her that, lame eye or not, nothing could keep me away.

The morning of December 10, we gathered one more time on the floor of TV-3 just off the newsroom. This was the place where I'd taken that late-night call from Peter Jennings disagreeing with my decision to do a prime-time special on Princess Diana; the place where I'd spent all those election nights over nearly fourteen years; the place where I hovered near the anchor desk to talk with Peter during short breaks in our 9/11 coverage; the place where Tim and I had spoken to the troops the day after Peter had died. For me, there was a lot of history and a lot of emotion.

Anne led off, describing the thorough search she'd made to find my successor and why she'd chosen Ben. Then I took the opportunity to speak to the friends and colleagues with whom I'd been through so much over almost fourteen years. After I thanked Anne for her support, this is what I said:

> This will go in a different direction than it otherwise would have . . . Part of that's because the times will be different. My times were different from Roone's, and you have to respond to those times. Part of it is because Ben's a different person. He comes with different interests, different orientation, different attitudes. That is a healthy thing. I look forward to that. Any healthy organization needs new blood and new ideas . . .
>
> Having said that, I want to move on to [talk about] all of you, because I know you, I think, pretty well—individually and, more important, collectively . . . I know what you can do. We've been through a lot together. Some of it in this room. I know how committed you are; I know how searching you are; I know how passionate you are. Passionate in the pursuit of truth—as much truth as you can find, recognizing that there will always be some truth left to discover. You'll never have it all. So, it's a relentless job that requires you to keep pushing all the time.
>
> And you do that. You ask questions that other people don't ask; you cover stories other people don't cover. It's what makes you great and gives you the capability to be greater still. This was true under Roone; it was true under me—because of you, not because of me; and it will be true under Ben. So, even as you have all these changes, there will be some things that remain the same . . .
>
> It's about time. In three weeks it will be time for me to get off the playing field. I've been here long enough. But I'm going to be up in the stands. I'm going to continue to be your biggest fan. And, Ben, now I'll be your biggest fan. Congratulations and best wishes.

With that, I shook Ben Sherwood's hand and headed back for some more laser treatment on my ailing eye. It was difficult. It was emotional. And it felt completely right.


I spent nearly fourteen of the best years of my life at ABC News, but that hardly gives me answers to all the important questions journalism faces today. By the time I left, it seemed that every week we heard about new rounds of cutbacks at news organizations—from the largest and most prestigious newspapers in the country, to some of our best-known news-magazines, to television-station groups, to the broadcast networks. Where does it all end?

I don't know. One of the important things I learned from my time at ABC was how little anyone can know about what's around the corner. Just consider how much happened that I would never have predicted back in March 1997. No one could have known the president would be im-peached, or that we'd have a tied presidential election, or that we'd suffer a major terrorist attack on U.S. soil, or that the economy would go into a tailspin worse than just about anyone could remember. And I certainly didn't know how much I would come to respect and love the news and the people devoted to reporting it. So I've come to take with more than a grain of salt many of the sweeping predictions experts make all the time about the future of news—television or otherwise. The world changes too fast and there's too wide a range of opportunities and risks for anyone to plot any certain course for the future of the news industry.

But there are some things that I'm pretty confident about.

First, as much as the technology and the ways we get our news change, people don't change. Not fundamentally. Human beings have an insatia-ble appetite for news and information. Since the beginning of recorded time, people have craved news, and they've craved stories about their world and the people in it. The overall appetite for news continues to grow even as the audience (or readership) for any particular news outlet shrinks.

Second, each news provider's slice of the growing pie may be getting smaller, but that doesn't mean there's any single source of news and infor-mation that's come along to rival the size and reach of the traditional news providers. The days of people structuring their time around sitting in front of the television to get "the news" from a single source such as Walter Cronkite on CBS or Chet Huntley and David Brinkley on NBC or Frank Reynolds on ABC are long gone. But there are still a lot more peo-ple tuning into Diane Sawyer and Brian Williams and Scott Pelley than there are turning to any other source.

To say that people will continue to want and need news and informa-tion doesn't mean necessarily that they'll continue to turn to the traditional news providers to satisfy that need. But even with all they've been through, the major news organizations still have some big advantages over the newer alternatives. They have concentrations of talented people who know how to work together to gather and vet and produce the news. They have rich archives of video and text going back through the years. Perhaps most important, they have long-standing relationships with millions of people. They have, in short, news brands that can be particularly valuable in an increasingly cluttered and confusing world.

The third thing I'm certain of is that the major news organizations will have to pay even closer attention to the economics of the business if they're to continue to be important sources for our news. Anyone who truly cares about journalism has to care as well about how news organizations can afford to invest in the work of reporters. I undertook a major restructuring of ABC News because of my deep commitment to serious journalism, not simply because of the bottom line. There remain important areas that cry out for better, more-in-depth coverage. The country needs and deserves good people who work full-time to give us this sort of coverage, telling the rest of us things that we'd never otherwise find out—either because we just don't have the time or because there are powerful people who don't want us to know. We need paid professionals to dig below the surface of news stories to get to what is really going on.

This sort of journalism does not come cheap. It requires years of investment in reporters who get to know their beats, who develop their sources, and who know enough to judge when they're being spun and when they're being told the truth. It requires spending money on stories that in the end may go nowhere. No one can bat a thousand when it comes to the really important enterprise stories. Precisely because this sort of valuable reporting takes time and money and patience, I see nothing on the Internet today that can provide it with any consistency. The blogosphere and citizen journalists can do a lot of good. But bloggers and citizen journalists just aren't in a position to accumulate the resources and commit to making sure that we get all the valuable original reporting we need. For that we have to turn to at least some large, more traditional news organizations with the resources and people required to support the most important enterprise journalism.

So I'm afraid that I see no relief in sight from the relentless efforts to control news costs—not just to keep the costs down, but to make sure that the money is being spent on journalism that provides the original reporting that we aren't getting anywhere else. You can't cut a business to success, and important parts of the news business need to grow, not contract. I saw fundamental, even dramatic changes in news during my tenure, and there's every reason to believe the pace of change will continue—or even accelerate. It's up to the major news providers to adapt to whatever new technologies may bring and to make sure they're growing to meet the public's increasing appetite for news. They have to respond even more quickly and effectively to changes in the ways people want their news.

For me, the question isn't so much whether the great news organizations have a future, but rather what they will do with that future—whether they will continue to serve the good of our democracy overall, that need for an informed citizenry that Justice Powell talked about in his chambers over thirty years ago. Most journalists recognize the duties they owe the public. They owe you their best efforts to find the truth and tell it. They owe it to you to be straight about what they're doing. (Are they telling you something because they believe it to be true, or are they trying to persuade you of their point of view? They can do either, but they owe it to you to make the difference plain.) And they owe it to you not to underestimate your appetite for serious news. The fact that they can get a big audience with a salacious murder story doesn't make it wrong to cover the story; but it also doesn't justify simply doing all murder, all the time. There were too many times at ABC when a substantive report on a serious subject defied all odds and drew a very large and very engaged audience. Journalists owe it to the people to continue serving up this fare—and then letting the people decide whether they want more of it.

There is a way to be passionate—and to generate passion—in the center. There are stories, important stories, that people care about deeply but that don't have a partisan tilt. Stories about corporations that ignore and then try to cover up defects in their products that could hurt their customers. Stories about waste and fraud in government, not just at the federal level but at the state and local levels as well. Stories about people triumphing over adversity and about our fellow citizens doing extraordinary things that change the world.

Michael Bloomberg, as mayor of New York, has generated a good number of great stories that generate passion without being partisan. The ban on smoking that he pioneered and that has spread across the country and to Europe wasn't a partisan issue. It was a public health issue. Yet it generated a great deal of heat. His quest for reforming our public schools isn't a matter of whether you're a Republican or a Democrat. It's a matter of the future of our children. Some of the best stories, the stories that got the strongest reactions from our audience during my time at ABC News, had nothing to do with a partisan perspective. They simply revealed to people something they didn't know about an issue that was very important to them. It got them thinking and, ideally, got them acting differently than they otherwise would have.

Which takes me to the last thing I'm certain of. Perhaps the thing I'm most certain of. Ultimately, the public will decide the future of news. There is great journalism being done every day by people working at the major news organizations, whether in print or in video. There could be more, and the country would be the better for it. But the starting place is to recognize that strong, substantive news reports are there for the finding. Whether there are more such reports, whether they even continue, depends most critically not on what the journalists want to do but on what the audience wants to watch and read. The public is a partner with the news organizations in deciding what gets covered, how it is covered, and how much it is covered. Better, more substantive reporting of the news requires a joint commitment of the journalists and the public.

There can be a bright future for great news organizations like ABC News. And it's important for the country that there is such a future. A democracy is stronger if at least some of the news reaching the people is coming from dedicated men and women who spend their lives working on beats and developing sources and finding the truth and telling it. The good news I took from my time as president of ABC News is that we continue to have many, many such dedicated people who work hard to do just this every day. All of us rely on these people; we need them. And if we want to continue to benefit from what they have to tell us, we have to recognize their work for what it is, giving it the time and attention that it deserves.

## | Acknowledgments

That this book ever saw the light of day is because of a host of supportive, helpful people who deserve credit—but none of the blame. I'll save that for myself.

Several friends gave me advice and encouragement, both of which I needed. These included Sir Harold Evans (whose passion bore me along), Peggy Noonan (who gave me the title), Walter Isaacson (who'd long encouraged me to write my own book), Bob Iger (who talked with me about the idea of the book and then gave me valuable early reactions), and my sister, Rebecca (who gave me her thoughts and, much more, her support, the way she always has).

I wouldn't have wanted to do this book without asking a range of my former colleagues to go over various sections to make sure I had them more or less right. Thank you to Clark Bentson, Marc Burstein, Amy Entelis, Mark Halperin, Kayce Freed Jennings, Ted Koppel, Phyllis McGrady, Vinnie Malhotra, Dan Merkle, Diane Sawyer, Ben Sherwood, Kerry Smith, Sandy Sidey, Robin Sproul, George Stephanopoulos, Katie Thomson, Chris Vlasto, Barbara Walters, Betsy West, and Bob and Lee Woodruff. You did far more than check my recollection; you gave me valuable comments and suggestions that made it a better book than it otherwise would have been. I'm especially indebted to Tom Nagorski, a gifted writer and editor, for taking the time to go through the entire manuscript and give me a detailed line edit. And to Cathie Levine, who also read a complete draft and offered sage advice on some key points.

I had the pleasure of working with two talented researchers over the course of my writing: Rebecca Lee got me started, and then Scott Norville did the lion's share of the checking and rechecking. They saved me from various errors, for which I thank them.

When I decided to seek a publisher for my book just before I left ABC News, I turned to Bob Barnett to guide me through the process, which he did expertly. Most important, he brought me to Sarah Crichton and her colleagues, particularly Dan Piepenbring and Susan Goldfarb. I could not have wished for a better, smarter, or more collegial editor than Sarah, or for more support from a publisher.

None of this would have been possible without my colleagues and friends at Capital Cities and ABC. At Steve Weiswasser's urging, Tom Murphy and Dan Burke plucked me from a Washington law firm and gave me every opportunity in the new (to me) media world. A few years later, Bob Iger gave me the opportunity to run a great news organization. And my colleagues at ABC News welcomed me (at least after a time) into their very special, very exclusive club. They allowed me the great privilege of being their leader through good times and bad. To all of them, I owe a great debt of gratitude.

Finally, I owe the most to those who gave me the most: my family. To my children, who tried their best to understand why I wasn't always there when they wanted me—or why I was too often distracted when I was there. And to my wife, Sherrie, who went over several drafts of the book and gave me wise advice. Much more, she lived through the triumphs and the disappointments of nearly fourteen years, feeling it all even more than I did, as all great spouses do.

# Index

ABCNews.com, 39, 99, 200
ABC News Investigative Unit, 113
ABC News Radio, 15, 39, 90, 99, 200
ABC Sports, 5–6, 22, 114
*ABC 2000*, 59, 68
*Abraham Lincoln* (aircraft carrier), 135, 136
absentee ballots, 85, 94, 98
Abu Ghraib prison (Iraq), 50
Academy Awards, 58
Afghanistan, 108
    war in, 4, 50, 73, 126, 128, 131, 136, 157, 177, 183, 193, 197, 198
African Americans, 151, 174–75
AIDS, 26
Ailes, Roger, 69, 207–208
*Air Force One* (film), 67
Air National Guard, 50–51, 135, 157
Alarcón, Ricardo, 36
Albright, Madeleine, 41
Allbaugh, Joe, 82
al-Qaeda, 78, 108, 128–29, 131, 132
Altman, Roger, 202
Amanpour, Christiane, 206
American Airlines Flight 93, 115–16
American Bar Association, 5
*American Lawyer, The* (magazine), 44
Annan, Kofi, 128
AOL–Time Warner, 207
Appalachia, poverty in, 28

Arledge, Roone, 5–8, 45, 51–52, 220, 221
    and ABC News anchors, 178, 203–305
    ABC Sports run by, 5, 6
    and coverage of Princess Diana's death, 21–26
    and Lewinsky scandal coverage, 38–39
    and millennium program, 59
    strategic relationship with CNN advocated by, 207
Arlington National Cemetery, 144
Armonda, Colonel Rocco, 190
Army, U.S., 184
    Third Infantry Division, 145
    Fourth Infantry Division, 180–82
    Special Forces, 131, 197
Ashcroft, John, 79
Associated Press (AP), 51, 63, 84, 85, 91, 97, 111
*Atlantic, The,* (magazine), 145
Austria, 78
*Avatar* (film), 58


Baghdad, 53, 54, 145, 166, 179, 182, 195
Bair, Sheila, 202
Baker, Gladys, 51, 52
Balad (Iraq), military hospital in, 177, 183–84, 187, 191–94

*Baltimore Sun,* 43
Bangladesh, 136
Banner, Jon, 206
Barksdale Air Force Base (Louisiana), 120–21
Bashir, Martin, 215, 216
Ba Thanh, 163
Bay of Pigs invasion, 73
Bednar, Rudy, 214, 217
Beirut, ABC's Middle East Bureau in, 20
Belgrade (Yugoslavia), 197–98
Bentson, Clark, 197–98
Berkowitz, David (Son of Sam), 23
Berlin Wall, 4
Berman, John, 83, 206
Bernanke, Ben, 202
Bethesda Naval Hospital, 185, 189–91, 194
Bettag, Tom, 39, 40
bin Laden, Osama, 108–10, 128–30, 132
biological weapons, 165
blacks, *see* African Americans
Blair, Jayson, 50
Blair, Tony, 34
Blankfein, Lloyd, 202
Blasi, Vince, 72
Bloom, David, 185
Bloom, Melanie, 185, 190
Bloomberg, Michael, 224
Bob Woodruff Foundation, 194
Boccardi, Lou, 51
Bono, 71
Boortz, Neal, 141
Bosnia, 72
Boston, 214
    Democratic National Convention in, 160
    hospitals in, 214
Bozell, Brent, 141
Bradley, Bill, 83
Brill, Steven, 44, 45, 48
*Brill's Content* (magazine), 44
Brinkley, David, 6, 20, 178, 206, 222

Britain, 102, 148, 166, 215
    in Iraq War, 54
    Press Complaints Commission, 74
British Broadcasting Company (BBC), 17–18
Brokaw, Tom, 96, 115
Brown, Aaron, 17
Bruno, Hal, 113
Bryant, Kobe, 142
Buchanan, Pat, 96, 207
Burkett, Bill, 51
Burns, John, 189
Burstein, Marc, 93, 112
Bush, George H. W., 82
Bush, George W., 53, 125, 142–43, 172, 161
    in Air National Guard, 50–51, 135, 157
    and Iraq war, 135, 136, 140, 143, 172, 179
    on 9/11, 111, 114, 120–23, 143
    in presidential election of 2000, 81–84, 88, 90, 92–95, 98–99, 101, 143, 157
    State of the Union address by, 179, 180, 190, 191, 198
Bush, Jeb, 82, 99
Bush, Laura, 121
Bush, Prescott, 82

Cable News Network (CNN), 44, 54, 104, 107, 207–209
    Gulf War coverage on, 7
    9/11 coverage on, 107
    presidential election of 2000 coverage on, 90, 91, 93, 97
    reports on Princess Diana's death on, 14
Calcutta, funeral of Mother Teresa in, 34–35
Cambodia, 158
Camden (New Jersey), poverty in, 28
Cameron, James, 58

Canada, 124

Capital Cities/ABC, 5–8, 21

Carter, Bill, 62

Carville, James, 42

Casey, General George W., 183

Castro, Fidel, 36, 75–77

CBS, 215

 News, 8, 19, 20, 22, 35, 43, 50–51, 84, 90–93, 97, 105, 126, 203, 222

Centers for Disease Control, 201

Central Intelligence Agency (CIA), 53

*Chariots of Fire* (film), 15

Charles, Prince of Wales, 14, 34

chemical weapons, 53, 145

Cheney, Dick, 114, 121, 122, 127

Chertoff, Michael, 132, 133

Chiarelli, General Peter, 183, 196

*Chicago Tribune*, 92

China, 166, 173

*Christian Science Monitor*, 43

Chung, Connie, 32–33, 178

Citigroup, 202

Civil War, 144

climate change, 72, 167–69, 213

Clinton, Bill, 17, 77, 82, 84, 142, 166

 cloning research banned by, 8

 DiCaprio interview with, 58–72, 74, 79–80

 Lewinsky scandal and impeachment proceedings against, 4, 33, 36–49, 51, 54, 57, 58, 81, 83, 153–54, 222

Clinton, Hillary, 46, 154

Clooney, George, 71

Cold War, 3

Colonial Williamsburg, 5

Columbia University, 43, 202

Comedy Central, 138

Committee of Concerned Journalists, 49

Compton, Ann, 120–22

Condit, Gary, 32–33, 106

Congress, U.S., 47, 71, 92, 109, 157

 annual dinner for reporters covering, 63–64

 and coverage of presidential election of 2000, 97, 99–101

 and Customs Service security failures, 55, 79

 evacuation on 9/11 of, 114

 resistance to enaction of federal "shield" laws in, 73–74

 *see also* House of Representatives, U.S.; Senate, U.S.

conspiracy theories, 46, 169

Constitution, U.S., First Amendment to, 4, 9, 72, 125

Consumer Product Safety Commission, 55

Costner, Kevin, 67

Council on Environmental Quality, 63

counterterrorism, 111

CourtTV, 44

Crash of 2008, 4, 202

Cronkite, Walter, 20, 178, 222

*Crossfire*, 207

C-SPAN, 65

Cuba, 36–40, 46, 60, 173

 Bay of Pigs invasion of, 73

 Castro interviewed by Walters in, 75–77

 Pope's visit to, 18, 36, 39, 40

Cuomo, Chris, 59, 60, 149–50, 206

Curry, Ann, 71

Cusack, Lawrence, 52–53

Customs Service, U.S., 55, 78–79

Cyprus, 136


Dahler, Don, 107–108, 110, 115

*Daily Show, The*, 71

Daley, William, 41, 95

Darfur, 72

*Dark Side of Camelot, The* (Hersh), 51

*Dateline*, 76

Decision Desk, 85–86, 88, 91, 93, 94, 96, 97, 99, 101

Defense Department, U.S., 111

Democratic Front for the Liberation of
    Palestine, 115
Democratic Party, 81, 156, 160, 162, 225
de Moraes, Lisa, 141
desegregation, 5
Dewey, Thomas E., 92, 98
Diana, Princess of Wales, 13–19, 35, 70,
    215, 220
    Jennings and coverage of death of,
        13–14, 18–19, 21, 23–27, 33–35,
        220
    public fascination with, 25, 31, 33
DiCaprio, Leonardo, 58–72, 74, 79–80, 96
DiFranco, Don, 118
digital technology, 68, 210, 212, 214,
    217–19
Dimon, Jamie, 202
Dion, Celine, 64
diversity, 25, 151–52
Dixville Notch, New Hampshire, 84
Donaldson, Sam, 62, 65, 66, 82, 204
Donvan, John, 17
Dowd, Maureen, 58, 65
Downs, Hugh, 206
Drudge, Matt, 41, 42
*Drudge Report*, 50
Dubai, 217
Dunn, Commander James, 190
Duvall, Jed, 162–63


Earth Day, 59, 60, 67
Eisner, Michael, 120
El-Erian, Mohamed, 202
Elizabeth II, Queen of England, 34
Ellis, John, 98–99
Emmy Awards, 38, 137
England
    Norman invasion of, 102
    *see also* Britain
Entelis, Amy, 204, 206
environmental issues, 60–63, 67–70,
    72, 80

ESPN, 150
ethnic diversity, 151
Evans, Don, 106
Evercore, 202
exit polls, 84, 87–89, 92, 98–99


Fallujah (Iraq), 136
Farrow, Mia, 71
Fayed, Dodi, 14–16, 21
Federal Bureau of Investigation (FBI),
    43, 79, 110, 131–33, 201
Federal Communications Commission,
    152
Federal Deposit Insurance Corporation
    (FDIC), 202
Federal Reserve, 202
federal shield law, proposed, 73–75
Feinstein, Dianne, 79
Feldstein, Martin, 202
Ferrer, Christy, 119
Fleischer, Ari, 127, 129
Florida
    Bush in, on 9/11, 111, 120, 121
    presidential election of 2000 in, 81,
        82, 88–101
    shark attacks off coast of, 31, 104
Foot, Michael, 148
Forbes, Steve, 202
Fox News, 7, 69, 141, 164, 207–208
    American flag lapel-pin policy of,
        123, 125–26
    fitting news to overall narrative for
        audience of, 65
    presidential election of 2000 coverage
        on, 84, 92, 93, 97–99
    Radio, 132
    right-of-center bias of, 143, 148,
        209–10
France, 166
Franks, General Tommy, 173
Freedom Forum Media Studies
    Center, 43

Friedman, Paul, 93, 113
Friendly, Fred, 126
Frost, David, 74
*Frost/Nixon* (film), 74
Fukuyama, Francis, 3

Gadahn, Adam, 131–33
Gallup Organization, 102
*Gangs of New York* (film), 63
Gannett Foundation, 43
*Gannett v. DePasquale* (1979), 4, 9
Gaza, 179
General Motors, 202
Germany, 166, 186, 188
   U.S. military hospital in, 183–86,
     188–92, 194
   in World War II, 5
Gibson, Charles, 106–109, 113, 116,
     186–87, 191, 204–207
Giles, Robert, 43
Ginsburg, William, 43
Giudice, Barbara, 15–17
Giuliani, Rudolph, 120
global warming, 167–68
   *see also* climate change
Goldenson, Leonard, 6
Goldman Sachs, 202
Goldston, James, 206, 215–17
Golodryga, Bianna, 150, 206
González, Elián, 60, 65, 68
Goodman, Roger, 112
*Good Morning America (GMA)*, 16,
     106–107, 132, 170, 188, 203–205,
     220
   9/11 coverage on, 107
   reviews of Disney films on, 150
   Sawyer on, 186, 187, 204–207
   *Weekend*, 176
Google, 179
Gore, Al, 82–84, 87, 89–92, 94–96, 98,
     101
Graham, Phil, 27

Gralnick, Jeff, 59
Grassley, Charles, 79
Great Depression, 4, 202
Grunwald, Henry, 69
*Guardian, The*, 148
Gulf War, 7, 207
Gurbst, Mimi, 182, 185

Haiti, 72, 198
Halabja genocide, 165
Hall, Arsenio, 71
Halperin, Mark, 83, 86, 93, 95
Harris, Dan, 196, 206
Harris, Katherine, 96
Harrods department store, 15
Harvard University, 202
Hasan, Lama, 152, 206
Hayes, Woody, 149
Hemingway, Ernest, 36
Hersh, Seymour, 51, 52, 54
Hirashiki, Tony, 119
Homeland Security, 132
*Hook* (film), 15
*Hopkins 24/7*, 68, 214, 217
Hotel Ritz (Paris), 15
House of Representatives,
   U.S., 92
   Commerce Committee, 34, 97
Hughes, Karen, 82, 122
Hume, Brit, 125
Huntley, Chet, 20, 178, 222
Hurricane Katrina, 4, 139, 151

Iger, Bob, 7, 38, 119–20, 140, 146, 177,
     211, 220
improvised explosive devices (IEDs),
     177, 182, 183, 185, 189
*In an Instant* (Woodruff), 193
India, funeral of Mother Teresa in,
     34–35
Indonesia, 78

Internet, 4, 87, 125
  leaks on, 87
  news sources on, 72, 131, 169, 179,
    209–10, 223
  polls on, 154
Iran, 167
Iran-Contra affair, 156
Iraq War, 4, 30, 53, 126, 135–46, 157
  abuses at Abu Ghraib prison
    during, 50
  Bush's "mission accomplished"
    proclamation on, 135–37
  journalists injured in, 176–96, 198, 202
  *Nightline* special on, 135, 138,
    140–45, 155
  U.S. government charges of bias
    against press coverage of, 73, 143,
    146, 173
  weapons of mass destruction as
    justification for, 48–50, 165–67, 172
Isaacson family, 104, 106
Isham, Chris, 108
Isikoff, Mike, 37, 40
Islam, 151
Israel, 146, 166, 179
  attack on 1972 Olympic team from,
    20, 114

Jackson, Michael, 30, 142, 144, 216
Jakarta, 217
Jamieson, Bob, 119
Jefferson, Thomas, 72
Jennings, Chris, 118
Jennings, Lizzie, 118
Jennings, Peter, 20–28, 51, 53, 104,
    109–11, 120–24, 165–67, 206
  accused of left-of-center bias, 143,
    146, 173
  Canadian citizenship of, 124
  and coverage of Princess Diana's
    death, 13–14, 18–19, 21, 23–27,
    33–35, 220

in Cuba, 36
  death of, 178, 181, 188, 201, 215
  and DiCaprio's interview with
    Clinton, 61, 62
  documentaries by, 28
  existence of Saddam's weapons of
    mass destruction questioned by,
    26, 165–67
  Kerry and, 157
  in Middle East, 20, 114, 151, 166–67
  millennium program anchored by, 59
  9/11 coverage anchored by, 111,
    113–18, 121–23, 143, 220
  on PBS seminar panel, 126
  presidential election of 2000 covered
    by, 81, 82, 86, 88–90, 92–95, 97–98
  *World News Tonight* anchored by, 6,
    15, 20–21, 36, 39, 42, 108, 131–32
Jiang Zemin, 106
John Paul II, Pope, 18, 36, 39, 40
Johns Hopkins Hospital, 68, 214, 217
Johnson, Lyndon, 105
Johnson, Tim, 188, 189, 201, 220
Joint Chiefs of Staff, 109, 111, 193
Jolie, Angelina, 71
Jones, General James L., 109
Jordan, 136
Jordan, Michael, 106
JPMorgan Chase, 202
Judd, Jackie, 36, 38, 39, 43, 45
Justice Department, U.S., 37, 47, 119, 132

Kabul (Afghanistan), 131, 194, 195
Karl, Jon, 206
Keane, General Jack, 183
Keller, Bill, 147, 188
Kelly, Jim, 137
Kelly, Michael, 145
Kennedy, John F., 51–52, 54, 73, 76
  assassination of, 104–105
Kennedy, Robert, 51–52
Kenya, 71

Kerry, John, 156–64, 166, 167, 169, 171, 174
Khashoggi, Adnan, 15
Khrushchev, Nikita, 76
Kimmel, Jimmy, 138–40
Kinsley, Michael, 207
Kissinger, Henry, 49
Knight Ridder newspaper chain, 167
Koppel, Ted, 39, 40, 77, 206
   departure from *Nightline* of, 211, 215, 216
   and DiCaprio's interview with Clinton, 61, 62, 80
   Iraq War dead special presented by, 135, 138, 140, 142–45, 155
   9/11 coverage by, 113, 116
   swift boat allegations refuted by, 156
   in Vietnam, 119
Korean War, 144
Kosovo, 197
Kovach, Bill, 127
Kristof, Nicholas, 71
Kristol, William, 65, 141
Krulwich, Robert, 16, 17
Kurds, 165
Kurtz, Howard, 61
Kuwait, 145
Kyl, Jon, 171

LaMay, Roger, 125
Landay, Jonathan, 167
Landstuhl hospital, 183–86, 188–92, 194
Langer, George, 81, 93
Laos, 44
*Larry King Live*, 207
leaks, 48, 54, 62, 87, 129, 154
Lee, Mike, 15–17
Lelyveld, Joe, 188
Leno, Jay, 138, 216
Letterman, David, 138, 215, 216
Levin, Neil, 119
Levy, Chandra, 32–33, 106

Lewinsky, Monica, 4, 36–49, 51, 58, 81, 83, 153–54
   blue dress of, 36, 41–45, 47–49, 54, 57
   Condit's comments on Clinton and, 33
*Life* magazine, 138, 139
Limbaugh, Rush, 122, 123
Lippmann, Walter, 70–72
Los Angeles, 152, 179, 198
   port of, containerized shipping through, 78
   2000 Democratic Convention in, 84
Lustig, Chuck, 182, 196
Lutz, Bob, 202
Lynch, Jessica, 50

Macedo, Magnus, 177, 184
Majid, Ali Hassan al- (Chemical Ali), 53–54
Malhotra, Vinnie, 177, 184–85, 187, 192
*Man Show, The*, 139
Marine Corps, U.S., 109, 179
Mayer, Jane, 67
McCain, John, 64, 83, 141, 161
McClure, Jessica, 26
McFadden, Cynthia, 206, 216
McGrady, Phyllis, 16, 18, 23, 59, 182, 204, 214, 215
McKay, Jim, 114
McLoughlin, Sean, 185
McWethy, John, 110, 111, 118
Media Research Center, 141
Medicare, 170
*Meet the Press*, 6, 42
Memorial Day, 141
Merkle, Dan, 97
*Miami Herald*, 92, 93
Michigan, University of, 149, 150, 176
Microsoft, 7
Middleton, Kate, 30
Miller, John, 108, 110, 115
Miramax, 63

Miron, Jeffrey, 202
Mitchell, Andrea, 75, 77
*Monday Night Football*, 5
Monroe, Marilyn, 51
Mora, Antonio, 106
Moran, Terry, 124–25, 127, 206, 216
Morse, Andrew, 163
Moscow, 198
Mozambique, 136
MTV, 71
Muir, David, 206
Mullen, Admiral Mike, 193
Mumbai, 217
Murdoch, Rupert, 7
Murphy, Bob, 185, 188, 192, 215
Murphy, Jim, 206
Muslims, 108, 151

Nader, Ralph, 93
Nagorski, Tom, 34n, 137
Nairobi, 217
Nance, John, 111
National Basketball Association
  (NBA), 83
National Broadcasting Company
  (NBC), 6–7, 19, 215
  CNBC, 141
  MSNBC, 7, 75, 92, 148, 203, 207–209
  News, 6, 16, 20, 35, 71, 75, 84, 92, 93,
    97, 178, 185, 203, 207, 220, 222
National Intelligence Estimate, U.S.,
  166
*National Review*, 161–62
National Security Council, 121
Navy, U.S., 159–60
New Delhi, 217
New Hampshire primary, 83
New York City, 151
  all-staff meetings in, 218–19
  Archdiocese of, 52
  news anchors in, 178, 179
  Police Department, 110, 201, 214

  port of, containerized shipping
    through, 78
  Son of Sam serial killings in, 23
Newman, Kevin, 14–17
News Corporation, 7
*News of the World* scandal, 74
*Newsweek*, 37, 40
*New Yorker, The*, 67, 130
New York-Presbyterian Hospital, 192
*New York Times*, 50, 58, 62, 71, 73, 102,
  129–30, 147, 160, 188–89, 193,
  195, 205
  Washington bureau, 127
*Nightline*, 6, 39–40, 62, 113, 116, 135
  Iraq War coverage on, 138–46, 155
  Koppel's departure from of, 211, 215,
    216
  swift boat allegations refuted on, 156,
    161–64, 174
*Nightly News*, 6
Nissen, Beth, 16, 17
Nixon, Richard, 37, 73–75, 160
Nolan, Peter, 64
North Atlantic Treaty Organization
  (NATO), 197
nuclear weapons, 83

Obama, Barack, 71, 150
  election of, 4
Obenhaus, Mark, 51–53
Office of Management and Budget
  (OMB), 150, 202
Offutt Air Force Base (Omaha,
  Nebraska), 121, 122
Ogletree, Charles, 126
Ohio, presidential election of 2000 in,
  88, 101
Ohio State University, 149
Oklahoma City bombing, 121
Olmstead, Larry, 92
Olson, Barbara, 119
Olson, Ted, 119

Olympic Games, 5–6
    Munich (1972), 20, 114
O'Neill, John, 159, 163
Operation Sealords, 158
Operation Tailwind, 44
O'Reilly, Bill, 141
Organization of News Ombudsmen, 127
Orszag, Peter, 150, 202
Osunsami, Steve, 206
Oswald, Lee Harvey, 105

Pakistan, 131
Palestinians, 115, 152, 179
Panama Canal, 19
Pandit, Vikram, 202
Paris, death of Princess Diana in,
    14–17, 21
Pataki, George, 120
patriotism, 106, 120–27, 129, 130, 140,
    141, 155, 172–73
Patrol Craft, Fast (PCF) boats, 158
    see also swift boat allegations
Pax Americana, 4
Pearl Harbor, Japanese attack on, 122
Pelley, Scott, 222
Penn, Sean, 72
Pennsylvania
    crash of American Airlines Flight 93,
        115–16
    presidential election of 2000 in, 88, 101
Pentagon, 131, 136, 196
    terrorist attack on, see September 11,
        2001, terrorist attacks (9/11)
Pentagon Papers, 46, 73
People magazine, 25
Peres, Shimon, 77
Pérez Roque, Felipe, 76
Perry, Bob J., 161
Peterson, Laci, 142
Peterson, Scott, 142, 144
Pew Research Center, 25, 102, 208
Philadelphia Inquirer, 63

PIMCO, 202
Planet Earth 2000, 67
Planned Parenthood, 171, 172
Pollack, Ken, 165
Polling Unit, 86
Port Authority of New York and New
    Jersey, 119
poverty, Sawyer's documentaries on,
    28–29
Powell, Lewis F., 4–5, 9, 10, 154, 224
Poynter Institute, 125
presidential elections, 4, 139
    Bush v. Gore (2000), 34, 60, 68,
        81–103, 222
    Bush v. Kerry (2004), 50, 156, 163
Presley, Elvis, 19
press conferences, presidential, 30
Primetime Live, 6, 16, 22, 204
Pruett, Kyle, 117
Public Broadcasting System (PBS), 126

Qatar, 152

racial diversity, 151
Raddatz, Martha, 182–83, 188, 206
Radio and Television Correspondents'
    Dinner, 58, 63–64
Raines, Howell, 130
Rather, Dan, 22, 50–51, 115, 157, 178
Reagan, Ronald, 18, 37
Reasoner, Harry, 22, 178
Redeker, Bill, 16, 17
Reiter, David, 137
Reno, Janet, 37
Republican Party, 51, 161, 162, 225
Reynolds, Frank, 20, 178, 222
Rice, Condoleezza, 82–83, 128–30, 132
Riley, Richard, 41
Rio de Janeiro, 217
Ritter, Bill, 17
Rivera, Geraldo, 44

*Rivera Live*, 44
Robaina, Roberto, 36
Roberts, Cokie, 36, 62, 65, 86
Roberts, Robin, 206
Robinson, Max, 20, 178
Rockefeller, John D., Jr., 5
Rogoff, Kenneth, 202
Roosevelt, Franklin D., 81
Ross, Brian, 78, 79
Rove, Karl, 82, 90, 122–23, 127, 143,
    146, 155
Rumsfeld, Donald, 54, 136
Russell, Bill, 83
Russert, Tim, 6
Russia, 83, 166
    Communist, *see* Soviet Union

Sachs, Jeffrey, 71, 202
Saddam Hussein, 26, 48–49, 53, 145
    and weapons of mass destruction,
        165–67, 173
*Salon*, 63, 67
Salpêtrière Hospital (Paris), 16
Sandhurst military academy, 15
San Francisco, 179
Sarah, Duchess of York, 106
Sawyer, Diane, 80, 182, 186–87, 220, 222
    coverage of Princess Diana's death by,
        13, 18, 23–25
    documentaries by, 28–29
    Elián González interviewed by, 60,
        65, 68
    on *Good Morning America*, 186, 187
        204–207
    Kerry and, 157
    9/11 coverage by, 106–109, 116, 151–52
    on *Primetime Live*, 22, 204
    Starr interviewed by, 77
Schembechler, Bo, 149
Schneider, Jeffrey, 108, 123, 128
Schultz, Howard, 202
Schumer, Charles, 79, 120

Sciutto, Jim, 186, 206
Secret Service, 82, 121, 123
Senate, U.S., 4, 46, 92, 171
    Foreign Affairs Committee, 156, 159
    Judiciary Committee, 73
    Select Committee on POW/MIA
        Affairs, 156
Seoul, 217
September 11, 2001, terrorist attacks
        (9/11), 4, 31, 104–26, 134, 136,
        154–55, 220
    Bush's statements on, 111, 121
    conspiracy theory about, 169
    coverage on *Good Morning America*
        of, 107–109
    expressions of patriotism after,
        120–26, 150, 172
    inadequate security of containerized
        shipping after, 77–78
    Jennings anchors coverage of, 111,
        113–18, 121–23, 220
    on-the-scene reporting on, 107,
        110–11, 118–20
    viewpoints of American Muslims
        after, 151–52
Serbia, 197
Sesame Workshop, 181
Shalala, Donna, 41
Sherwood, Ben, 200, 220–21
Shipman, Claire, 106, 111, 120, 206
Sievers, Leroy, 135, 136, 138, 145, 155
Sinclair Broadcast Group, 141, 142, 144,
        146, 155
*60 Minutes*, 18, 22, 50, 54, 157, 204
slave trade, 102
Slavin, Paul, 176, 178
Sloan, David, 206
Smith, David, 141
Smith, Kerry, 79, 96–97, 117
Snow, Kate, 176, 206
Snow, Tony, 132
Social Security, 170
Southeast Asian tsunami, 4, 197

Soviet Union, collapse of, 3, 78
   fissile material in former
      republics, 78
Sproul, Robin, 41, 125, 128
Stanford University, 82
Staples Center (Los Angeles), 84
Starbucks, 202
Stark, Lisa, 104
Starr, Ken, 37, 41, 43–45, 47, 48, 77
State of the Union addresses, 30, 179,
   180, 190, 191, 198
Steele, Bob, 125
Stephanopoulos, George, 77, 84, 86, 95,
   182, 206
Stewart, Jon, 71, 79
Stiglitz, Joseph, 202
Strategic Air Command, 121
Strobel, Warren, 167
Sucherman, Stuart, 204
Sudan, 71
Summers, Larry, 202
"Super Tuesday" primaries, 159
Supreme Court, U.S., 4, 73, 95, 154
Sweeney, Anne, 177, 218, 220–21
swift boat allegations, 156–64, 166, 167,
   169, 171, 174

Taji (Iraq), 176, 177, 180, 182, 196
Taliban, 131
Tapper, Jake, 206
Tauzin, Billy, 97, 98
Telecommunications Act (1996),
   152–53
Telegraph, The, 148
Television Critics Association, 45
Teresa, Mother, 34–35
terrorism, 73, 78, 79, 107–10, 131, 132,
   157, 222
   at 1972 Munich Olympics, 20, 114
   see also September 11, 2001, terrorist
      attacks
Thatcher, Margaret, 148

This Week, 6, 62, 65, 168, 170, 182, 215
Thomas, Pierre, 206
Thornburgh, Dick, 51
Time magazine, 69, 137
Times of India, 65
Tin Cup (film), 67
Titanic (film), 58, 59, 64, 65
Today show, 6
Tonight Show, The, 215
traumatic brain injury (TBI), 188–89,
   193, 194
Truman, Harry S., 92, 98
Turkey, 78
Turning Point, 16
20/20, 18, 28
   Downtown, 59

Ultra Project, 5
Unfit for Command (O'Neill), 160, 163
United Nations, 128, 136, 166
   Millennium Project, 71

Vargas, Elizabeth, 116, 178–79, 186,
   187, 191, 206
V-chip, 152–53
Vieira de Mello, Sergio, 136, 137
Vietnam, 156
   war in, 138, 139, 144, 156–72, 174, 189
View, The, 71
Vlasto, Chris, 38, 51
Vogt, Doug, 176–96, 198, 202
Vogt, Vivianne, 177, 183, 186, 189–91
Voter News Service (VNS), 84–85, 89,
   91, 94, 95, 98
Vo Van Tam, 163

WABC-TV New York, 107, 110, 118–20
Wald, Richard, 43
Wallace, Mike, 126
Wallau, Alex, 119–20, 138–40

*Wall Street Journal*, 102

Walt Disney Company, 31, 38, 211, 212, 220
  ABC News charged with bias against Israel by director of, 146
  Capital Cities purchased by, 7
  *Good Morning America* reviews of films produced by, 150
  Miramax and, 63
  and 9/11 coverage, 120

Walters, Barbara, 16–18, 34, 67
  Castro interviewed by, 75–77
  coverage of Princess Diana's death by, 13, 17, 18, 23–25
  evening news co-anchored by Reasoner and, 22, 178
  Jiang Zemin interviewed by, 106
  Kerry and, 157
  specials of, 16

war crimes, 159, 160

Warren, Elizabeth, 202

Washington, D.C., 151, 154
  all-staff meetings in, 218–19
  antiwar protests in, 173
  news anchors in, 178, 179, 191
  news bureaus in, 41, 44, 61, 62, 66, 111, 125, 127, 198, 200
  Radio and Television Correspondents Dinner in, 58, 63
  sniper in, 50
  Vietnam Veterans Memorial in, 144

*Washington Post*, 27, 42, 61, 63, 102, 141–42, 161

Washington Wizards basketball team, 106

Watergate scandal, 44, 46, 47

*Waterworld* (film), 67

Watt, Nick, 196, 206

weapons of mass destruction (WMD), 26, 48–50, 165–67, 172, 173

Weight Watchers, 106

Weir, Bill, 206, 216

Wentworth, Ali, 182

Westin, Lily (stepdaughter), 117

Westin, Rebecca (sister), 14, 26, 33

Westin, Sherrie (wife), 15, 61, 119, 128, 177, 181, 182, 193

West Virginia, mine disaster in, 179

White House Correspondents' Dinner, 64, 142

White House Press Office, 63

Whitewater investigation, 37, 154

*Wide World of Sports*, 5

Wiener, Robin, 183, 186

Will, George, 113, 168, 170

William, Prince, 30, 34

Williams, Brian, 222

Wilmer, Cutler & Pickering, 5, 119

Woodruff, Dave, 185, 186, 190, 191, 194

Woodruff, Jimmy, 190, 194

Woodruff, Lee, 176–77, 180–81, 183, 185–93, 195

Woodruff, Mike, 190, 194

Woodward, Bob, 109

*World News Tonight*, 8, 16, 137, 152, 201
  anthrax in work space of, 201
  election coverage on, 83, 88, 174
  *with Peter Jennings*, 6, 15, 20–21, 36, 39, 42, 108, 131–32
  Woodruff and Vargas as co-anchors of, 178–79

World Trade Center, 104
  terrorist attack on, *see* September 11, 2001, terrorist attacks (9/11)

World War I, 144

World War II, 5, 144

Wright, David, 206

Wrong, Terry, 214

WTXF-TV, Philadelphia, 125

Yale University, 117, 158

Yates, Andrea, 106

Yugoslavia, 136, 197